M000159399

Fruit Trees *for* Every Garden

Fruit Trees *for* Every Garden

An Organic Approach to Growing
Apples, Pears, Peaches, Plums, Citrus, and More

ORIN MARTIN

WITH MANJULA MARTIN

Photographs by Liz Birnbaum
Illustrations by Stephanie Zeiler Martin

TEN SPEED PRESS
California | New York

Foreword

I have been a deep admirer of the work going on at the Chadwick Garden for decades now; even as I was starting my restaurant Chez Panisse in the early 1970s, I remember hearing about Alan Chadwick, the biodynamic farmer who had recently begun a radical new sort of teaching garden at the University of California at Santa Cruz. Alan Chadwick's approach to tending the land using French intensive gardening practices was both revolutionary and ancient, and through the decades it has profoundly influenced thousands of farmers, chefs, educators, and activists around the country, including me. It is regenerative agriculture at its purest—and at this moment in time, I believe there's nothing more important than passing this knowledge on and engaging students in this type of edible education. This one small organic teaching garden has become a living, growing, thriving model of how we can rebuild and nurture the land instead of stripping it of its biodiversity.

Orin Martin began working at the Chadwick Garden in 1972 and has been steeped in this revolutionary history. He now has more than four decades of experience with French intensive gardening, doing the hard work that leads to the great depth of knowledge presented here in this book. When I visited the garden recently, Orin walked me through it, and I was dazzled by the wonderland of biodiversity that coexisted happily in such a modest 3-acre plot: more than 120 different varieties of apple trees alone! It is a delight to witness Orin in his natural element, tending to the trees as if they are old friends. This bounty of varieties is a result of Orin's lifelong horticultural curiosity and his steady, meticulous approach to his work: "Gardening is very much a process of observation, decision, action, and reaction," says Orin. "Rinse, repeat."

It is this patient, slow, joyful work, year after year, that Orin so deftly captures in these pages. Some might be overwhelmed by the prospect of planting their own fruit trees, thinking the task of caring for an orchard too advanced or the rewards too unpredictable. But Orin eases the reader through the process; you can plant a fruit tree wherever you are, he reasons, with enough forethought and simple planning. Here you have all the practical tools to create your own orchard of any size—information on rootstocks, pruning, thinning, and a thrilling array of varieties—but moreover, you have Orin's wise and gently wry voice to guide you through it. (You can see his activist soul here, too: I love his idea of planting orchards throughout the campuses of Silicon Valley tech giants as a way to take the valley back to its agricultural roots!) Orin also reminds us that there's great beauty and pleasure in growing your own fruit trees; you need only flip through the book's lovingly done etchings of pluots, Comice pears, and Tompkins King apples to understand that.

Slow Food founder Carlo Petrini calls farmers the intellectuals of the land; they understand the workings of our planet better than anyone. I firmly believe this to be true, and this book is a perfect example. We all need to reconnect with nature. And it is only by listening to the farmers and the gardeners that we have a chance to do that and start building a sustainable future for ourselves. It is the only real way we can heal our planet.

—ALICE WATERS

Introduction

"You can't learn to farm by reading a book, and you can't tell somebody how to farm. Older farmers I knew used to be fond of saying, 'I can't tell you how to do that. But I can put you where you can learn.' "

—WENDELL BERRY, *THE WAY OF IGNORANCE*, 2006

The people of this planet have a long and storied association with trees. Put simply: the story of fruit trees is the story of us.

Some archaeobotanists argue that fig orchards once dotted the eastern rim of the Mediterranean Sea and eastward toward the upper Euphrates River Valley. These early orchards may have predated the wild progenitors of wheat, barley, oats, emmer, and other ancient grains that propelled humankind into farming some 10,000–11,000 years ago. Since then, we have benefited from the presence of trees in the immediate landscape and, more fundamentally and simply, trees on the planet.

Why grow fruit trees? Like soil stewardship, fruit tree culture is intergenerational. You are growing fruit trees for the next generation and the one after that, too.

Of course, people grow fruit trees for a variety of reasons—for fruit, shade, aesthetic beauty, and (perhaps in a fit of nostalgia for our primate pasts) climbing and swinging through them. Whatever your reason, it's heartening to remember that the act of tending to an organic orchard—whether it's one little peach tree or an entire acre of apples—can also be a chance to turn back the clock on some of the damage humans have done to the earth. Along with enhancing biodiversity in any garden, planting trees can aid in saving the planet—trees sequester atmospheric carbon, essentially modifying the environment and cooling it. When we garden, we should keep in mind that we are very much growing fruit trees in order to *grow more trees*.

A Paradise for Every Garden

For the past forty years, I've been teaching people how to grow fruit trees organically at the Farm & Garden at the University of California, Santa Cruz. The UCSC Farm & Garden is my office, classroom, curriculum, and lesson plan all rolled into one. The Garden, also known as the Alan Chadwick Garden, is about 3 acres perched on an impossibly steep south-facing slope in central, coastal California. It's been a teaching garden since 1967, when Chadwick, a pioneer of French intensive (organic) gardening, began it as an experiment at the newly founded university. Chadwick was both a formative force and a visionary pioneer in the world of organic growing. In a sense, he was the Rosetta stone for all that has unfolded subsequently in the field. His gardens and those he inspired were at the confluence of technique, science, art, and aesthetics. As organic gardeners, we owe him an extreme debt of gratitude.

I started as a volunteer at the Farm & Garden in 1972, and after serving as an apprentice in 1974–75, I became the manager in 1977. Skip ahead four decades: now I'm that old guy leaning on a spade, expounding on the merits of cover crops and compost to a group of idealistic, hardworking apprentices. Nowadays, our apprentices live in tent cabins (not tents, like they used to). In addition to the apprenticeship program, we sell vegetables, flowers, and fruit through a CSA, at a market cart, and to the cafeterias on campus, and we distribute free produce to food pantries on campus, helping to combat food insecurity among students. The program has graduated more than 1,500 apprentices who've gone on to found and lead organic farms, teaching gardens, and food justice projects around the country and the world.

My own fruit tree addiction started with apples. The apprentices tease me that after 40 years in the orchard, I still haven't gotten out of the "A" section of the fruit tree catalog. But why would I need to? One of the advantages of apple trees is that, thanks to an array of size-controlling rootstocks, they lend themselves to intensive plantings and small gardens. But after 10 years of specializing exclusively in apples (more than 120 varieties at last count), the Chadwick Garden orchard is now graced by a collection of stone fruits, including apriums, apricots, peaches, nectarines, plums, and pluots. The truth is, all fruits are great.

Earlier civilizations, from the Sumerians to the Egyptians to the Greeks, made a lush, fragrant garden the basic mythical setting of *paradise*, a word sharing the same etymological root as the word *garden* itself. More accurately, it was an orchard. An orchard as paradise . . . I suppose paradise is certainly a place where existence is positive, harmonious, even timeless.

From the beginning, I encourage you to think of yourself as an orchardist. It doesn't matter how many trees you have or how big your yard is; your orchard is your own slice of paradise. And while paradise is a place of contentment, it is not a place of luxury, and certainly not idleness. For there is much work and learning to be done, daily, out in the orchard, garden, paradise.

Putting You Where You Can Learn

Gardening is very much a process of observation, decision, action, and reaction. Rinse, repeat. Organic gardening is even more so, because each unique environment, each orchard, will have its own attributes and foibles. In conventional horticulture and agriculture, there are often exact answers to exacting microquestions, but the so-called solutions often provide more problems for the environment and planet. Organic gardening, by contrast, looks at the whole picture—the macro and the micro, all in your line of sight. In this book I'll encourage you to understand the ecological systems at work in and around your tree, so you can identify what decisions you need to make and then make them in the service of the tree.

Fruit tree growing is a managed craft, infused and informed by science. It's important to have meaning and intention behind the food you grow, but in farming, nothing happens without science. While it's true that growing trees is natural, the healthy, productive, aesthetically pleasing fruit tree ... isn't. What the tree might do in the wild often bears little or no resemblance to what you as an orchardist want or need the tree to do to produce a good quantity of quality fruit annually. In an unmanaged situation, a fruit tree's goal is to put fruit and seed on the ground in order to perpetuate its species. A fruit tree does not exist to produce large, annual crops of cosmetically clean fruit. That is the imperative of our particular species. You want good apples? Sweet, juicy pears? It's all about managed intervention, manipulation, behavior modification . . . but all toward a good end. Orchardists have evolved to be master manipulators, with the skills to constantly shape, direct, and redirect tree growth and fruiting with an exacting precision. Rather than manipulation, let's just call it tending trees.

Fruit Trees for All

This book will enable you to select, plant, grow, and manage healthy, productive fruit trees organically, from soil management to irrigation, feeding, and pruning, no matter the size of your orchard. More than just a task list or manual, this book is designed to help you learn to identify the choices you need to make, and then to make good choices. In order to alter the natural growth and fruiting habit of a fruit tree, you will need a thorough understanding of *how* trees grow—their structure, physiology, biology, and growth patterns—so you can be equipped to do what you need to do to the tree *when* you need to do it, *with what, how,* and *why.* Along the way, you'll get a strong foundation in French intensive organic gardening—learning to care for and improve your soil through cultivation, compost, cover crops, and green manure. (You can apply this knowledge to any type of gardening, but here we're applying it to growing fruit trees.)

The first sections of the book use deciduous fruit trees as your testing ground—specifically, pome fruits (apple, pear, quince) and stone fruits (peach, nectarine, apricot, aprium, pluot, plum, cherry). The truth is, most of what you need to know about fruit trees you can learn from pome and stone fruits. The rest are...well, they're easier. Some of my other favorite fruits to grow—citrus, pomegranates, persimmons, and figs—have their own considerations later in the book.

When I was growing up in New England, everybody had to take Latin, a subject with which I was entirely disinterested. (Baseball was more my thing.) But in the years since, I've schooled myself up a bit. There's a Latin phrase I often translate for my apprentices: *a posse ad esse.* It means (variously) "from the possible to the actual," "from being possible to being actual," or "from being able to *being.*" As applied to our goals here, the theory goes a little something like this: Of course it is *possible* to grow fruit trees. Of course it is advisable. But this book will make that real. It is both lexicon and road map. Let's get into it.

I

Getting Started

Whether you're growing one tree, ten, or even a thousand, the guiding principles for good growing are about the same. To start, we'll look at what you need to do before you plant a fruit tree: how to pick the right site, assess your soil's fertility, and other considerations.

The first impulse people often have is to grab a tree, grab a spade, dig a hole, and plant the darn tree. In reality, the *last* thing you want to do is plant the darn tree.

Many mistakes with fruit trees are made before the trees are even planted. These mistakes are hard to rectify once your tree is in the ground; you can't reverse engineer yourself out of them. Don't get me wrong. I'm all for planting fruit trees, more fruit trees all around! But planting a fruit tree is, or at least should be, a considered act involving a well-thought-out plan with a set of goals. In a sense, you don't simply *grow* a tree—you *design* it through the choices you make about the site, rootstock, variety, size or height, and pruning or training systems. Planning ahead will give you time to assess your site; improve your soil; set up good irrigation practices; and make sure your garden is a biodiverse environment for your trees to thrive in.

There's an old gardeners' joke that goes like this:

Q: "When is the best time to plant a fruit tree?"

A: "Twenty years ago."

They say patience is a virtue; be virtuous. In an ideal scenario, consider at least 1- to 3-year lead time before you plant a fruit tree. Yes, you heard me right: 1–3 years. This is mainly so you can improve the quality of your soil before planting. Of course, not all scenarios are ideal. If like most people you're not the patient type, you'll want to plant *now*; the multiyear planting hole (see page 110) offers a hybrid approach to planting and soil improvement so you can begin sooner. But even if you insist on planting tomorrow, you will still need to improve your soil in subsequent years. And maybe you'll start to see the value in slowing down along the way. It's worth the effort.

Site Selection

The first question to ask: can you grow fruit trees where you live? What can grow where is largely dictated by climate and weather. Some people use the two words interchangeably, but *climate* is the way the atmosphere behaves—the weather conditions over a long time period (30 years). Climate does change; for instance, in 2012, the US Department of

Agriculture (USDA) added 5°F to the low temperature readings for all of its climate zones. When we talk about *weather*, it's more about the specific conditions (rain, fog, temperatures, wind, and sun) over a short period of time: today, the 3- to 5-day forecast, seasonal forecasts.

CLIMATE

The USDA assigns each type of fruit a cold hardiness zone, which indicates where in the United States that fruit can be grown. These hardiness zones account for the average *low* temperatures for different areas. You can figure out what USDA hardiness zone you live in at http://planthardiness.ars.usda.gov/PHZMWeb/.

While USDA zones won't tell you all you need to know about the ability of a particular variety of fruit to thrive in your location, they will at least help you set the parameters for what you can grow in general.

Zone 5b
−15 to −10 F.

USDA HARDINESS ZONES	
APPLES	ZONES 3-9
PEARS, QUINCE, PEACHES, NECTARINES, APRICOTS, AND APRIUMS	ZONES 4-9
EUROPEAN PLUMS	ZONES 4-10
SWEET CHERRIES	ZONES 5-7
ASIAN PLUMS AND PLUOTS	ZONES 5-9
FIGS	ZONES 5-10
PERSIMMONS	ZONES 7-10
POMEGRANATES	ZONES 7-10 EASILY, ZONES 5-6 POSSIBLY
CITRUS	ZONES 8-10

Hardiness zones are pretty cut-and-dried: below X temperature, the tree will die. But heat is also a factor in a tree's growth. Heat triggers faster, greater growth and fruit development and high sugar content.

Although heat is desirable, too much can be harmful. A sustained series of days with temps higher than 92°F–95°F will be problematic. Particularly in mid- to late summer, a heat wave in excess of 4–5 days will cause the tree to need more water and also can cause heat stress, which makes trees more susceptible to pests. Too much sunlight can sunburn leaves, fruit, and branches. That doesn't mean you can't grow fruit trees; overall, the deleterious effects of heat are more subtle than those of cold. (One of the typical ways people deal with the problem of heat is to allow the tree to develop a thick canopy. This offers more shade for the fruit and branches and can minimize heat damage. Another trick of the trade is to sprinkle the trees with water overhead on mornings when it's expected to be hotter than the mid-90s. The resulting evaporative cooling effect can lower the tree canopy's temperature by 8°F–10°F.)

Wherever you live, you should find out what has been grown successfully in your area—recently, as well as historically. If something grows well in your neighborhood or county, you can likely make it grow well for you, too. The best way to understand what grows in any region is to talk to locals (home gardeners, orchardists, homesteaders). Walk around and look at what your neighbors are growing. Search online for nearby land grant universities, which have mandates to educate the public about agriculture. These are usually state universities, and most have Cooperative Extension Systems (CES) that put out excellent websites, workshops, or talks accessible to the public. As biologist Roger Payne wrote in his book *Among the Whales*: "Any observant local knows more than any visiting scientist. Always, no exceptions." When it comes to growing things, any well-informed, tuned-in local knows more, in a more nuanced manner, than most or even any so-called outside expert. As you ask around, don't forget that land values can affect crops, too. For example, an area that used to have apple orchards may now be full of vineyards, strawberries, or higher-dollar crops (or, perhaps, summer homes for the wealthy). But chances are, apples will still grow well there.

CHILL HOURS

To produce fruit, deciduous fruit trees need bountiful sunshine, but they also need sufficient cold weather. When a tree is dormant in wintertime, it requires a certain number of hours when the temperature is between

32°F and 45°F in order to enforce a period of rest, before the tree breaks dormancy and resumes growing in the spring. Orchardists call these chill hours. During dormancy, a tree will not resume growth until it has received its required chill hours. This adaptive strategy gives trees the ability to resist outside environmental cues to grow during warm winters or "false thaws," and to wait until favorable growth conditions occur in spring. It's important that the varieties you intend to grow match the chill hours in your area.

Chill requirements are more quickly and easily achieved with a continuous rather than alternating chill; temperatures greater than 60°F will undo some of the chill hours a tree has achieved.

Chill Hours in Different Regions

The chill needs of a deciduous tree usually reflect the climate of that fruit's origins. For example, apples are originally from Kazakhstan and Uzbekistan, plums came from northern Europe, and peaches, nectarines, and apricots hail from northwest China. Their required chill hours correspond to the climate of those regions. Pick varieties that have about the same chill hour requirements you are likely to get in your area. Choose wisely.

Generally, different growing regions have different predictable chill hours.

REGIONAL CHILL HOURS	
COASTAL NORTHWEST	1,000–1,500 HOURS
UPPER NORTHWEST INLAND	2,000–3,000 HOURS
NORTHERN CALIFORNIA	1,000–1,800 HOURS
COASTAL CENTRAL CALIFORNIA	500–900 HOURS
SOUTHERN CALIFORNIA, FLORIDA, AND THE GULF COAST STATES	100–200 HOURS (SOUTH FLORIDA, COASTAL LOUISIANA, AND TEXAS AS LOW AS ZERO HOURS)
ROCKIES	1,600–1,800 HOURS
SOUTHWEST	800–1,600 HOURS (EXCEPT LOWEST AREAS, WHICH HAVE FEWER)
MIDWEST AND GREAT PLAINS	1,000–1,400 HOURS
UPPER MIDWEST, NEW YORK, NEW ENGLAND	GREATER THAN 2,000 HOURS
MID-ATLANTIC STATES	1,000–1,500 HOURS
SOUTHEASTERN STATES	600–1,000 HOURS

Note that I said "predictable" chill hours. Who knows what the future holds? The Central Valley of California produces about 90 percent of the nation's deciduous fruits. If average temps in the Central Valley rise by 1°F–3°F, deciduous fruit tree production will become nearly impossible. As growers, we must constantly notice and adapt to the changing climate around us. Adapt or perish, as they say . . .

Similarly, different fruit species have different chill requirements. (Citrus are not categorized using chill hours, as they are a "tropical" fruit.) The chart that follows shows the general ranges for different species. In the next chapter, we'll get into the chill hour needs of individual varieties (see page 47).

FRUIT SPECIES CHILL REQUIREMENTS	
POMEGRANATES	100–150 HOURS
PERSIMMONS	100–200 HOURS
FIGS	100–300 HOURS
APPLES AND PEARS	100–2,200 HOURS
APRICOTS, APRIUMS, PEACHES, AND NECTARINES	200–1,100 HOURS
QUINCES	300–500 HOURS
ASIAN PLUMS AND PLUOTS	300–1,500 HOURS
SWEET CHERRIES	400–800 HOURS
EUROPEAN PLUMS	500–1,700 HOURS

To find your area's chill hours, consult your local authorities—neighbors, nursery workers, community garden members, etc.—or do a quick internet search—for example, sites like getchill.net allow you to search for your chill hours by zip code.

WEATHER

In addition to the macrolevel climate, you need to have an understanding of the minute weather patterns in your specific yard or piece of land. This is where you become your own best expert. Embark on a project of regularly observing your prospective site. I recommend setting up a small homemade weather station. It's easy and inexpensive, and it can be good nerdy fun. Go down to the hardware store and grab a high-low outdoor thermometer (about $40), a small rain gauge ($5 or so), a simple, cheap wind vane, and a blank journal or notebook. Observe and record what's happening.

Keep track of the high, low, and average temperatures in your orchard. This will help you understand your cold and heat parameters. Note how many hours of direct sunlight your site gets (see "Sunlight," page 18). Are there prevailing winds? Wind can be hard on plants. Exposed sites may need extra attention or even windbreaks—perhaps a hedge. Be aware of the date of your first and last frosts of the year, especially the last frost in springtime; these dates define your growing season. Frost during the bloom period (early spring for most deciduous

Take Back the Valleys for the Heart's Delight

Here's an interesting fact: before it was home to massive tech companies and feral venture capitalists, California's Silicon Valley was known as the more poetic Valley of the Heart's Delight. As such, it was the leading fruit-producing region *in the world* from the mid-1800s until the 1960s, known for its prunes, plums, apricots, and cherries. What changed between then and now?

Over the last 50 years, the number of chill hours in Silicon Valley, a.k.a. Santa Clara Valley, has decreased from 1,200 to 400. This radical reduction makes it virtually impossible to grow the varieties of fruit that formerly graced the valley landscape.

Such drastic change was brought about by an effect often referred to as urban heat islands. Previously, the open ground of the fields and orchards absorbed heat in the daytime and reradiated it back into the night sky, significantly cooling the air on the valley floor. But because the valley floor is now primarily made up of asphalt, cement, and building materials—and because of the geometry of tall structures and roads and the heat generated by vehicles and industrialization—heat is retained by all these things at a greater rate than, say, by trees. The climate of the valley has been substantively changed.

In his song "Ruby and Rosie," the folk musician Keith Greeninger (think Jackson Brown with snarl and attitude) tells this story in persuasive rhetoric with a more poetic twist. Greeninger and his musical partner Dayan Kai sing of the highways and buildings replacing orchards as the crops of Santa Clara Valley—but these new crops don't fruit. Somewhere beneath all this "progress," there's soil rich enough to feed the world.

When Apple, Inc's "spaceship" headquarters were constructed in Cupertino, one of my apprentice program grads was contracted to plant 600 apple trees in the "courtyard" (it's actually 6 acres). I was kidding him when I said 1) apples for Apple, eh? and 2) yeah, it's part of a new grassroots movement: occupy and take back the Valley—one small piece of ground at a time.

Then I got to thinking (always a dangerous proposition and generally frowned upon by higher-ups): why not? Start in the south, in Los Gatos, and work our way up the mid-Peninsula to Palo Alto and toward San Francisco. Knock on the corporate front doors of Facebook, Google, Amazon, Intel, Netflix, Hewlett-Packard, Agilent, Cisco, Oracle, Stanford Research Park, and the like, and propose/respectfully demand, that they, too, plow down their lawns and start organic orchards, with a community educational focus and a fruit share for community members in need. (You know how the old slogan goes—*from each according to their means, to each according to their needs.*)

Yeah, let's take back the valleys with fruit trees, this time with lower chill varieties. This would perhaps necessitate further changes in the landscape to swing the pendulum back in the direction of real life versus virtual reality, to seek a new equilibrium—a move away from dry, impermeable landscapes and a return to a terrain that was once moist and receptive. A place that, while paying tribute to the startling progressive gains of technology, still remembers and values (and benefits from) a community and culture rooted in the soil. It's a project not unlike that old activist sentiment from the 1970s—*"Terre primum! Terre primum! Earth first! Earth first!"* But in a slightly gentler manner, in the form of fruit orchards.

trees) will damage your blooms—no crop. And if you live in an area with late spring frosts, you'll want to stay away from varieties that bloom and ripen early in the season. At the fall end of the growing season, it's less of an iron curtain, but a significant frost can still injure fruit and get you in trouble.

Collecting and tracking this kind of weather data will help you lock in to where you live, in your own yard and beyond, and get in touch with it. This will allow you to figure out not only where to put your trees, but how best to tend them once they're planted.

SUNLIGHT

From the time they bloom through harvest, fruit trees require a *minimum* of 6–8 hours per day of full sunlight. Period. And 8–10 would be better. Why so much sunlight? No light, no photosynthesis.

Sunlight also generates heat, which is important during the bloom period and encourages insect activity and pollen viability (flow).

Go outside and look around. Pace about. Track the sun—morning, noon, and late in the day. Track it at the spring and fall equinoxes and at both summer and winter solstices. This will take time—a year. But fortunately in the age we inhabit, there are tools and aids to help you do this faster. Try websites like findmyshadow.com, suncalc.net, and sollumis.com. The University of Oregon has a cool sun chart feature on its Solar Radiation Monitoring Laboratory page. Or try the apps Sun Surveyor and Sun Seeker. All these kind folks will do the math for you and map the sun's path across your property.

Sun is life. Make sure your chosen site has enough.

THE LAY OF THE LAND

In analyzing the topography of the spot where you plan to grow, the two main considerations are flat ground versus sloping ground.

What is the key advantage of flat ground? Well, it's flat. That is, it's much easier to work. It is also less erosion prone. Often flat ground will have deeper, darker, more fertile soil, especially if it is at the base of a slope or is river bottomland (and it's potentially wind protected).

And the cons? Well, your area of flat ground could be a frost pocket, especially if it's on a valley floor. Cold air is heavier than warm air, and like water it drains downslope and accumulates at the bottom. Such topography is to be avoided. Frost during the bloom period will cause poor fruit set or even lead to being "frosted out"—no crop. Flat ground

"Photosynthesis is foundational, our only true wealth. Without it we devolve. Poor land leads to poverty, hunger, social unrest, cultural deprivation, inhumanity, and war. So we must wonder why the biological health of the planet is not our number one priority."

—GRETEL EHRLICH, from the introduction to *Cows Save the Planet* by Judith D. Schwartz, 2013

Photosynthesis

Plants are autotrophs (*auto* = "self," *troph* = "food"). They make their own food or fuel. And they do it via that old staple of biology classes throughout the ages: photosynthesis (*photo* = "light," *synthesis* = "putting together").

Photosynthesis is the most important reaction on the planet. It gives us first the food chain and then the food system, and its role in balancing carbon dioxide (CO_2) and oxygen (O_2) in the earth's atmosphere is essential to human survival. In our efforts as orchardists, most of what we do is done in support of photosynthesis, from site selection to pruning to fertilizing to watering.

Through photosynthesis, plants take sunlight energy and combine it with carbon dioxide from the atmosphere and hydrogen from the water molecules in the soil to make carbohydrates (mostly sugars, in the form of glucose). These carbohydrates are the building blocks for a plant's structure and function at every level. The glucose produced by photosynthesis also stores energy, which can be used to fuel growth and development immediately or stored as carbs for future use. Think of a tree's leaves as solar collectors. Sunlight equals fruit, so *fiat lux*!

Have you ever noticed how the air in a forest seems vital, fresh? It's not your imagination—the air is highly oxygenated. Trees take in carbon dioxide through tiny openings on the underside of the leaves, called stomata. Inside the leaves are structures called chloroplasts and a pigment called chlorophyll, which captures sunlight and its energy for photosynthesis (chlorophyll is also responsible for the "green" in leaves). Ironically, the tree regards oxygen as a waste product. It "kicks" it out, or exhales it back into the atmosphere. This is a good thing and it's lucky for us. It gives us the very air we breathe.

may also have drainage issues. As an old farmer once joked to me, this makes it great for growing hay; trees, not so much.

Sloping ground is your other option. With sloped sites, the slope and direction of the soil surface create a microclimate and subtle, even significant differences of soil and air temperatures. The direction of the slope is referred to as aspect.

A gentle south-facing slope (less than 4–8 degrees) is probably the most favorable of sites if you live in the Northern Hemisphere. (In the Southern Hemisphere, it is the reverse: north facing is favorable.) South-facing slopes, along with southeast- and southwest-facing slopes, offer a warmer microclimate and are less prone to frosts.

South-facing slopes allow cold air to drain downslope, and blossoms and fruit are more protected. South slopes warm more quickly in spring, are warmer in summer, and stay warmer longer in fall. And because they're slopes, they usually feature good soil drainage. Drawbacks of the south-facing slope include potential wind exposure and the possibility of thinner, nutrient-poor soil.

Slopes and Sunlight

SOUTH-FACING SLOPE
Concentrated heat; warmer air and soil temperatures

FLAT GROUND
Diffuse and dispersed rays; cooler air and soil temperatures

NORTH-FACING SLOPE
Coolest; potentially shorter growing season

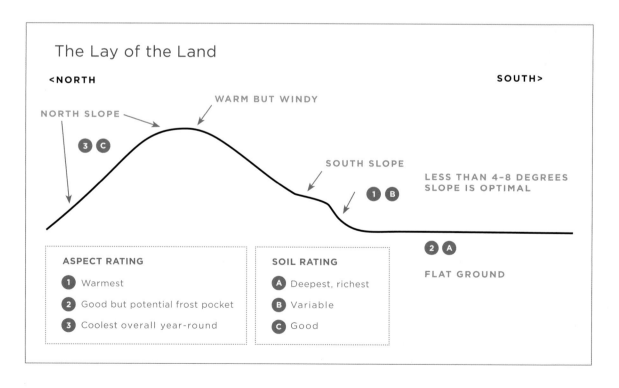

The Lay of the Land

<NORTH

SOUTH>

WARM BUT WINDY

NORTH SLOPE

3 **C**

SOUTH SLOPE

LESS THAN 4–8 DEGREES SLOPE IS OPTIMAL

1 **B**

2 **A**

FLAT GROUND

ASPECT RATING
1 Warmest
2 Good but potential frost pocket
3 Coolest overall year-round

SOIL RATING
A Deepest, richest
B Variable
C Good

A caveat about the legendarily good south-facing slopes: some say they are amiable; others call them sacred. Certainly they're advantageous. But in northern regions, the warmth of a south slope can force bloom too early, making flowers and fruit subject to potential early frost. Also be wary of windy conditions at the top of slopes. Wind is generally hard on plant growth. It increases evapotranspiration (water loss) from both the soil and the plant. Plants that are constantly buffeted by wind put more energy and reserves into creating thicker, more sturdy stems and leaves. They do this at the expense of vigorous shoot growth. So if you're bemoaning the lack of a south-facing slope on your land, don't be too taken aback. You can still grow fruit trees.

Southeast and southwest slopes offer similar heat advantages to south-facing slopes, but to a lesser degree. Southeast slopes offer both warmth and quicker recovery from nighttime frosts as well as quick-drying foliage after night rains and even dew. Quick drying of foliage minimizes leaf fungal diseases. Southwest slopes stay warmer longer into the day as well as longer into the fall.

North-facing slopes offer the coolest of all directional microclimates. The more oblique angle at which the sun strikes the ground causes the sun's rays to be spread over a greater area, and thus they don't transfer as much heat energy. Simply put, north slopes are cooler overall and delay the break from dormancy. This can be a good thing for some early-blooming varieties in areas that have late spring frosts and rains, as it will delay the bloom until after the damaging weather events. The soil on north slopes can be deeper, often has higher organic matter percentage than on south slopes, and retains soil moisture longer. A north slope may be a boon in extremely hot summer areas, as sites *can* have too much heat (maybe not too much sun, but too much heat). If you're planting on a north slope, you'll have a shorter growing season. But it's doable.

ASSESSING YOUR SOIL

Although we tend to take it for granted, human society is principally possible only because the earth's crust is dusted with a thin and often fragile layer of life-supporting material on which we can grow food: the soil. Soil is often thought of as an inert substrate, useful in propping up plants and a mere vehicle for applied fertilizer and water. But soil is a distinct ecosystem—a system formed by the interactions between a community of organisms and their physical environment. If soil is the portal to growing, *good* soil is the portal to good growing.

Microclimates

Different slopes, corners, or areas of your property might have different climate advantages. One early pomologist who knew this was "founding farmer" Thomas Jefferson, who was an astute and persistent observer and recorder of the natural world around him. Much of the horticulture done at Monticello was truly groundbreaking for its time and locale. Jefferson and his orchardists—a staff made up of slaves, paid European immigrants, and Jefferson's family members—made innovative use of Monticello's microclimates.

Jefferson watched his site as you would do well to observe yours prior to planting. He kept a natural history–like journal with entries about the weather: daily high and low temperatures, dates of first and last frost, their severity and duration, prevailing winds, and more. As a result, his orchards enjoyed much greater success than those of his neighboring landowners in the rich bottomland soils.

Although situated in Charlottesville, Virginia (within USDA zone 7A), Jefferson's southeast exposure at an 800-foot elevation created a distinctive microclimate, one that was the equivalent of that of northern Florida (USDA zones 9 and 10) several hundred miles to the south.

His microclimate produced a situation bordering on Mediterranean! It allowed him to grow figs, almonds, pomegranates, apricots, and even peaches, which are notoriously frost susceptible, as they bloom early in the season. In fact, the slope of Jefferson's "fruitery" was a bit too warm for the species—apples, pears, gooseberries, and currants—that require a little more winter chill. This explains his siting of those species at another site, a north-facing slope dubbed the North Orchard. By making creative use of the different microclimates available, the crews at Monticello were able to extend the warmth of the growing season by two months and to dodge damaging frosts.

Horticulturalists often wax rhapsodic about Monticello, and with good reason. But in acknowledging Jefferson's horticultural legacy, it's important to also acknowledge that his "ethic" of farming was one that included forced labor. As actor and musician Daveed Diggs, who portrayed Jefferson in the Tony Award–winning Broadway musical *Hamilton*, told *Time* magazine, "I think if you embrace all of [Jefferson's] contradictions, you can end up with a lot of things about him that are great—but you still have to remember that he was a slave owner."

As part of assessing a potential site for your trees, it is critical to assess your soil and make plans to improve it. Many tree species will live longer than 75–100 years, and you only have one shot at prepping the soil they'll live in. Studies show it is two to three times more expensive to farm poor soil compared to fertile soil. For every 0.5 percent rise in the soil's organic matter content, there are approximately 15–20 percent more nutrients present and available to the tree. Select a spot with decent soil, or allow yourself enough lead time to improve it. Ideally, you will need 3–5 feet of good topsoil, although 2–3 feet with a rigorous soil improvement program should suffice.

There are two ways to understand your soil: a quantitative assessment and a qualitative one. Do both.

Quantitative Soil Assessment

Take a soil sample and get a lab analysis. I like A&L soil labs (see Resources, page 266), but any lab will accept mail samples and provide instructions for collecting and mailing them. Get a complete analysis. It costs $35–$40 and is well worth the expense. Tell the lab that you are growing organically and state what crop you are growing, and ask them to include nutrient recommendations in their report.

The lab will send you a report that tells you what texture of soil you have (clay, sand, silt) and analyzes your soil's nutrient levels (nitrogen, phosphorous, potassium, etc.). This is why I recommend sufficient lead time before you plant: for soil to be ideally fertile, each nutrient needs to be up to a certain threshold, which varies by nutrient.

There is no alchemy in soil science; you can't make somethin' from nothin'. If even a single nutrient is below a certain threshold, plants will not grow optimally. If your lab report says a nutrient is not up to threshold, you must apply that nutrient via fertilizers or organic matter. A good lab will give you specific amounts of specific amendments you should apply to your soil to correct deficiencies, for instance, "apply rock phosphate at a rate of 3 pounds per 150 square feet." Once you have added the recommended amendments, you should do another soil test the following year to see if your adjustments were adequate and retest periodically thereafter.

On subsequent soil tests, some signs that your soil is improving might include:

- Organic matter percent is steady or rising over time.

- Estimated nitrogen release (ENR) is greater than 70–80 pounds per acre and/or rising over time. ENR is a scientific guesstimate based on the percent of organic matter. It predicts how much nitrogen will become available to the plant in a growing season.

- A low bulk density reading, preferably between 0.8 and 1.4. Bulk density is a measurement of the weight of a volume of soil, solids and pore space included. If your cultivation practices are good, you have a well-aggregated soil with good structure. Such a soil will have a lot of pore space and thus be lighter and give you a lower bulk density reading. A soil with plentiful pore space will hold more air and water and be easier for roots to penetrate as they forage for water and nutrients.

In chapter V, How You Grow a Tree, you'll learn more about the building blocks of your soil and how to improve it through the use of double digging techniques, cover crops, green manure, and compost.

Qualitative Soil Assessment

This simple process is largely visual and tactile. Look at your soil and feel it. This skill will help you learn to develop and manage your soil's fertility in the long term.

Generally speaking, an ideal soil for fruit trees is one that is open, friable (loose and crumbly—you could say you want a "crumb-y" soil), and well drained to a depth of 3 feet. Such a soil should also be well supplied with both organic matter and nutrients at depth.

The word *tilth*, a composite of several soil science terms, is generally used to describe the physical characteristics of soil: structure, permeability, consistency, drainage, aeration, and water-holding capacity. But as growers we also define tilth as the workability of a soil. Basically, it's this: When you grab a handful of soil, does it have good structure? Is it crumbly but not too sticky? Structure largely depends on soil type, but in general you want a soil that you can ball up, but still has porous spaces that air and water can move through. Next, check for evidence of soil life, such as earthworms, sowbugs, millipedes, centipedes, mycelial strands (webby, rootlike evidence of beneficial fungi). These are all desirable critters, and they contribute to your soil's fertility. Smell the soil—does it have that rich, "earthy" aroma? If so, it is probably chock-full of beneficial organisms. That earthy aroma is the by-product of actinomycetes, otherwise known as good bacteria.

Look at the visual elements of your soil. What color is the soil surface? Darker soils indicate higher organic matter content with associated nutrients, which is what you're going for. Are there already plants growing in the soil? Do they look healthy? Does your soil have a crusty surface versus open (or permeable) surface? Open surface soils are preferred, as they allow entry of water and air exchange between the atmosphere and the soil. This is vital. A crusted surface soil will puddle and be prone to erosion. Is the soil compressed and compacted, either on the surface or at depth? If it is, you'll have hardpan (a stiff layer of difficult-to-penetrate soil) and will need to

Determining Soil Texture

Your lab test will reveal your soil's texture. You can also do a simple field/feel test called ribboning. Grab a handful of soil, get it really wet, and form it into a ball. Then try to make a ribbon by pushing out the soil between a thumb and forefinger, so it's shaped a bit like a cigar. If the ribbon is longer than 2 inches, it's a clay. Anything less than that is silt or sand. To determine which, rub a pinch of soil between your thumb and forefinger. If you feel grit, it's sand. If it feels silky smooth and talc-like, it's silt. Other signs of a clay soil are a sticky, tacky texture that will stain your palm.

Sandy soils usually have low nutrient- and water-holding capacity, and accordingly they have a lower organic matter content. On the plus side, sandy soils drain well, warm quickly, and allow early cultivation and planting in the spring. Clay soils are the opposite: they hold high levels of nutrients and water, but are often difficult to work. *Loamy* refers to a soil that has approximately equal amounts of sand, silt, and clay—the result being a very good soil.

If you have an extreme soil texture—a "sieve-y" sand or adobe clay—be of good cheer, for as Alan Chadwick once said, "All soils are beautiful." I've amended that statement: "*however*, at the present time some soils are more beautiful than others." Any soil can be radically improved by the addition of organic matter and skilled, timely digging or plowing.

---

cultivate deeply. Compaction restricts root growth as well as reducing pore space, which is vital in supplying oxygen to plant roots and soil microbes and improving drainage.

A lot of what you're doing by asking all these questions is simply learning to tap into your own common sense: *Does this dirt seem like something plants would readily grow in?* Your answer is probably in the general vicinity of correct.

You also need to learn how your soil drains. Do a simple percolation test by digging a hole the size of a 1-gallon container when the soil is moist, but not wet. (If necessary, water the soil and let it dry out for a day or two before digging.) Fill the hole with water, let it drain, then fill it again. It should drain, ideally, in 3–4 hours, but at least within 8–10 hours. You don't want your soil to hold water like a puddle—trees don't like wet feet—nor do you want the soil to drain out too quickly.

You might consider digging a soil profile to see what's going on beneath the surface. A pit about 2–3 feet deep and 2–3 feet wide will allow you to view the soil layers, top to bottom. Go ahead, stand in it. From that vantage point, you can evaluate the visual elements of the soil as you did with your handful.

PLANNING YOUR SOIL IMPROVEMENT REGIMEN

Use what you learn from your quantitative and qualitative soil assessment to begin a soil improvement program. Again, I recommend doing this *before* you plant. But even if you've already planted, you can still vastly improve the soil around and between your trees with a rigorous soil improvement routine.

As you'll read in chapter V, How You Grow a Tree, the act of improving your soil is at the core of what organic gardeners do. It can be a lifelong process, if we're lucky. And it is deeply satisfying to look at your soil after a few years and be able to see a difference in its quality, color, and fertility. (Your fruit trees will like it, too.)

If you are just beginning to grow, a good 1- to 3-year soil building program should include but not be limited to the following:

- Deep or double digging a bed before planting your tree and/or deep digging the beds or areas around your tree after it is planted (see page 134).

- Adding a legume and grass cover crop that is turned back into the soil as a green manure. It is possible to do this three to five times in one calendar year, as needed (see page 144).

- Liberally applying compost with each digging of the soil (see page 138).

- Adding mineral fertilizers to correct nutrient deficiencies discovered in your soil test (see page 152).

What combination you do is up to you—it depends on the state of your soil, your patience, your desire for thriving and productive trees, and your time, labor, and budgetary capabilities. Even with the most wretched of dirts, 2–3 years of intensive soil building using a combination of the above techniques will catapult soil fertility and structure forward and yield a plantable, fruit-worthy soil.

WHEN THE SITE PICKS YOU

As a home grower, you often may find that the site selects you and not the other way around. Although your options may be limited, you must put a premium on sunlight. Your trees need to be sited far enough away from the house or other buildings to receive the requisite 6–8 hours of sunlight per day.

The Top Foot

The upper 2 feet of soil typically contains more than 50 percent of the available water and nutrients that plants use to feed themselves. Much of that 50 percent is in the top foot. Additionally, a high percentage of the beneficial microbes in the soil are in the top foot, with up to 80 percent of them in the top 6–8 inches. This is principally because it's warm, moist, and well oxygenated. A high percentage of a fruit tree's roots are also in the top 1–2 feet. This is true regardless of tree size. Most of a fruit tree's effective roots are shallow: 12–18 inches deep. The old mystical adage, *as above, so below,* may be indicative of the grand nature of the universe, but it is patently false when applied to tree roots; the fruit tree's canopy has a much greater volume than its root system. To zoom in even closer, the rhizosphere is a very small zone right around the feeding root tips of a tree. This is where all the action—biochemically—is. So while the total volume of your soil is vast and not unimportant, you should be very focused on the upper regions of that subterranean landscape, especially for the purposes of tillage, fertilizing, and watering. By cultivating and nurturing this zone, you can radically improve the physical, chemical, and biological properties of your soil.

Additionally, try to site your tree in a spot where you will go daily. Proximity leads to prosperity. If you see your trees daily, you can keep an eye on them and give them optimum, well-timed care. What's that old phrase—out of sight, out of mind? Don't let that be you.

Contemplate the pleasure of siting, thus seeing, your trees where they can be viewed through the lens of your life, out the window. This allows you to witness seasonality and its subtle but sometimes dramatic changes, through the growth of your trees. Think of the sun creeping across your yard, slowly illuminating the trees each and every day. The early morning's light imparts a subtle but almost glowing hue to the trees as you fix a cuppa. Then at day's end, perhaps while enjoying an adult beverage, with the soundtrack of your choice in the background, there's the effect of the fleeting, fading glimmer of sundown and long shadows . . . the gloaming.

This is the landscape of your life. In the end, what to grow and where to site it are a function of multiple hard-and-fast criteria. But maybe Wendell Berry says it best, in the aggregate: "What will nature allow us to grow here? What will nature help us to do?"

Planning and Layout

Once you've decided on your site, determine the size of your planting. Many online tree nurseries have spacing charts that assist in calculating the number of trees per area, based on the spacing of trees in a row and the distance between rows. Adams County Nursery in Pennsylvania has a great one (see Resources, page 266). For vigorous species like Asian plums, apricots, and cherries, whatever the rootstock, a good 10–12 feet between trees is recommended, maybe even 15 feet. For apples, pears, peaches, and European plums on semidwarf rootstocks, 8- to 10-foot spacing can work. Alley width—the spacing between rows of trees—depends on what needs to get up and down the alleys. If a vehicle is involved, the alley should be slightly wider than the wheelbase. For pedestrian access, 6–8 feet should do the trick.

If you have a row of trees (three or more), try to orient rows so that they run north-south for better, more even sun exposure. If slope and erosion are of concern, run tree rows cross slope (rather than up and down).

Only have room for one or two trees? That's great. Only plant one or two, but make sure to read about pollination (see page 43). Have half an acre? That's a nice little orchard you've got there.

If you are lucky enough to be planting a larger orchard, you can figure out the number of trees per acre by multiplying the distance between trees in a row by the distance between rows. Divide that number into 43,560 (43,560 square feet equals 1 acre). For example, say you have an acre. The distance between trees in each row is 10 feet, the distance between rows is also 10 feet, and 10 times 10 equals 100. Divide 43,560 (an acre) by 100 and you get 435.6 trees. Round down.

While the specific architecture of your garden is entirely up to you, there are a few things you can do to ensure your fruit trees grow vigorously and productively. When "designing" your trees, you should think about size manageability and order accordingly. One way to help out the pollinating insects that will be assisting your trees in making fruit is to plant in rows and/or in a rectilinear or square grid pattern. This draws more pollinators to a small area. If you live in an area with deer, you'll need a fence high enough that deer can't jump it. And you'll need to set up your irrigation method of choice.

Irrigation Systems

Water is essential to the life of plants, the orchard, and the earth. Being a good water manager is an important skill, and setting yourself up for a good management system is a smart thing to do ahead of time. If you want an irrigation system, it pays to plan before you plant.

There are several options—overhead systems, drip systems, and good old-fashioned hand watering. You might already have one of these in your garden. Each has possibilities and constraints (which would make a great name for a garage band—Possibility and The Constraints).

OVERHEAD WATERING

The term *overhead watering* refers to watering a tree by spraying it with a sprinkler from above or, in the case of micro sprinklers, from beside or below. Overhead watering wets a wide area, which encourages roots to expand and encourages beneficial soil microbe populations. It also cleans dust and dirt off leaves, enabling photosynthesis, and exerts a cooling effect on hot days. The downside of overhead watering systems is that even under ideal conditions, with the exception of micro sprinklers (see facing page), only 80 percent of the water emitted in overhead watering ever gets in the soil; the rest is lost to evaporation and blow-off from the wind. When trees are in bloom, overhead irrigation can cause both leaf and fruit fungal diseases. And these systems need high water pressure—greater than 40 pounds psi. To get around these constraints, water in the cooler parts of the day (early or late), when there is little or no wind, as this radically increases efficiency. Due to concern about disease, I avoid overhead watering early in the season from bud break through flowering and early fruit set, but I will give the trees an overhead watering several times in mid- to late summer simply to clean off the leaves.

Oscillators

Oscillators are sprinkler systems that feature durable gear-driven overhead sprinklers capable of rotating on a 180-degree adjustable arc, with a coverage range from approximately 10 by 40 feet to 25 by 60 feet. The small water droplets that oscillators emit are conducive to easy soil infiltration and minimize puddling, crusting, and runoff. Of the many brands of oscillators, give me the best—on a home garden scale, Gardena is the one. This German company has been making and distributing garden oscillators for three decades. It's an accurate and durable product.

High-Impact Sprinklers

These are commonly referred to as "Rain Bird" sprinklers, which is the leading brand (and an excellent one at that). High-impact sprinklers feature rotating sprinkler heads mounted on risers (small-diameter piping from 6–18 inches tall) that rotate and cover a large area in a circular pattern. Like oscillators, they apply a very fine droplet at a low rate (0.5–2.0 gallons per hour hour). While this minimizes puddling and run off, the droplets can be blown off target or evaporate in air with windy conditions.

Micro Sprinklers

Micro sprinklers are just that—small sprinklers mounted on 6- to 8-inch spikes. They provide a nice intermediate solution to some of the above issues with overhead systems. Because water is projected close to the ground, almost 100 percent of the water applied is delivered to the root system. The application pattern is wide and even, and, unless it

Irrigation system with micro sprinklers

is windy, on target. And there is a good application rate to infiltration rate, meaning there's no surface puddling. However, with micro systems, spray is easily blown off target when winds are greater than 7–10 miles per hour. (This problem is not insolvable—water when it's not windy.) On the negative side, the emitters and spikes are fairly expensive and easily damaged when working among the trees in the summer, when you tend to be looking up and then feel the disconcerting crunch of boot on plastic. After much trial and error, I am in love with a micro sprinkler called the AquaMaster 2005 made by NaanDanJain.

DRIP TAPE AND IN-LINE DRIP SYSTEMS

Water can also be applied by dripping, rather than spraying. Drip tape and in-line drip systems consist of a main line with emitters that allow the water to slowly drip into and onto the soil at the base of the tree. Drip systems offer probably the most efficient way to irrigate, as the water is delivered directly with little chance of blow-off. These systems are also well suited to low-water-pressure situations, even down to 3–5 pounds psi. However, drip systems can be tricky because it's hard to spot leaks. If you miss a leak, you're not watering evenly around a tree, potentially restricting the full development of the root system.

Drip Tape Systems

A drip tape (commonly called T-Tape after the leading brand) is a piece of flat plastic tubing that has emitter holes spaced in increments throughout the tubing (usually at 4, 6, 8, or 12 inches apart—any of those works well). The water drips out of the holes and directly into or onto the soil. Drip tape systems are efficient (100 percent when slightly buried) and cheap.

In-line Drip systems

In-line drip systems consist of $\frac{1}{2}$-inch poly tubing that has internal no-clog drip emitters. The tubing can be connected to a threaded swivel connector and then screwed into a hose. In-line drip emitters are designed to be nonclogging and have pressure compensation for slopes. My preferred brand is the Netafim Techline CV with 12-inch spacing. Even with particulate well water, it never clogs, and the $\frac{1}{2}$-inch poly tubing resists UV-ray deterioration.

HAND WATERING

Hand watering with a garden hose is effective if you have one to a few young or small trees. It has the added dividend of being contemplative and meditative. However, hand watering can be time and labor consumptive, and the method is susceptible to human error and inconsistency. You can only hand water effectively for young trees, 1–2 years of age. For hand watering to be successful, make sure you are wetting the entire root zone. Try to avoid wetting the leaves, although every now and then an occasional shower to wash off dust can be useful. My preferred brand of hose is the ½-inch-diameter Gilmour Heavy Duty Flexogen. With it, you can use any generic cheap watering wand.

Generally, I check soil moisture every 5–7 days and water as needed once a week. For information on assessing your soil moisture, see "Watering," page 156.

Once you've planned your site and started prepping your soil, the fun really starts: it's time to pick which fruit trees to plant. You'll need to decide what rootstocks you want your tree on, pick your varieties, and make sure they have access to sufficient pollination.

II

Selecting Pome and Stone Fruit Trees

Choosing Rootstocks and Scions

The managed, temperate-zone, deciduous fruit tree is composed of two genetically distinct parts that are fused together: the *scion* and the *rootstock*, collectively referred to as the stion. You won't get the same variety of apple tree by planting a seed from an apple and growing it; apples don't reproduce true to type. Instead, you buy a young or bare root tree, which consists of a scion that has been grafted onto a rootstock. Different species of fruit (apple, pear, plum, peach) have a number of rootstocks to which scions can be grafted or budded.

The scion and the rootstock are the two most important choices you'll make about your new tree. To make that choice, it helps to understand where they come from and what genetic qualities or characteristics they impart to the tree.

SCION BASICS

The scion refers to the fruit-bearing or top portion of the tree. You may also hear a scion referred to as a *variety* or *cultivar* (short for cultivated variety): the scion Fuji apple; the variety Fuji; the cultivar Fuji. They're all the same apple.

The scion you choose is all-important in that it determines the fruit variety and its characteristics: flavor, aroma, texture (coarse, crisp, or melting flesh), ability to keep (both on and off the tree), uses (fresh, juice, cooking), season of ripening, and disease and pest resistance or susceptibility. The scion also determines a tree's growth habits—upright versus spreading, weak or strong growth, whether the tree is a lateral bearer of fruit or a stem bearer, if it has strong or brittle wood—and it is a secondary contributor to tree height. (Rootstock is the principal determinant.)

In addition, the scion determines flowering and fruit patterns: light, heavy, annual, or biennial. And several independent genetic scion characteristics influence the size and shape of a tree.

Fruit tree scions generally come into existence as chance or volunteer seedlings; through breeding programs; or by chance mutations, often referred to in the trade as bud sports. Once a scion's characteristics have been noted by breeders, it is then cloned or reproduced asexually by budding or grafting. That's how clones are created and designated, for instance, the Fuji apple clone. Cloning ensures genetic (and performance) uniformity and reliability. So, while there are literally millions of Fuji apple trees worldwide, there is really only one Fuji tree, genetically. This is good for reliable production, but perilous if disease or pest problems enter the clone, as there is little or no resistance due to a limited gene pool. The Irish potato famines of the 1840s are a graphic example of overreliance on a limited gene pool for a staple food crop.

Many scions are the result of conscious breeding programs, often at university or agricultural experiment stations, such as Cornell University's station in New York and the PRI collaborative program between Purdue, Rutgers, and Illinois universities that has bred disease-resistant and -immune apple varieties for more than 50 years. (Fun fact: PRI varieties usually have the letters PRI consecutively in the name, for example, William's Pride, Prima, Pristine, and Enterprise.) It can take up to 30 years to breed and successfully introduce a new variety of fruit. A fruit tree breeder might spend his or her life in the profession and never have a successful introduction. The process includes raising and discarding tens of thousands of seedlings to assess their performance, pest and disease resistance, fruit quality, and storage capability, among other factors. Then there are decades of grower and consumer trials.

For example, the omnipresent Fuji apple was bred in 1930 but not named and released to the public until 1962. Fuji is a cross between Ralls Janet (an old Virginian apple preferred by Thomas Jefferson) and Red Delicious. It is one of many releases that originally stemmed from an ambitious Japanese apple breeding program launched in the early 1900s. One of the most notable of these releases was Mutsu (also known as Crispin), which was raised in 1930 and released in 1948 but took until the 1970s to catch on with Western consumers. I often refer to varieties with Mutsu genes in their parentage as "sisters of Mutsu," for example, Kinsei, Sayaka, Tsugaru, Shizuka, and Orin (a sweet but late-maturing Mutsu, a fact that my wife, Stephanie, doesn't dispute).

Many excellent varieties also occur as chance seedlings in the wild or in the field. One such volunteer is Hudson's Golden Gem, arguably the biggest and most sugary of the rough, dull-skinned, russeted apple types. Hudson's Golden Gem is a found seedling, discovered in the 1920s in a fencerow near Hudson's Wholesale Nursery in Tangent, Oregon. It is thought to be an open-pollinated seedling of Golden Delicious. And Golden Delicious itself is probably a chance seedling

cross from Grimes Golden and an old (circa 1600s) European apple, Golden Reinette. It sprouted on a farm owned by Anderson Mullins of Clay County, West Virginia, in the 1890s. In 1914, he sold the tree to Stark Brothers Nursery of Missouri. The Stark Brothers cloned it and named it Golden Delicious (resembling Red Delicious in shape but, thankfully, not in taste or genetics). Golden Delicious has gone on to become the second-leading commercial apple in the United States (after Red Delicious) and enjoys a loyal following in central and northern Europe.

Unfortunately, there are no reliable compendia of information describing scion characteristics. Ferreting out such important information involves trial and error; reading between the lines in fruit tree catalogs (for instance, "Galas have long, arching branches" equals vigor!); and chatting up your local orchardist or hobbyist fruit grower. In the section "Varietal Recommendations: Pome Fruits," page 50, I'll introduce you to some of my particular favorites.

ROOTSTOCK BASICS

Rootstock choice is probably the most critical and dominant factor in the type of fruit tree you'll end up with, as it influences both tree size and the ratio of tree canopy to fruit.

Rootstock describes the lower, or basal, portion of the tree—it's made up of the root system and the trunk below the graft or bud union. As with scions, rootstocks result from naturally occurring seedlings, chance mutations, or conscious breeding programs and are reproduced asexually by cloning.

A classic example of a naturally occurring rootstock from antiquity: Around 400 BCE, Alexander the Great sent back to Macedonia a rootstock found in Persia (now Iran). This apple rootstock was naturally very dwarfing, productive, self-rooting, and thus easy to maintain and propagate. It came to be known as the "Paradise" rootstock, and some of its genes have been bred into modern-day dwarfing rootstocks.

The rootstock is all-important in tree choice because it controls tree size. It also controls the roots or root system, transport and partitioning of resources, yield efficiency, precocity, and longevity of the tree. Different rootstocks can have different adaptations for soil types, soil pests and diseases, or cold.

I recommend growing only dwarfing or semidwarfing rootstocks. Your back and neck will thank you for it later.

DWARFING ROOTSTOCKS

If your image of an orchard includes a tire swing and a picking ladder, you may be surprised to find that rootstock breeding efforts have trimmed fruit trees down to a more manageable size. A relatively new trend in the United States, the "pedestrian orchard" full of compact trees with extremely dwarfing rootstocks, where all work can be done without ladders, has been popular with commercial orchardists in Europe for decades. Similarly, dwarf trees enable home gardeners to plant a small orchard in almost any yard. Dwarfing rootstocks limit overall tree size—to 6–12 feet tall—by reducing shoot growth in the scion. (Note that the term *dwarf* also refers to semidwarf trees.)

Trees on dwarfing rootstocks actually have a higher production efficiency than tall trees and come into bearing much earlier in life. Much like Mozart was a precocious lad and wrote symphonies while still a child, dwarf trees begin producing fruit at the age of 3–5 years compared to the 8–10 (or more) years a standard-size tree requires. The more dwarfing the rootstock, the earlier in life the tree enters its fruiting phase. And because trees on dwarfing rootstock can be spaced closer together, they produce more fruit than bigger trees on a per-area basis.

Dwarf rootstocks also have an effect on how the tree takes up nutrients and distributes them. A tree's roots are its winter storage sites for carbohydrates, which are then shuttled to leaves, flowers, fruits, and shoots. Dwarf rootstocks manufacture and store fewer carbohydrates. Their roots are narrower in diameter and hence are less efficient at taking up and transporting water and nutrients to the top part of the tree during the growing season. And the roots tend to be brittle, constantly breaking off at the feeding tips, which limits their ability to explore and forage for nutrients and water. With dwarf rootstocks, fewer of the chemical messages that promote vegetative growth and vigor are manufactured and transported to and from the tree's "antipodes." The tree gets the message: *Grow less rampantly, fruit earlier in life and abundantly as life goes on, and, oh yeah, exhaust your reserves and live less long.* Granted, this statement is both reductive and anthropomorphic, but it is nonetheless graphic and true.

The practice of using dwarfing rootstocks dates back to the Greeks of the third century BCE, and even earlier on the eastern rim of the Mediterranean basin. In northern Europe (principally France), dwarf deciduous fruit growing was a refined art by the sixteenth century. English horticultural writings of the nineteenth century reveal interest in dwarfing rootstocks by both amateurs and commercial growers throughout Europe. As you get into growing fruit trees, you'll begin to see that much of the theory (and some of the plant material) used in modern intensive orcharding has its roots in antiquity. *Vive la histoire!*

APPLE ROOTSTOCKS

ROOTSTOCK	TREE HEIGHT	DESCRIPTION
SEMIDWARFING ROOTSTOCKS		
MM111	15–20 feet	Adapted to a variety of soil conditions; tolerates drought. Rootstock has fibrous roots—produces a heavy-bearing, well-anchored tree. Excellent for spur-type cultivars.
MM106	14–18 feet	Adapted to a wide range of soil temperatures. Should not be planted on poorly drained soils.
M7	11–16 feet	One of the most popular rootstocks. Exceptional winter hardiness; performs best on deep, fertile, well-drained soils that retain constant moisture. Susceptible to woolly apple aphid; moderately resistant to fire blight. May lean with heavy crops on windy sites—it's advisable on such sites to support lower trunk to a height of 3 feet in early years.
DWARFING ROOTSTOCKS		
M26	8–14 feet	Roots well and is better anchored than M9, though still needs support. Very productive and early bearing. Recommended for use on all but badly drained soils. Rather shallow rooted; pay careful attention to irrigation management. Subject to burr knots.
M9	8–12 feet	Very precocious with high yield efficiency; susceptible to fire blight and woolly apple aphid. Most extensively planted rootstock worldwide.
Bud 9 or B9	5–8 feet	Extremely dwarfing rootstock bred when Russia was the Soviet Union. Both Russian and Polish breeding focus on cold hardiness and small trees, one goal being to breed trees shorter than the average annual snowpack (snow is a huge insulating blanket), and so it goes with B9. Photos of "Siberian creeper orchards" show people bending down to harvest. Precocious; heavy crop for its dwarf size.
G935	6–8 feet	From Cornell University's station in New York, somewhat new on the commercial scene. A little more dwarf than M7 and very fire blight resistant. Way more cold hardy than M7. More productive than M6 and M9.
G30	6–8 feet	Tried and true. Shorter M7 type that is much more cold tolerant and resistant to fire blight and collar rot. High yield efficiency.
Mark	8–10 feet	Very precocious with high yield efficiency. Trees on Mark require support to produce full-canopied tree. Extremely hardy; tolerates numerous soil types. More resistant to fire blight than M26. Heavy bearing in early years stunts tree—thin fruit to avoid this.
EXTREMELY DWARFING ROOTSTOCKS		
M27	4–6 feet	Very precocious with high yield efficiency. Requires support. Less susceptible to fire blight than M9 and M26. Well suited for growing in container or small yard. Thin or remove fruit first year or two to encourage growth. Very exacting—requires frequent inputs of water and nutrients because of restricted root system.

PEAR ROOTSTOCKS

There are no effective, truly dwarfing rootstocks for pears.

ROOTSTOCKS	TREE HEIGHT	DESCRIPTION
Winter Nelis, Betulaefolia, Calleryana, Bartlett Seedling	25–40 feet	Don't even think about it. These are monstrous trees that can take 5–8 years to even begin fruiting.
Old Home x Farmingdale 333 (OHxF 333) and Old Home x Farmingdale 513 (OHxF 513)	10–18 feet	About as semidwarf as pears get. Resists woolly apple aphid. Resists collar rot, pear decline. Tolerates wet, heavy soils. Farmingdale 333 and 513 perform similarly, but 513 is slightly more precocious.
Pyrodwarf series	6–15 feet	Reportedly keeps pears at 6–10 feet, although my experience with it is 10–15 feet. This rootstock does not promote heavy fruit set and is somewhat susceptible to fire blight. It is weak rooted and intolerant of water fluctuations. Plus, it's almost impossible to find. But other than that, it's great.

STONE FRUIT ROOTSTOCKS

Compared to pome fruits, rootstock options are more limited.
There are no truly dwarf stocks—the only choices are full size and semidwarf.

ROOTSTOCK	TREE HEIGHT	DESCRIPTION
Lovell	Greater than 15–20 feet	Seedling rootstock compatible with all peaches, plums, and some almonds and apricots. Susceptible to root knot and root lesions, also to oak root fungus, crown rot, and bacterial canker. Good drainage; tolerates wet soils better than other peach stocks.
Nemaguard	Greater than 15–20 feet	Compatible with peaches, plums, and some nectarines. Resistant to root knot but not root lesion nematodes. Susceptible to oak root fungus, crown rot, and bacterial canker. Avoid wet soils; likes well-drained loams.
Citation	10–15 feet	Semidwarf; compatible with peaches, nectarines, plums, apricots, pluots, and apriums. Resists root knot nematodes. Susceptible to oak root fungus, crown rot, and bacterial canker. High tolerance for wet soils; not drought tolerant. Warning: Peaches and Citation have a delayed incompatibility. Tree grows and fruits quite well for 5–6 years, then takes a nosedive.
Marianna 2624	10–15 feet	Plum rootstock that can be used for some almonds and apricots, but not peaches and nectarines. Pest susceptibility unknown. Moderately resistant to oak root fungus and crown rot. Susceptible to bacterial canker. Does very well in wet soils and tolerates a variety of soil types, including heavy soils.
Krymsk1	8–12 feet	Semidwarf, a plum stock. Imparts precocity to peaches, nectarines, plums, and apricots. Pest and disease susceptibility unknown. Grows well in heavy soils with drainage issues.
NEW ROOT-1	8–12 feet	Best dwarfing rootstock for sweet cherries to date. Floyd Zaiger introduction. Good in clay soils. Early bearing.

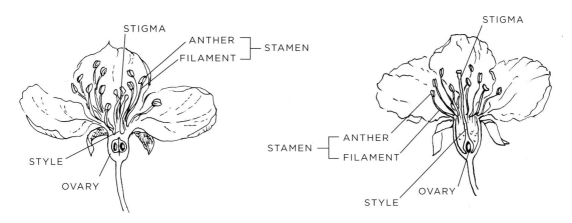

Apple

STIGMA
ANTHER ⎤
FILAMENT ⎦ STAMEN
STYLE
OVARY

Apricot

STIGMA
STAMEN ⎡ ANTHER
⎣ FILAMENT
STYLE OVARY

Pollination

For your tree to successfully fruit, you must be aware of whether the varieties you've chosen are self-pollinating or cross-pollinating.

Self-pollinating fruit trees, also called self-fruitful, include apricots, apriums, peaches, nectarines, quinces, pomegranates, figs, and persimmons. Self-pollinating trees can accept the transfer of pollen from the flower's anthers to the flower's stigma of the *same variety* of fruit, whether on the same tree or another tree of the same variety. Because they can accept their own pollen, you need only plant one tree of each of these fruits. When it comes to pollination, these fruits are low maintenance; you're good to go.

But many fruit trees are cross-pollinating (also called self-unfruitful), including apples, pears, plums, and pluots. This means that to pollinate and produce fruit they need pollen from a *different variety* of the same fruit *that blooms at the same time*. For example, a Yellow Newtown Pippin apple tree cannot pollinate either itself *or* another Yellow Newtown Pippin tree. But, a Yellow Newtown Pippin tree can pollinate a Golden Delicious apple tree and vice versa. When it comes to cross-pollinating species, for each fruit you will need at least two trees that are different varieties from each other: two different apples; two different pears; two different plums. And remember, the pollen donor (pollenizer) tree needs to bloom at the same time as the other tree. As exceptions to their species, Queen Cox apples, Bartlett pears, and Shiro plums are thought to be self-pollinating, but they have not yet been proven to be so, and I wouldn't recommend winging it with just one tree. Some apple varieties are triploids, meaning they can't pollinate another apple tree at all. Make sure to check your pollinators.

Unfortunately, there is no complete compendium of pollination partners. Almost every fruit tree catalog worth its salt will have reliable pollination charts at the end of each fruit section that tell you what varieties of cross-pollinating trees are best planted together. The website orangepippintrees.com is an amazing resource, too. In its pollination checker database, you can select just about any variety of any fruit species and punch in "pollination partner" and, violà, you will find a long list of suitable partners for your tree to do-si-do with. (Orange Pippin Trees will also source and sell you trees of just about any variety of fruit.) I also like the pollination charts from Raintree Nursery in Washington, Adams County Nursery in Pennsylvania, and the University of Missouri agriculture extension, all easily accessed online (see Resources, page 266). This whole internet thing might just catch on after all.

It's best if your compatible pollenizer is located within 20–30 feet of the variety to be pollinated. Studies have shown that bees, particularly honeybees, work up and down rows 80 percent of the time and cross-row only 20 percent of the time. But if you have just a few trees, you can plant them in almost any pattern, and if they are in close proximity, the pollinators will find them. If you have room, by planting four, five, six varieties of the same fruit you will likely have your bases covered. And if you live in an area where other people have gardens,

Peach blossoms being pollinated

it is likely that you will have a suitable pollinator nearby, as pollinating bees can range 2–3 miles or more.

Finally, multigraft trees are available. A multigraft tree has several pollen-compatible varieties of the same fruit grafted together. These trees are more expensive than regular trees, but for some home gardeners, they could be a good solution for cross-pollination.

CRABAPPLE: A UNIVERSAL POLLENIZER FOR APPLES

Apples can be a little more problematic in choosing pollinators than all other fruits, as they bloom over a much longer period than any other fruit (often 6–8 weeks from earliest to latest bloom). If you're planting apples, consider planting a crabapple alongside. Crabapples have come a long way from their bitter reputation. They offer the profusion and beauty of their flowers in spring, a rich source of pollen for all types of bees and some beneficial insects, and fruit to eat, cook with, and press for cider. And they provide pollination services as well. Just about any variety of crabapple will pollinate just about every other variety of apple that blooms at the same time. White-flowered varieties of crabs offer much more pollen than red-flowered types. Crabapples tend to be compact growers and thus manageable, especially on dwarfing rootstocks.

While most crabapples can be eaten, they have a reputation for being very acidic and are usually used for cooking, jams, sauces, and ciders. However, several varieties are sweet enough to eat fresh. One that stands out is Wickson. I carry a few around in my pockets in the fall and snack on them throughout the day—yum!

CRABAPPLE VARIETIES OF NOTE

CENTENNIAL (midseason ripening) Sweet fruit, naturally dwarf tree.

CHESTNUT (midseason ripening) Excellent pollenizer. Produces small, pale yellow fruit that is sweet, crisp, and nutty in flavor.

CRIMSON GOLD (late-season ripening) Attractive in appearance, looks like a mini Gala. Coarse fleshed, high juice quotient. Sweet taste hangs around for a long time in your mouth. Highly productive.

DOLGO (mid- to late-season ripening) Excellent early pollen source. An old Siberian variety, hence cold tolerant. Vigorous grower with big, fragrant white flowers followed by 1- to 2-inch bright red, oval fruit. Makes a good jam or jelly.

EVERESTE (midseason ripening) The most disease resistant of all crabs. Originally from France, bred in 1974. An edible ornamental: the tree in bloom is an avalanche of fragrant white flowers top to bottom. Produces hundreds of small round tart fruits annually. (Leave some fruit on the trees for hungry winter-foraging birds!) Good for cider making, jellies, and pickling. Truly a tree of merit.

HEWES (mid- to late-season ripening) Very long bloom period. Makes a dry cinnamon-flavored hard cider. Preferred cider apple of Thomas Jefferson.

WASHINGTON STATE UNIVERSITY PUGET SPICE (midseason ripening) Abundant pollen source for midseason apples.

WHITNEY (midseason ripening) Profusion of pink or white blossoms. Reasonably sweet fruit.

WICKSON (mid- to late-season ripening) My fave. A little sweet meat with a little acidic kick. And truly, I get a kick out of 'em.

Chill Hours by Variety

As you learned in Chapter 1, "Getting Started," the climate and weather in your area dictate which species of fruit trees you can grow. Each individual variety of fruit also has recommended chill hours, and it's important to make sure that the varieties you select match the chill hours in your area (see page 15). Chill hours for each variety are usually listed on tags at the nursery or in catalogs alongside the varietal description. For easy reference, the chart that follows is a complete list of the chill hours for every variety of fruit mentioned in this book (plus a few reliable varieties I'd additionally recommend if I had unlimited space and time).

RELIABLE FRUIT TREE VARIETIES AND THEIR CHILL HOUR REQUIREMENTS

APPLES

Golden Delicious and Its Offspring	
Pink Lady	400
Mollie's Delicious	500
Gala, Mutsu, Pristine	600
Arlet, Golden Delicious	700
Jonagold, Lodi, Yellow Transparent	700–800
Chehalis, Elstar	800–1,000
The McIntosh Family	
Beverly Hills	300–400
Belmac, Freedom, Liberty, Macoun, Paula Red, Shay, Spartan, William's Pride	600–800
Empire, McIntosh, Rodger's McIntosh	800
Cox's Orange Pippin Tribe	
Cherry Cox, Fiesta, Freyberg, Holstein, Kidd's Orange Red, Queen Cox, Piñata (a.k.a. Pinova, Corail, or Sonata), SunCrisp	600–800
Alkmene, Cox's Orange Pippin, Rubinette	800
Favorites of Mixed Parentage	
Granny Smith	500
Aroma, Braeburn, Gravenstein	700
Hauer Pippin, Yellow Newtown Pippin	700–800
Russeted Apples	
Russet Beauty	600–800
Ashmead's Kernel, Belle de Boskoop, Egremont Russet, Golden Russet, GoldRush, Hoople's Antique Gold, Hudson's Golden Gem, Roxbury Russet, St. Edmund's Pippin	800–1,000
Additional Recommended Apple Varieties	
Arkansas Charm	400
Cameo, Fuji, Pink Pearl	600
Sierra Beauty	700–800
Honeycrisp, Idared, Razor Russet, Spitzenburg	800
Bramley's	800–1,000

EUROPEAN PEARS	
Summer or Butter Pears	
Bartlett, Bella di Guigno, Dawn, Honey, Seckel, Tyson	500–600
Ubileen, Warren	600
Buttira Precoce Morettini, Red Clapp's Favorite	600–800
Winter Pears	
Bosc	500–600
Comice	600
D'Anjou, Orcas, Rescue	800
QUINCES	
Aromatnaya, Karp's Sweet, Orange, Pineapple, Smyrna	300–500
PEACHES	
Old School Varieties	
Babcock, Giant Babcock, Sweet Bagel	250–300
Avalon Pride	300–400
Donut	400–500
Rio Oso Gem	500
Mary Jane	600
Suncrest	700
Loring	750
Elberta strains	700–800
Baby Crawford, Early Red Haven, Red Haven	800
New School Varieties	
MP1	600–700
Q1-8	600–800
Arctic Supreme, Frost	700
White Lady	800
Starfire Freestone	850
NECTARINES	
Double Delight	300
Arctic Glo	400–500
Fantasia	500
Heavenly White	650
PLUMS	
European Plums	
Italian Prune, Schoolhouse, Seneca, Valor	600–800

Asian Plums	
Beauty	250
Santa Rosa, Late Santa Rosa, Satsuma, Mariposa	300
Catalina	400
Laroda	400–500
Elephant Heart	500–600
Shiro	600
Emerald Beaut	600–700
Hiromi Red	600–800
Damson Plums	
Blues Jam, Damson, Jam Session, Shopshire	800
Greengage Plums	
Bavay's	700
Cambridge, Coe's Golden Drop, Early Laxton, Kirke's Blue	700–900
APRICOTS	
Blenheim	400
Autumn, Moorpark	500
PLUOTS	
Flavor Grenade	300–500
Dapple Dandy, Flavor King, Flavor Queen	400–500
Flavor Supreme	700–800
APRIUMS	
Cot'n Candy, Flavor Delight	200–300
SWEET CHERRIES	
Stella	400
Lapins	500
Craig's Crimson	800
POMEGRANATES	
Ambrosia, Early Wonderful, Granada, Sweet, White, Wonderful	100–300
FIGS	
Black Mission, Brown Turkey, Celeste, Chicago Hardy, Desert King, Kadota, Osborne Prolific, Panache, Peter's Honey, Violette de Bordeaux, White Genoa	100–300
PERSIMMONS	
Hachiya Varieties	
Chocolate, Hachiya, Tamopan	100–200
Fuyu Varieties	
Fuya, Giant Fuyu, Izo, Jiro	100–200

"To have the best fruit you must grow it yourself."

—EDWARD A. BUNYARD,
The Anatomy of Dessert, 1929

Varietal Recommendations: Pome Fruits

Among the thousands of fruit varieties in the world to choose from, which is best for you? Here I'll recommend some of my favorite pome fruit varieties (apple, pear, quince), followed by stone fruit varieties (peach, nectarine, apricot, plum, pluot, aprium, cherry). Later chapters will get into fruits that have different care needs—citrus, figs, pomegranates, and persimmons.

Loosely grouped by family association and my own preferential quirks, these varieties represent some of the best in flavor, size, shape, reliability, parentage, and history, plus that irresistible je ne sais quoi that makes you obsess over a particular fruit. Welcome to the insane, amazing world of fruit tree varieties. It's one of my favorite places on earth.

The principal pome fruits are apples, pears, and quinces. As with stone fruits, these three principal genera are members of the rose (Rosaceae) family.

The origin of the name *pome* (pronounced with a long "o," as in *poem*) is somewhat shrouded in the mysteries of the history of language. Pome means "small seeded." *Pome* or *pomum* in Latin simply means "fruit," but more specifically it refers to apple. In French, the word for apple is *pomme*. And *pome* is also seen in ancient literature in reference to the Roman goddess Pomona, who watched over fruit orchards and gardens and was often depicted wielding a grafting knife. An excerpt from a Roman prayer to Pomona reads, "may your gentle touch make our trees grow strong, free from blight and heavy with healthy fruit."

Pome fruits are climacteric fruits; that is, they can be picked mature but green and then brought to full ripeness and sweetness off the tree. *Climacteric* derives from the Greek root meaning "critical point" or, literally, "rung of a ladder," implying a major turning point or critical stage—in this case, pre-senescence, a.k.a. the tragic turn from ripe to overripe. These fruits store their sugars in the form of starches that are converted back to sugars by enzymes and by warm (65°F–75°F) temperatures off the tree. Thus, they can also be held in cold storage for many months and then brought out and ripened at room temperature. This trait allows for longer seasons of enjoyment and availability.

Because pome fruits hail from more northerly climes, they require and can tolerate more cold than stone fruits. Consequently, they can be grown over a much wider geographic span than stone fruit. They also require less heat to ripen the fruit on the tree.

Pomes are much longer-lived species than "stoners," but they take longer to come into bearing. Interestingly for the home orchardist, because there is a longer history of pome fruits having been grown, observed, and researched, there is correspondingly more research-based cultural information, better-articulated pruning and training systems, and a wider range of size-controlling rootstocks available.

Quince, although botanically similar to apples and pears, is an outlier in both behavior and care; I've included special considerations for quince where applicable.

APPLES

Malus domestica

You haven't truly experienced the peak of flavor until you've eaten an apple fresh out of hand in your own garden. And to take advantage of all the apple has to offer, you need to grow a variety of varieties.

Let's take a moment to travel across the arc of time, along the trajectory of geography, by the banks of rushing streams straight out of paradisiacal shepherd's tales, into the foothills of Kazakhstan's Heavenly Mountains (Tian Shan) and up hillsides bedecked with deciduous trees: mélanges of wild apples, pears, grapes, and nut trees amid flowering, fragrant vines and shrubs twined like garlands up wilding trees—there rests the hearth and home of our modern-day apple.

The apple is both storied and well traveled, from its dynamic origins in Kazakhstan to the shelves of international supermarkets. It is, no doubt, the most widely grown, distributed, and eaten deciduous fruit on the planet. There are more varieties of apples (more than 7,500 named, cultivated varieties today) than any other fruit. And although apples are grown extensively in the temperate and cooler Mediterranean zones of the world, I think it's safe to say that apples know no geographical bounds. In North America, they can and are being grown in central Florida, in the Louisiana basin (low-chill varieties), along the coasts of both Nova Scotia and British Columbia, and everywhere in between. They offer the longest season of harvest and an astonishing array of looks, tastes, and uses. If you are just wading into the waters of fruit tree growing, apples are a sure bet. Get 'em and grow 'em, and they will reward you.

As a backyard grower faced with choosing which varieties to plant, you always need to ask, What do you want in a fruit? What's your bias? Sweet, tart, fresh eating, cooking, juice blends, fine flesh, chunky coarse flesh, red, mottled, russeted, yellow, green . . . no other fruit species offers the spectrum of tastes, textures, and uses and the length of harvest season (June to January) as *Malus domestica*, the modern-day apple.

Apple tastes can be grouped into families, with characteristic flavors that reflect a common parent. Even though there are thousands of varieties of apples, a large percentage of the dessert apples one sees in markets are descended from just a handful of varieties: Red Delicious, Golden Delicious, Cox's Orange Pippin, McIntosh, Jonathan. And throw in a few of the russeted types, too.

Apple flavor depends on the relationship between sugars and acids. Acidity in particular contributes to fullness of flavor; too little makes for a bland, almost watery taste. Some aspects of taste are built-in, or genetic; a Red Delicious will always look good but taste like juicy sawdust. Taste is also a result of cultivation practices, for example, sunlight distribution within the tree, water, nutrition, disease control, and thinning. The weather that year also plays a role—for instance, cool summers give Gala a flat, insipid taste, but warm temperatures impart full sweetness. Finally, time of picking and handling can change a variety's flavor. A Golden Delicious is neither golden nor delicious if picked early, and it's not the same apple after more than three months off the tree, despite the technological marvels of cold storage.

Seasonality is another concern when selecting apples to grow. If you choose wisely, you can set yourself up to be eating fresh-picked apples for most of the season.

Early-season varieties generally ripen from late June through early September. A light, sprightly taste characterizes these apples. The taste sensation doesn't last long, and the flavor tends to be mono as opposed to the Dolby surround sound of mid- and late-season apples. Early-season apples don't possess the complexity of flavors (the balance of sugars and acids) that distinguish their late-season counterparts. Instead, they tend to be either sweet or tart. As a group, early-season apples don't hold well, either on or off the tree. Two varieties that are particularly notorious for preharvest drop, in which apples fall from the tree before they're ready to harvest, are McIntosh and Gravenstein. Early varieties also have thin skins, which are great from an eating perspective but contribute to both easy bruising and very short storage life (usually fewer than 3 weeks).

Midseason apples ripen from mid-August through early October and offer the most plentiful and versatile varieties. They possess a more complex balance of sugar and acids than early-season apples, and the taste lasts a longer time on the palette. Often midseason varieties can be both sweet and tart, with one flavor predominating over the other. For example, Elstar is tart over sweet at harvest but will reverse itself to sweet over tart after a month in storage. Midseason varieties feature good cooking, juicing, and dessert apples. Some of the highest-quality aromatic varieties mature in midseason. They hold well on the tree (up to 3–4 weeks) and store well off the tree (2–4 months).

Late-season varieties ripen from mid-October until January 1 (depending on your local climate) and are the best keeping apples. They feature thick, tight, sometimes chewy skins that contribute to longevity both on and off the tree. The flesh is generally coarse and chunky, quite the opposite of the melting, soft flesh of early-season offerings. While these apples take complex flavors to the limit, they are usually more tart than sweet. As the summer season winds down and the apple season wanes, late-season varieties are savored. Appreciation increases with the knowledge that soon there will only be store-bought, cold-storage apples, which lack vitality and pale in comparison to homegrown, tree-ripened apples plucked on the run from your yard as you finalize your fall vegetable garden and sow those all-important cover crops.

If you want a safe bet for apples, there are a few recommended varieties that tend to satisfy all comers. These are all relatively grower friendly, with low pest and disease pressure, reliable annual bearers, good size and quality, and chill hour requirements of 500–900 hours: Chehalis, Braeburn, Cox's Orange Pippin, Queen Cox, McIntosh (especially Empire Mac), Gala, Fuji (September Wonder is 2 months earlier, great for colder climates), Golden Delicious, Hudson's Golden Gem, Jonagold, Mutsu, Pink Lady, Pink Pearl, Spitzenburg, Yellow Newtown Pippin, Honeycrisp, Pristine, Golden Russet, Early Gold, and Valstar.

But there are so, so many more. A few of my favorite "families" of apples follow, grouped loosely by genetics. These varieties run the gamut, from those commonly found in supermarkets to those offered at more adventuresome farmer's market stalls, to those you will only savor if you grow them yourself. Let's get into it.

All apples are cross-pollinated: in order to produce fruit, they need to be near a different apple variety that blooms at the same time. I've included a few suggestions for pollination partners with the varietal groupings in the next section. Universal pollinators for apples include Yellow Newtown Pippin, Granny Smith (that's about all it's good for—and pies!), Golden Delicious. and white-flowered crabapples. These varieties have abundant pollen and an extremely long bloom period. When in doubt, plant a crabapple (or three . . .).

Golden Delicious and Its Offspring

In the spring night the petals are luminous and look like stars,
each tree a pulsing, bright nebula. Summer, the limbs sag
with the weight of apples, *golden delicious* hanging like globes
of small suns, a fusion of sugar in their core. The windfall apples
are crushed and pulped into a cider, the liquid a rich amber
the color of the moon rising slowly in the thick, autumn dusk.

—HAN SHAN (China, seventh to eighth century BCE), from
  "The Orchard," translated by Joe Stroud, 1998

The Golden Delicious variety is one whose brand has been degraded, disparaged by attempts via sophisticated cold storage to make it a 365-day, on-the-shelf commodity. Consequently, most people view Golden Delicious as a dull-skinned, soft, even mealy apple, lackluster at best. But not so fast, my friend! Almost any apple bred with Golden Delicious in it is a winner, especially if you are a sucker for a crisp, sweet apple.

When it is grown at home, given full hang-time, and picked at the peak of maturity, the Golden Delicious will delight. It is crisp, chunky or coarse fleshed, and loaded with sugar, but with only a little balancing acidity. In essence, it eats well. It makes a mean pie and a sweet cider, too. As breeding stock, Golden Delicious breeds with almost any other apple, producing outstanding progeny. And Golden Delicious offspring can keep you in apples all throughout the growing season.

Suggested pollination partners for the following Golden Delicious family selections include (but are not limited to) Granny Smith, Yellow Newtown Pippin, Chestnut and Dolgo crabapples, Honeycrisp, Fiesta and many other Cox's types, and most McIntoshes. Note: Golden Delicious will *not* pollinate any variety that has Golden Delicious in its parentage.

VARIETIES OF NOTE

ARLET (700 chill hours/midseason ripening) Also known as Swiss Gourmet, this is a Swiss crossbreed of Golden Delicious and Idared. A very intensely flavored, complex apple, it starts out with a slightly tart "twang" and finishes sweet with a spicy undertone. Possessing a distinctive perfume, it resembles in looks and shape both Gala and Elstar; in taste it drifts toward Elstar. Tree is of moderate vigor and easy to shape and train.

CHEHALIS (800–1,000 chill hours/early-season ripening) Found seedling from an abandoned homestead in Oregon. It is everything you like about Golden Delicious, but bigger, lighter, and sweeter, and it ripens 6–8 weeks earlier. This large conical-round apple starts out light green and matures to a light, almost translucent yellow. It sets a heavy crop reliably year in and year out. Scab-free and relatively resistant to codling moth damage. Chehalis bakes up into an excellent pie and makes great juice. If you only grow one early variety, this is the one to choose.

ELSTAR (800–1,000 chill hours/midseason ripening) Ripens just on the heels of Gala, with some overlap. It is a Gala with gusto. This cross between Golden Delicious and Ingrid Marie (a Cox's Orange Pippin offspring) looks like a Gala but is larger, with a more elongated shape that colors into a brighter red. Introduced in Holland in the 1950s and rivals Golden Delicious as one of northern Europe's leading dessert apples. An intensely flavored apple, it has more acidity than Gala and sweetens better, even in cool summers. Some years, it has a tart over sweet taste; in others, sweet over tart. It has a crisp, denser, cream-colored, juicy flesh and bakes into an excellent pie. One of my favorites.

FREYBERG (600–800 chill hours/midseason ripening) See description on page 65.

GALA (600 chill hours/early-season ripening) Often thought of as one of the better "new" commercial varieties, bred in 1934 and named in 1965 by J. H. Kidd, an amateur fruit breeder and farmer in New Zealand. Breeding a new apple variety gets you into the Apple Hall of Fame. Of the twelve to fifteen leading commercial varieties introduced in the last 15–20 years, two or three are the result of breeding, and twelve or thirteen are chance mutations, known as sports or bud sports. If, as J. H. Kidd did, you breed three varieties (J. H. Kidd, Gala, and Freyberg) in a span of 6–7 years, you're the Albert Einstein, Stephen Hawking, and/or Steph Curry of your field.

Gala apple

A beautiful conical apple, with a warm orange-red blush in the foreground and a deep yellow background. At full maturation, it almost glows. The mild, sweet flavor is lighter and more sprightly than Golden Delicious. It is thin skinned, fine fleshed, crisp, and juicy, with pale creamy-white flesh. Overall, the tree is grower friendly and bears heavy annual crops. Minimal scab and mildew and only moderate codling moth damage. It holds well for 3–4 months in cold storage; after that the apples look good but taste bland and mushy.

Gala is, by genetics, a small to medium-sized apple, although its size can be increased by thinning early and aggressively to one apple per cluster and 8 inches between fruits. Or you can grow 'em small for your kid's lunch box. Coastal situations yield excellent color; inland warmth imparts higher sugar content.

A multipick apple, Gala yields three to five picks over 3–4 weeks. It is a very vigorous grower with especially brittle wood. I shudder remembering how many times I've snapped branches while engaged in a tree-training exercise or demonstration.

JONAGOLD (700–800 chill hours/midseason ripening) Golden Delicious and Jonathan cross, bred in 1968 at Cornell University. Large, high-quality dessert apple with dense flesh, a high juice content, and a decidedly sweet over tart rich flavor. Also makes a great pie. Jonagold is triploid, and hence not a pollinator.

Jonagold is the quintessential example of what's wrong with US apple buyers. Although it's a great apple, its ambiguous color—red foreground with yellow stripes—has never caught on in markets. America buys with its eyes, preferring totally red apples, sweet apples (some say overly so), and all-purpose apples—one variety that can be eaten fresh, used for all methods of cooking, and juiced as well. In England and Europe, apples are revered for their eating qualities first, and Europeans prefer varieties used exclusively for one purpose— cooking, eating, or juicing. Thus small apples with russeted or mottled skins, à la Cox's Orange Pippin, are appreciated.

LODI and **YELLOW TRANSPARENT** (700–800 chill hours/very early-season ripening) Virtually identical varieties, with Lodi being a bit less acid and less prone to bruising. Yellow Transparent was bred in southern Russia and introduced to the United States in 1870. The apples are large and yellowish green with a soft creamy-white flesh. Acidity and juiciness are the main components of taste. This apple only lasts 7–10 days on the tree, 3–5 days off the tree. Best use is for cooking, especially for sauces and purees. While it is not the world's greatest apple, I don't know of an earlier variety.

MOLLIE'S DELICIOUS (500 chill hours/very early-season ripening) Big apple (10–12 ounces) that bridges the gap between Chehalis and Gala. Cross between Golden Delicious and Red Gravenstein developed at Rutgers University in 1966. Its taste and thin skin (which bruises easily) make it a characteristic early-season apple. This is a pleasantly mild, sweet, juicy apple with red striping over a yellow background. As the apple is big, so is the tree.

PINK LADY (400 chill hours/very late-season ripening) Outstanding long- and warm-season apple from Australia, among the top five apples I've ever tasted. Midsized apple that is red with a pink blush and creamy white flesh. Taste is crisp, juicy, and sweet with a spicy-tart finish. Region adaptable, it does well in California, eastern Washington, and in and around Southern Pennsylvania.

PRISTINE (600 chill hours/very early-season ripening) New offering from the PRI disease-resistant apple-breeding program (see page 37). Pristine is weak and twiggy, and thus the trees can be grown very close together, as close as 3–5 feet apart. It produces an abundant crop of midsized yellow apples that are sugary sweet (despite the catalog descriptions that say tart) with a crisp, juicy aspect. Scab resistant.

The McIntosh Family

Growing up in New England, I thought two things were ordained (in addition to the parish priests):

- The Boston Celtics *always* won the NBA title.

- All apples were McIntosh—at that time in New England (1950s–60s), it was just about a certainty.

But time moves on. Horizons broaden. Opinions and trends change. The Golden State Warriors end up winning my allegiance. And an onslaught of new apple varieties always pop up to pique people's curiosity—all for the better. The McIntosh apple probably derives from an older French apple, Fameuse (a.k.a. Snow apple, owing to its pristine, fine-grained white flesh). Fameuse is written of in France as early as the 1500s. Now that's an old apple! It remains an excellent apple to this day. Fameuse was imported into Quebec in the 1600s. In the early 1800s, a Fameuse tree sprouted a seedling on a farm belonging to John McIntosh along the St. Lawrence River. At the time, it was called Granny's Apple. It was later renamed Red McIntosh and eventually McIntosh (known in the parlance as Mac). The original tree was damaged in a fire in 1894 but lived on until 1910. McIntosh became and remained a regional favorite until its spread to New England and upstate New York orchards in the 1900s.

The winter of 1933–34 was, as they say in Boston, wicked cold—even by northeastern standards. Most of the leading commercial apples of the time—Baldwin, Northern Spy, and Rhode Island Greening—succumbed to the cold. McIntosh proved much hardier and grabbed market share for the next 40–50 years. Eventually it was supplanted by the ubiquitous varieties of supermarket fame, Golden and Red Delicious.

In part, McIntosh's popularity was due to its pretty red (sometimes almost black-red), shiny look. It also responded admirably to moderate New England summers with cool or cold night temperatures during the last month of growth. These conditions raised the soluble solids (carbs) and expressed the sugar content.

McIntosh (800 chill hours/midseason ripening) is an excellent eating and juicing apple for both hard cider and sweet apple juice. When cooked, it turns to mush—though sweet mush. It is medium sized, round, and conical. Some Mac offspring are quite small. The skin is bright red, if unevenly colored. The stem is quite short, making hand thinning difficult to near impossible, but the apples must be thoroughly thinned to attain even decent size. The skin, while pretty, is tough to penetrate and irritatingly chewy.

McIntosh has a perfumed smell even before eating—a hint of very ripe strawberries. After the skin is punctured, the pure white flesh is soft and melting. Some people dislike this. It is distinct from mealy, mushy, overripe flesh, and also different from modern varieties that place a premium on crisp, breaking, chunky flesh. Don't blame the apple—it's supposed to be that way. The flavor is characterized by what I call Mac Twang (not to be confused with Mark Twain). The taste is at once spicy, sweet, and sprightly with an acid or tangy kick. If the apple is not dead-on ripe, it will have metallic, even phenolic overtones—now *that* will get your attention. Either you love it or loathe it (a lot like feelings surrounding cilantro). Californians can usually take it or leave it (laid-back approach). For most easterners, it is to die for. Isn't it amazing how nostalgia can activate the taste buds? Truth is, eastern transplants are merely eating a memory, as California-produced Macs can never rival eastern Macs. This is not regional chauvinism, but pure climatics.

Suggested pollination partners for the following McIntosh family selections include (but are not limited to) Hudson's Golden Gem (and many other russets), Granny Smith, Yellow Newtown Pippin, and Wickson (and many other crabapples).

VARIETIES OF NOTE

BELMAC (600–800 chill hours/midseason ripening) "New" from Quebec, originated as a seedling at the Ottawa Research Station in 1968. Medium to large Mac with a shiny, deep-red coloring. Sweet-tart combination a lot like Spartan but bigger. Disease resistant.

BEVERLY HILLS (300–400 chill hours/very early-season ripening) Melba-McIntosh cross. This very vigorous tree produces an abundant crop of large, oblate-shaped apples that are heavenly sweet and scented like strawberries. Thin skinned, with a soft, melting, fine-grained flesh and a sweet, aromatic taste. William Henry Chandler, UCLA's preeminent pomologist, bred this apple in 1939—back when Beverly Hills had farms and orchards! Like most early varieties, this one is here today, gone tomorrow, lasting only 10–14 days on the tree.

EMPIRE (800 chill hours/midseason ripening) Cross between McIntosh and Red Delicious. Probably the "best for the West" of all Mac types. But don't worry—all it gets from Red Delicious is a little more fruit size, unfortunately not enough size, especially if not thinned well. Dark red, round-conic fruit. A sweet, crisp, breaking flesh that is coarse and chunky (for a Mac). Not the soft-melting, fine-textured flesh typical of most Macs. Empire is not subject to the extreme (70–90 percent) preharvest drop that plagues most Macs (especially in warm districts). Virtually disease immune. Royal Empire is simply a redder, more uniform strain.

LIBERTY and **FREEDOM** (600–800 chill hours/late-season ripening) Two very similar varieties from the late 1960s and early 1970s from Cornell University's station in New York. The names refer to freedom and liberation from scab via breeding resistance, and thus from spraying. These varieties are, however, somewhat subject to mildew. Both are dark red, intensely colored, and intensely flavored (sprightly, spicy, sweet) medium-sized (at best) Macs.

MACOUN (600–800 chill hours/midseason ripening) Named after a Canadian fruit breeder, W. T. Macoun. Arguably the best tasting of the Macs and very popular in upstate New York and New England, where it excels climatically. This small black-red apple with a dusty bloom is juicy, crisp, very sweet, with hints of strawberries. (Here, bloom refers not to flowering period, but to fine hairs on the fruit that give the appearance of dust—similar to dark red and black plums.)

PAULA RED (600–800 chill hours/early- to midseason ripening) Found seedling from Sparta, Michigan, in 1960. About the biggest of the Macs, along with Beverly Hills (above)—two radically different geographies and cultures. Very sweet with firmer, crisper flesh. Usual Mac hint of strawberries. Widely grown as a commercial apple in Michigan, upstate New York, and the Tyrolean Alps of northern Italy. Excellent eating quality, good juice and cider potential.

SHAY (600–800 chill hours/midseason ripening) Also called McShay. Absolutely well-behaved tree and disease-immune Mac. Elongated red fruit hangs heavy on the tree. Nice open structure to the tree allows sunlight to reach and color fruit in the center of the canopy.

SPARTAN (600–800 chill hours/mid- to late-season ripening) McIntosh–Yellow Newtown Pippin cross from British Columbia, dating to 1936. Glossy red, almost mahogany in color. Highly aromatic. Sweet with hints of both strawberry and melon.

WILLIAM'S PRIDE (600–800 chill hours/very early-season ripening) Relatively new (1976) McIntosh type bred at the PRI breeding program (see page 37). Midsized, round, slightly oblong apple with red stripes over a yellow background. Typical Mac type with thin skin; fine, pure white flesh; and a slightly tart, spicy taste with plenty of juiciness. The tree is a reliable annual bearer and a very vigorous scion. Suffers 50–60 percent preharvest drop. Scab immune.

Cox's Orange Pippin Tribe

Cox's Orange Pippin apples (800 chill hours/midseason ripening) are widely revered as flavorful, aromatic, sweet, rich, tender, unsurpassed, and generally one of the greatest. They are also one of the more difficult apples ever grown—definitely not grower friendly! But so worth it.

Pippin was a term used in eighteenth- and nineteenth-century England to describe apples with excellent characteristics. *Pip* refers to the small nature of the apple seed. It probably derives from the French word *petit* (small). Cox's Orange Pippin was originally planted as a pip of the sharper and more strongly flavored Ribston Pippin by retired brewer and horticulturist Richard Cox in Buckinghamshire, England, in the 1820s.

Owing to its small size and intense flavor, it was elected the best nineteenth-century dessert apple. By the 1890s, Cox's Orange Pippin was the leader in English apple sales. But by the early 1900s, it had fallen from grace, due to its extreme and extensive problems with disease. It was resurrected in the 1920s with the advent of lime-sulfur sprays to control fungal problems.

Its fame persists to the present day, not only in England, but in Holland, Germany, Belgium, and New Zealand . . . and in my garden as well. That this variety has remained popular for a couple of hundred years despite its demerits is a testament to its outstanding taste.

Cox's is a small apple, oblate in shape, with an unassuming dull color—a weak orange-red flush over a greenish yellow background with patches of small dots and russeting (a toughening of the skin) over the top half of the fruit. It is aromatic, even perfumed, and has an intense flavor range: spicy, rich, honeyed, with a hint of nuttiness. The flesh is coarse and chunky, sometimes evoking pearlike qualities. The blend and complexity of sugars and acids give it an unsurpassed tender juiciness that lingers on the tongue.

The demerits of Cox's go on almost endlessly: it cracks and splits, especially in cool, wet, gray spring and early-summer weather (think England; Santa Cruz, California; and the Pacific Northwest west of the Cascade Range). The first time I observed this phenomenon, I thought someone had gone through the tree with a knife and slit every fruit once, twice, three times. The stem basket (the sunken area surrounding the stem) is deep and collects a lot of water, often russeting to the point of cracking. This syndrome is most pronounced in the first 5–6 years

"If any one wonders at the absence of 'eating' apples from my diet let me explain that this is one case where I have spoilt my palate with an aristocratic taste. I can eat only Cox's Orange Pippins, and am in mourning applewise from April to October."

—IRIS MURDOCH,
The Sea, the Sea, 1978

of fruiting and then only in wretched springs. Mildew also weakens the tips of the shoots, causing dieback, in which the tips of the shoots die. Heat, high sunlight levels, and humidity are anathema to Cox's, inducing sunburn, bark burn, and turning it to mush.

The scion is weak, arguably the weakest of all scions. And yet the fruit load is consistent and heavy. This results in a tree that needs constant prodding to grow vegetatively. Be proactive on an annual basis in applying more compost and perhaps more high-nitrogen fertilizer, such as ½ pound blood meal at 12 percent nitrogen or ¾ pound Suståne at 8 percent nitrogen.

In coastal areas, Cox's is also subject to papery bark disease, a devastating syndrome wherein the bark exfoliates (beautiful on Sierran granite, not so on apple trees) for no other reason than you decided to reside near the ocean.

Cox's is a basitonic (from the Latin *basi*, which means "low" or "wide") tree, often wider than tall. This growth habit makes the development of the upper part of the tree frustrating if not fruitless. On rootstocks weaker than M26, most of the Cox's tribe tend to be productive bushes (4–5 feet tall) that can be spaced close together (3–4 feet apart).

Cox's Orange Pippin's eating intrigue begets a loyal, almost cultlike following and tastes that are to die for. It is both precocious (bearing at an early age) and promiscuous (it will mate and breed with almost anything *Malus*). Thus the list of chance-occurring seedlings and intentional breeding products is extensive and delicious.

Suggested pollination partners for the following Cox's Orange Pippin family selections include (but are not limited to) Akane, Elstar, Egremont Russet (and most other russets), Gala, Granny Smith, Yellow Newtown Pippin, and most white-flowered crabapples, especially Chestnut and Dolgo.

VARIETIES OF NOTE

ALKMENE (800 chill hours/midseason ripening) Cox's Orange Pippin cross from Germany. Same sweet-tart flavor as Cox's but more lively, rich, and honeyed. Popular commercial variety in Germany and Holland. Rivals Cox's for lack of tree vigor.

CHERRY COX (600–800 chill hours/midseason ripening) Discovered as a seedling or mutation of Cox's Orange Pippin in Denmark in 1942. Just like Cox's, with a cherry-red blush and matching flavor.

FIESTA (600–800 chill hours/midseason ripening) Latest, best-behaved, and thus most marketable of all Cox scions. Virtually crack, scab, and mildew immune. The fruit can be twice as big as the original, with a slightly rounded shape. Color is 75–80 percent red over a green-yellow background and quite pretty. It has a good deal of the full Cox's flavor but is a bit more sprightly and juicy. Easier to sell and almost as good to eat.

FREYBERG (600–800 chill hours/midseason ripening) Another J. H. Kidd winner from New Zealand (see page 57), this variety was introduced in 1958 and is a cross between Golden Delicious and Cox's Orange Pippin (aren't they all?). Small, russeted-type apple. Moderate tree vigor and very upright. Arguably the most complex tasting of all apples. When it is at full ripeness, you have to sit down, contemplate, and assimilate all the components of its taste. George Delbard, famous French nurseryman, waxes poetic about this variety: "A veritable cocktail of flavors with the merest hint of anise and producing a juice that resembles the taste of apple, pear, and banana." Freyberg is variable in color—a yellow, almost chartreuse that tends toward porcelain when fully ripe on the tree. An aromatic apple that has juicy, medium-fine, cream-colored flesh. This is an apple you have to grow to experience the fullness of its flavor, as you will never see it in any market. Unfortunately, nothing about the tree is grower friendly; it fruits only in alternate years, is codling moth ridden, and is a weak and awkward grower. Raintree Nursery is about the only US source.

HOLSTEIN (600–800 chill hours/midseason ripening) Thought to be an open-pollinated seedling of Cox's Orange Pippin out of Hamburg, Germany, in 1918. A bit like a Cox's pumped up on performance enhancers. Base color is a deep yellow overlaid by an orange-gold flush with some russeting. Unfortunately, it often produces a very light crop. Texture is even more coarse and chunky (this is a good thing) than Cox's. Creamy yellow flesh with lots of juice and an aromatic flavor similar to Cox's, but bigger, bolder, and sharper (acidity).

KIDD'S ORANGE RED (600–800 chill hours/midseason ripening) Yet another breed from so-called amateur J. H. Kidd (see page 57). A typical "amateur" (from *amore*, Latin for "love of") effort of triumphant passion that crossed Cox's Orange Pippin with the useless Red Delicious in 1924. (Kidd also bred Gala and Freyberg.) Bigger than Cox's and conical in shape like the Red Delicious, with yellow skin flushed orange. Tolerates warm climates better than Cox's. Flavor is a rich blend of sugar and acids with the aroma of violets—wow!

QUEEN COX (600–800 chill hours/midseason ripening) Whole tree mutation discovered in Berkshire, England, in the early 1950s. A bigger, cleaner, prettier Cox's. It is reported—but not reliably proven—to be self-fruitful. So pair it with a pollinator and it's a sure bet to set fruit, even under wretched weather conditions. The tree itself is even weaker than the standard Cox's.

RUBINETTE (800 chill hours/midseason ripening) Another Cox's Orange Pippin and Golden Delicious cross raised in Switzerland (where it's called Rafzubin) in the 1960s. Dwarf, low-spreading tree bears small fruit with light, dull red striping over a yellow background, slightly russeted. Despite its recent vintage, it has the looks and taste of an old-time variety. Taste is nutty and sweet with aroma.

RUSSET BEAUTY (600–800 chill hours/very early ripening) See description on page 76.

SUNCRISP (600–800 chill hours/midseason ripening) Introduced in 1994 from Rutgers University. Cox's and Golden Delicious cross that is cleaner, bigger, and more conical in shape than either parent. It possesses an impressive aromatic sugar to acid ratio. The tree is very dwarf and not spreading, thus further slowing tree development. Reliable and heavy cropper.

A VARIETY IN SEARCH OF A NAME (PIÑATA) (600–800 chill hours/midseason ripening) A variety that is starting to resemble Odysseus's 10 years of trials, travels, travails, and condemned wandering before arriving home safe in Ithaca, this apple is alternately called Pinova, Corail, Sonata, and Piñata. First released in 1986 from the Pilnitz, Germany, fruit-breeding station. The distinctive parentage—Golden Delicious, Cox's Orange Pippin, and Dutchess of Oldenburg (an older European pie apple)—accounts for both sweet and tangy taste sensations. The apple is crisp, rich, and aromatic. The look is a thing of great beauty, with a glowing blush of pinkish red over a solid orange-yellow background. Medium sized with a slightly conical shape, not unlike Golden Delicious. The flavor combinations make it a distinctive eating experience.

The tree is of low vigor. On M7 rootstock, it is only 5–6 feet tall; MM106 or MM111 gives it a boost to 7–10 feet. Thrives in cool coastal areas, where the color is enhanced. Virtually scab resistant. It is very similar in both appearance and taste to Gala, Honeycrisp, SunCrisp, and Sunrise, although the eating experience is superior to all these varieties. I fear it will never catch on with consumers due to lack of name recognition. Too bad (for them). It is easy to buy and grow on your own. Perhaps it can be shepherded through the rocky straits of Scylla and Charybdis . . .

Favorites of Mixed Parentage

Breaking out of the familial groupings, here's a varietal grab bag of sorts, a loose assortment of apples, not necessarily any relation to one another, that I just happen to love.

VARIETIES OF NOTE

AROMA (700 chill hours/early-season ripening) Cross between Ingrid Marie (Cox's Orange Pippin seedling) and Filippa (possibly a Danish seedling of Gravenstein) introduced in 1973. Ripens on the heels of Gravenstein. Very large (10–14 ounces), multiple-flavored, aromatic apple with creamy, soft melting flesh. The juice quotient is high. Eating an Aroma can be a sublime experience. Typical of one parent line (Gravenstein), it has problems with preharvest drop (greater than 70 percent). Pick 'em, put 'em in a bowl, ripen, enjoy. Again, like Gravenstein, coloring is variable and much aided by full sunlight in the center of the tree. Thankfully, the tree has an open habit, with strong yet graceful arching branches. With requisite sunlight, Aroma attains a rich red-over-yellow stippled look. And like Gravenstein, it is a shy bearer. Suggested pollinators: Akane, Chestnut and Dolgo crabapples, Gala.

BRAEBURN (700 chill hours/late-season ripening) Unsung late variety from New Zealand that excels when sampled fresh off the tree. Conical apple of good size, with a green hue with red stripes in the foreground. Firm and crunchy texture and tangy flavor both mildly sweet and slightly tart. The most outstanding taste component of a dead-on ripe Braeburn is a "bring you to your knees in appreciation" spicy finish. Braeburn is thought possibly to be self-fertile. Suggested pollinators: Akane, Chestnut and Dolgo crabapples, Gala.

GRANNY SMITH (500 chill hours/very late-season ripening) Discovered as a volunteer seedling from Australia in the 1860s. Generally a hard, crisp, mild (slightly acidic) green variety that develops both sugar and orange-yellow blush on the shoulders at full maturation. To me, it is a very ordinary apple whose only redeeming quality is the time of year it ripens (late fall to early winter). In July to October, it's a "spitter"—take a bite to test it, spit it out, and move on. But in December and January, it's not a bad apple. It's also utilitarian, it crops reliably, and it's a great pollinator for most apple varieties. Suggested pollinators: Akane, Alkmene, Chestnut and Dolgo crabapples, Gala, Golden Russet.

GRAVENSTEIN (700 chill hours/very early-season ripening) Old apple (400-plus years), with a storied and conflicted past. It has a cult following owing to its early ripening (late July–mid-August) and distinctive tangy-sweet flavors. The ivory-white flesh is both crisp and juicy, yet soft and melting. The thin skin is a yellowish green with variable red striping. Favored for fresh eating, juice, pies, and applesauce.

This variety is thought to have originated in either Italy (the Tyrolian Alps), Germany, Russia, or most probably Denmark in the 1600s. It was transported to the Sebastopol, California, area by Russian immigrants from the southern Ukraine (*Sevastopol* area) in the 1800s. Gravenstein was a leading, although problematic, commercial apple into the early 1980s. At one time, it was the leading agricultural product of Sonoma County, California. Sadly, many of the commercial plantings have been abandoned for higher-dollar-value-per-acre wine grape crops—or, even more sadly, second homes for Bay Area professionals.

The distinctive flavors of Gravenstein coupled with its early-season maturation have created a loyal, almost feverish following, as in "Are the Gravvies in yet?" So what are its problems? A multitude.

It is one of the most vigorous of all apple scions. Unless planted on very dwarfing rootstocks, it'll be you and the high wire act of the Flying Wallendas at 25 feet above the ground. A perilous proposition. Try it on M9, B9, M7, or G30.

It is a shy and erratic bearer, setting a light crop. Some strains, Rosebrook and Red, are more consistent, as well as a bit prettier and sweeter. Because of the early bloom, sometimes the weather can negatively affect pollination and fruit set. So much of a successful year of fruit growing is dependent on weather conditions during a 10- to 14-day stretch in early spring. And as we all know, spring weather is nothing if not erratic.

It is a short-stemmed apple, and when it sets fruit, it always does so in clusters of three to five. If not thinned, the apples will push each other off the tree as they enlarge.

Gravenstein has a soft skin, which is good for eating, but simply look at it cross-eyed and it will bruise. That, coupled with a tendency to preharvest drop (more than 65 percent of the apples tend to fall preharvest), makes it a difficult apple for commercial farmers.

Gravenstein is a bit of a shape shifter. Some of the fruits are big, some small, some oblong, some round or elliptical, some ribbed, some smooth. Almost all are lopsided. They are good, though. In his tome *The Anatomy of Dessert*, Edward Bunyard said, "of Gravenstein it is hard to speak in mere prose. So distinct in flavor . . . so full of juice and scented with the very attar of apple . . . bringing to mind the autumnal orchard in yellow sunlight." (Attar is the fragrant oil from rose petals—an old Persian term.) Suggested pollinators: Alkmene, Braeburn, Dolgo and Wickson crabapples, Egremont Russet, Fuji, Gala, McIntosh, Tompkins King. Gravenstein is triploid, and hence not a pollinator.

HAUER PIPPIN (700–800 chill hours/very late-season ripening) Chance seedling originally selected by Peter Hauer in Corralitos, California, in the 1890s. Latest apple in the garden, typically ripening mid-December to mid-January, well after the tree is dormant. Green with an orange-red blush and white spots, it is a large, crisp, dense, tight-fleshed, tart apple. Keeps well into the spring in a cold room or garage. Suggested pollinators: Most white-flowered crabapples.

YELLOW NEWTOWN PIPPIN (700–800 chill hours/late-season ripening) Originated in Newtown, Long Island, in the 1750s. Often sold green in August and September, but reaches its full flavor and color peak in October into November. At maturation, this medium-sized variety is a warm yellow-green with a burnt-orange blush and is slightly waxy to the touch. One of the more complex, full-flavored apples, with a brisk, juicy, aromatic taste with hints of pineapple, strawberry, and guava. Often keeps on the tree well past leaf drop in the fall, making a striking sight and an easy target for birds. Suggested pollinators: Akane; Alkmene; Chestnut, Dolgo, and Wickson crabapples; Elstar; Fuji; Gala; Granny Smith.

Dry-farmed Yellow Newtown Pippin apples in winter as practiced by Everett Family Farm in Aptos, California.

Hidden Heirloom Gems: Russeted Apples

When recommending apple varietals, I always try nudge folks to break out of the Fuji, Honeycrisp, Jonagold, and especially Gala rut. It's not that these varieties aren't good, but it's time to open a new "door of perception," to quote Aldous Huxley.

Russeted apples are not a variety, but a type of apple consisting of many heirloom varieties that have common skin and taste characteristics. Russets harken back to colonial times when apple varieties were regional, giving true meaning to the much-championed "Buy Fresh, Buy Local" marketing slogan of the present. Generally, these apples had a short fresh market season. Back then, russets were renowned as keepers. Put them in a box and store them in a cool room (below 40°F) or a root cellar; under such conditions, they would keep in reasonable shape for 3–6 months.

Today's most popular market apples tend to be red, round, and smooth skinned. And they'd better follow suit with the superlatives: sweet, sweeter, and sweetest. And they'd better be big and oblong to conical in size and shape, à la Golden and Red Delicious.

Russets are anything but. Variety to variety, and even apple to apple on the same tree, almost everything about the look of russets— size, shape, coloring, and skin—is anomalous. Both texture and color of the flesh are variable. However, taste and aroma are somewhat uniform, combining "green" and sugary backed by acidity and a touch of nuttiness. Russets often drift toward subtropicality with hints of citrus, guava, and even pineapple. In the aggregate, they are a cut above—sublime.

Most russets are small to medium in size and have a shape that is classified as round or oblate. Often they are as wide or wider than tall. Two notable exceptions regarding shape are Hudson's Golden Gem and Hoople's Antique Gold. Both are either bud mutations or seedlings of Golden Delicious. As such they tend to be oblong or conical with five distinct knobs at the base, much like their parent. These varieties vary in shape apple to apple; this is especially true of Hudson's, which is more than occasionally lopsided.

The most unifying characteristic of russets is that they tend to either look or be rough to the touch. The skin can even be corky, bumpy, or warted. The Knobbed Russet takes this to an extreme—with its froglike skin, it's positively amphibian. They often look like they have a bad case of apple scab, a fungal disease. The topography of the skin even has peaks and valleys. Some varieties exhibit heavy and rough russeting, much like a baking potato or a Bosc pear. Still others have only an irregular, lightly webbed russeting and can actually be smooth skinned. These varieties—Ashmead's Kernel, Roxbury Russet, and Golden Russet—usually display a flushed cheek of copper, bronze, or orangish red coloration at full maturation.

In one sense, russets have a drab appearance, and yet they have a quiet, strong beauty. They are as they look, apples with both a story and a history, a personality and a depth of character—an apple lover's apple. Russets are truly beautiful as well as utilitarian, and eating a russet is a long, layered, thought-provoking experience. Sometimes, after first admiring and then consuming a Roxbury Russet or an Golden Russet, my conclusion: best darn apple I ever ate, or could ever eat.

While not all russets taste alike, they do share some taste characteristics. They usually start out sugary, followed by balancing acidity. Volatile aromatic oils usually factor in. The russet experience can make eaters feel they have taken a temperate zone, deciduous fruit and sailed off to subtropical latitudes where evergreen fruits rule supreme: citrus (especially lemon), guava, banana, and pineapple. At the same time, in sequence, you are experiencing the sugar, texture, and gritty cells of a pear. This last sensation is most pronounced with Hudson's Golden Gem.

Utilitarian is definitely the byword with russets. They are equally good fresh or stored for up to 6 months, dried, baked, or made into crisps or pies and rendered to cider—sweet and hard.

Potential pollination partners for the following russeted apple selections include Alkmene and most other Cox's types, Belle de Boskoop, Dolgo and Chestnut crabapples, Grimes Golden, Yellow Newtown Pippin, and most McIntoshes.

VARIETIES OF NOTE

ASHMEAD'S KERNEL (800–1,000 chill hours/late-season ripening)
Gloucester, England, 1700. Asymmetrical small apple with a flat-round
shape. Golden brown with a reddish orange, sometimes bronze flush
on the cheek. Crisp, coarse, and yellowish green flesh. The taste
is sugary enough, but with an assertive, aromatic acidity. Not an
apple for the faint of heart. Good in cider blends. Note: It's not a
strong grower and hence not recommended if you're only growing
a couple trees.

EGREMONT RUSSET (800–1,000 chill hours/late-season ripening)
Origin unknown but probably England, 1870s. Medium-sized apple
with a flat-round shape, sometimes almost blocky and rectangular.
Very rough russeting of the skin with a good deal of cracking, especially in the stem basket (sunken area round the stem). The dark
russeting can appear almost black with a gold or bronze background.
The skin, which is best discarded, is tough and chewy, giving way to a
greenish yellow, densely textured flesh that is nutty, sweet, and aromatic. Distinctive sweet-tart taste with some smoky overtones thrown
in for good measure.

GOLDEN RUSSET (800–1,000 chill hours/late-season ripening)
Likely, early 1800s, New York. A small round-flat apple with rough-
looking, streaked, uneven russeting and a cork-like quality around
the stem basket. The skin has bronzy hues with a copper splotch on the
sunny side and a golden green background color. Creamy yellow flesh
with a tinge of green at the core. The dense and fine-textured flesh is an
exception among russets. Intense and sugary taste at the outset, followed
by a balanced but pronounced kick. A slight oily, volatile aromatic
aspect to the latter part of the taste sensation. Mature fruit hangs on the
tree as late as leaf drop.

GOLDRUSH (800–1,000 chill hours/late-season ripening) Looks
old, but is of recent vintage (1992), introduced from the PRI disease-
resistant apple-breeding program (see page 37). Outstanding tart-sweet
apple fresh off the tree; sugary-tart after 1–2 months in cold storage.

Generally assertively tart when fresh picked; more than occasionally you can find a sweet one. The sugar can be credited to the Golden Delicious in its parentage. In size, it rivals Golden Delicious. Thinning to 6–8 inches between apples increases the size. The coloring is green-yellow, turning to a soft gold at full maturation. Some light russeting in the stem basket area and pronounced speckling. The skin is a bit tough and chewy. The flesh is both green and yellow.

Where this apple excels is in the boldness and complexity of the tasting experience. With the first bite, you become aware that you're on to something strong, long, and definitive. Initially the crisp, coarse flesh is palpable, then comes a strong bite of acidity coupled with and then extended by big sugar.

HOOPLE'S ANTIQUE GOLD (800–1,000 chill hours/late-season ripening) Meritorious apple from Mr. Harry Hoople of Hoople's Fruit Farm in Otway, Ohio. A weak scion and small apple with a big taste. Probably a bud mutation of Golden Delicious. In shape, Hoople's resembles its alleged parent. Antique refers not to its age, but the beauty and richness of its gold skin. The flesh is coarse textured and chunky. The taste is almost as sugary as Hudson's Golden Gem. Sweetness is the major chord, with crispness and acidity as the minor chord. I like it a lot, but all the more so because it is my wife's favorite apple.

HUDSON'S GOLDEN GEM (800–1,000 chill hours/midseason ripening) Found hedgerow seedling from Hudson's Nursery in Tangent, Oregon, 1931, probably an escaped seedling of Golden Delicious. Similar to its parent in shape: long, oblong-conical. Arguably the largest and definitely the sweetest of the russets, with an uncanny knack for throwing variable lopsided fruit. The skin is dry and rough to the touch. The color is a dull, soft faint yellow background with mottled, dotted russeting in the foreground. Sugary and juicy with a similar taste and texture as pears and a little nuttiness for good measure. Because it has that "pear cell grit," if you close your eyes you might be able to mistake a Hudson's Golden Gem for a pear.

Roxbury Russet,
America's oldest apple

ROXBURY RUSSET (800–1,000 chill hours/late-season ripening)
From the Roxbury district of my hometown of Boston, early 1600s,
thought to be the first cultivated, named apple variety in America.
Round to oblate in shape. Features creamy white flesh and thin
nonchewy skin. The flavor is very sugary, with translucent sugar swirls
in the flesh (actually a precursor to a storage disorder called water
core, which causes fruit to rot in storage). A slight lemon scent and a
following acidity and greenness that balances the initial sugary sensation. For a refined, smoother-eating experience, couple with sliced
extra-sharp Cheddar (of New England origin). But then, that recipe
works for all the russets.

RUSSET BEAUTY (600–800 chill hours/midseason ripening)
Thought to be a chance seedling of a cross between Cox's Orange
Pippin and Golden Delicious. Early September russet that is atypically
large fruited, round-oblate in shape. Uniform bronzy-golden fawn with
many small bumps. It has all the high flavor of Cox with an insane
amount of sugar (gets watery and soft if not picked promptly within
10–14 days). Firm texture if picked at perfection. Tree is spreading with
good vigor. This is often a favorite among the apprentice group and thus
disappears from the Chadwick Garden's trees with great alacrity.

ST. EDMUND'S PIPPIN (800–1,000 chill hours/very early-season
ripening) England, 1875. Also known as St. Edmund's Russet. About the
earliest ripening of the russets, which rivals Fall Russet for early cropping. An annual and heavy cropper. Fruit is medium sized, flat-round,
and wider than tall. Skin color is uniformly golden-fawn russeted. Flesh
is a pale creamy yellow, crisp, juicy, fine textured, and dense. Taste
runs to pear, even pear nectar, rich, sugary, subacid, and aromatic.
An impressive apple.

EUROPEAN PEARS

Pyrus communis

Pears have been cultivated for more than 4,000 years. Dried slices of cultivated pears have been unearthed in Swiss cave dwellings dating to 400 BCE. Records left by the ancient Greeks and Romans show pear propagation, cultivation, and appreciation as a dessert fruit. Most of today's quality varieties were first bred by French and Italian monks (1500s–1800s) and then their Belgium counterparts (1800s). What are known now as European pears (*Pyrus communis*) actually hail from regions of temperate Europe and western Asia (southern Caucasus Mountains into the northern mountains of Iraq and Iran, formerly Persia).

What makes the Queen of Fruits so sublime? It's not so much that pears, especially summer types, have more sugar than apples. Both are about 10 percent sugar by weight. However, pears have less acidity than apples (2 percent versus 8 percent). The sugar-acid ratio of apples is about 13:1; with pears it's 50:1. In fact, hard as it may be to fathom, pears have more sugar by weight than apricots and are about the same as peaches. It's all about the sugar-acid ratio. Those European monks of old really knew their science.

Commercial pear variety offerings are stuck in the same rut apple varieties were mired in until 20 or 30 years ago. With apples you could get any variety you liked as long as it was Granny Smith (green), Red Delicious (red), or Golden Delicious (yellow). These days, supermarket (including your local Big Organic Chain branch) pears devolve to Bartlett (early and yellow), Comice (midseason and the world's most popular mail-order gift fruit), D'Anjou (late and green), and Bosc (later still and a dull, bronzy russet color). It's not that these aren't exquisite pears at their peak of ripeness—it's just that so many other choices expand and extend the eating experience and season of ripeness.

Pear growing is not for the impatient, with standard-size trees taking up to 20 years to reach their stride and bear a sizable crop. Even semidwarf trees take 5–8 years to carry a good fruit load. There are no truly dwarfing rootstocks for pears, and it is hard to keep tree height under 12–18 feet. Fortunately, there are a few natural dwarf varieties: Seckel, Honey, Dana's Hovey, and Bella di Guigno.

A crucial aspect of choosing pear varietals is understanding how and when pears ripen. There are two basic classes of pears—summer and winter. Think of summer and winter pears as being as vastly different as summer and winter squashes.

Summer Pears

Summer pears, as the name implies, crop early (July–September) and sweeten and ripen on the tree. In size, they tend to be small (2–3 inches in length) or medium (4–5 inches). Two notable exceptions are the ubiquitous Bartlett (6 inches) and the Bulgarian-bred Ubileen (8 inches).

Summer varieties feature a very thin, delicate, and easily bruised skin that severely limits storage, shipping, and thus marketing. While they have limited commercial appeal owing to their fragility, they are an easy-to-harvest, sublime treat for the home grower. The taste experience goes something like this:

- Thin, dissolving skin

- Fine-textured flesh that is soft, melting, and often aromatic

- A rich, buttery sweetness with a slight background taste of mild acidity

Summer pears lack the characteristic grit, or stone cells, of most winter pears, whose cell structure imparts a gritty but pleasant component to the taste experience.

Pears ripen from the inside out. Because of the small size and the makeup of cell walls in summer pears, all can be ripened on the tree and can keep for up to 2 weeks in the refrigerator after harvesting. This is in contrast to winter pears, which require cold storage in order to ripen and can keep for months in the refrigerator (see below).

Here is how to determine ripeness with a summer pear:

- Taste it. As I often joke with apprentices, a reliable indicator of unripeness on any fruit is five to six pears at the base of the tree, each with one bite taken out of it.

- As the pear matures, color should brighten, even glow.

- When gently squeezed, fruit should give slightly, especially around the neck.

- Seeds should be dark brown to black.

- Fruit should be slightly aromatic, especially around the calyx (bottom) end.

Winter Pears

The *winter* here refers not so much to time of harvest (September to November) as to season of ripening (while off the tree) and distribution for mass marketing.

I think pears hold up better to cold storage than any other fruit. Winter pears require 3–4 weeks of cold storage to ripen (convert starches to sugars). Just put them in the vegetable crisper drawer of your refrigerator. If pears are left to ripen on the tree, the interior will be soft, mushy, and fermented by the time the exterior is sweet. If picked too early, they never sweeten and remain hard. The trick is when to harvest.

The technologies and tools available to large-scale commercial growers are beyond the scope and cost possible for home gardeners. Most winter pears are picked at the "green, mature stage" (maturity is a precursor to ripening), refrigerated, and then ripened at room temperature. When it comes to deciding when to pick winter pears, home gardeners have several less technical options than their commercial counterparts:

- By the calendar. Or, "Well, last year I picked my Comice starting around September 15. I picked in several rounds through October 5." This can work but also can be off by as much as 2–3 weeks either way, depending on the summer weather and temperatures.

- Noticeable color change. Bosc lose their green background tinge and become a dull bronze. Red varieties lose brightness and gloss. Comice and D'Anjou start to develop a little background yellow-gold hue.

- Seed color change. As pears mature, seed color goes from white, to beige, to dark brown or black.

- Cradle test. Gently grasp the bottom of a pear on the tree and slowly swing it from 6 o'clock to 9 o'clock and away from you in a twisting motion. It should easily separate, with the stem attached, at maturity.

> All pears are cross-pollinated; in order to produce fruit they need to be near a different variety of pear that blooms at the same time. Luckily, most pears bloom close together. Note: The varieties Bartlett and Seckel, however, will not pollinate one another.

SUMMER PEAR VARIETIES OF NOTE

BARTLETT (500–600 chill hours/very early-season ripening) World's most planted pear variety. Often associated with canned pears; also one of the best dessert pears. Goes from green to a warm yellow color at maturation (ripe). Very short holding period on the tree until it goes mushy (7–10 days at maturation), but matures in waves over 3–4 weeks (August–September). Juicy flesh with a sugary, musky flavor. Thought to be somewhat self-pollinating, but should be treated as cross-pollinating—sets a bigger crop, in both size and number, with a pollinator. Originated in Berkshire, England, in the 1700s as a chance seedling. Known then by its proper name—Williams' Bon Chretien—and still referred to as that or Williams' in Europe. It is astounding that a fruit variety has enough redeeming qualities to endure for more than 200 years as a leading commercial production variety. Moderately dwarf growth habit. Note: Bartlett can be treated as a summer or winter pear. The first 7–10 days of harvest lend to winter treatment; thereafter, summer treatment, that is, pick it ripe off the tree.

BELLA DI GUIGNO (500–600 chill hours/very early-season ripening) Hands down the earliest pear (*Guigno* is Italian for "June") and the smallest fruit (2–3 inches). Crisp, sweet over tart taste. Hard to sweeten before it goes fermenty—cute though. Sets a heavy crop annually.

BUTIRRA PRECOCE MORETTINI (600–800 chill hours/early-season ripening) Also known as Early Butter Morettini. Large tree, large fruit, large sweet, spicy rich buttery taste.

DAWN and **TYSON** (500–600 chill hours/early-season ripening) These two different varieties, with significant similarities, are the ultimate summer sweet-butter pears.

RED CLAPP'S FAVORITE (600–800 chill hours/early-season ripening) Originated in Michigan. Large fruit with deep red skin and abundant annual crops. Basically a Bartlett with spice.

Red Clapp's Favorite fruit buds with young pears

SECKEL and **HONEY** (500–600 chill hours/late-season ripening) Honey is also called Honey Sweet; Seckel is aptly nicknamed the "Sugar Lump." Two different varieties, with significant similarities. Naturally dwarf trees, these 5- to 8-foot "bushes" are loaded annually with small brown-red russet fruit.

UBILEEN (600 chill hours/midseason ripening) Unusually large pear from Bulgaria that is all sugar, no grit, exploding with juice and a soft, buttery texture. Heavy fruit set can induce branch breakage—thin to one fruit every 8–9 inches.

WARREN (600 chill hours/midseason ripening) Found seedling from Hattiesburg, Mississippi, by noted horticulturist T. O. Warren. Medium-large, asymmetrical teardrop–shaped, dull brown fruit that's not much to look at. But it's all about a smooth-as-butter, aromatic, sugary-sweet experience. If a pear can be too sweet, this one comes close, begging the question, Can there be too much of a good thing? Warren is a notoriously difficult pear to pollinate, but Bella di Guigno is a good pollination partner.

WINTER PEAR VARIETIES OF NOTE

Bosc pear

BOSC (500–600 chill hours/late-season ripening) Also called Beurré Bosc. The French have a penchant for preceding pear names with Beurré, Doyenne, or Dutchess D'. Large, long necked, and tapered with golden brown, russeted skin. Spicy, sweet, aromatic, and gritty good. Heavy annual crops. Originally from Belgium.

COMICE (600 chill hours/midseason ripening) Or more properly Doyenne (Queen) du Comice. Probably the world's most famous pear. Sugar balanced with acidity and smooth pear texture. Stores well for more than 5–6 months.

D'ANJOU (800 chill hours/mid- to late-season ripening) Also called Beurré D'Anjou and Red D'Anjou. Smooth texture, lemony flavor, not the sweetest pear.

ORCAS (800 chill hours/midseason ripening) Found seedling from Orcas Island, Washington. Yellow-carmine flushed skin. Large fruit, full flavor—sweet, acid, spicy.

RESCUE (800 chill hours/midseason ripening) Another Northwest favorite. Huge fruit with bright red-orange blush and sweet, juicy, smooth-textured flesh.

QUINCES
Cydonia oblonga

Quinces hail from the wooded slopes in the regions of Turkey, Armenia, and eastward in a geographic band through Iran and Afghanistan. They have been grown in Turkey and on the isle of Crete for the past 4,000 years and are now grown throughout the Mediterranean. The word *quince* is thought to be a variation of the name Kydonia, a city-state on ancient Crete.

Quinces certainly qualify as being both unsung and underappreciated. Until the decline and demise of the small family farm in the United States, almost every farmyard or homestead featured at least one quince. Yours should, too. If you want to experience the quince's subtle strength of form, foliage, and stunning flower, you'll have to grow your own, for they are seldom seen on farms or in markets.

We grow quinces at the UCSC Farm & Garden. We may occasionally fertilize them, and they get some water sometimes, maybe. We rarely if ever prune them, we never thin them, and we are almost always consistently rewarded with the dividend of a heavy fruit crop in September and October. They are essentially a managed or "benign neglect" species. Additionally, they are not too particular about soil and can tolerate wet feet. Coupled with their unique culinary qualities, what's not to like?

The ripe fruit has a fuzzy covering of fine hairs, which are easily brushed off. The fruits look like odd-shaped pears, flattened on one side, but they are suffused with a dull golden glow, as if they were small sun orbs, hanging at twilight. When first picked, they are leathery and tough on the outside. And if biting into them does not break a tooth, you will be "rewarded" with a taste that is astringent to the point of tasting like one part quinine, one part sandpaper, and one part cement mix, with a chaser of paint thinner.

You will pucker up and grimace. Relax. Put the fruit in a box, in a single layer. Set it in a warm but shaded room. Wait 3 weeks or so. And voilà—the fruit will have softened, but it will still retain a good deal of its astringency, and sugar is nowhere to be found.

The astringency in quinces is caused by tannins. Red wines also have tannins, but not with such wicked concentration. These tannins are heat, acid, and water soluble, so the highest and best use for the quince is to bake, stew, or poach it. During this process, the tannins are volatilized, and the starches are converted to sugars. The result is a soft but firm sauce with plenty of sweetness and aroma. Adding a bit of lemon juice also aids the process.

Quinces can then be used to make marmalade, jams, jellies, and chutneys. When I mention marmalade, you might think of citrus and the Brits, but the first marmalades are credited to the Spanish in the fourteenth century—and their substrate was quince. Try it; you'll like it. Quince paste, jam, marmalade, or chutney shines when paired with dry, sharp cheeses or savory dishes. Quince is also a good additive to apple and pear pies and sauces, contributing sugar and firmness and a flowery aroma. Put a couple or a few quinces in a bowl on a ledge or counter and the citrus-guava scent will waft out, filling the room and acting as natural air freshener.

Unlike apples and pears, the quince is self-pollinating—one tree will suffice (unless you want a whole lot of quince fruit, which is not necessarily a bad thing). All the following varieties require approximately 300–500 chill hours and ripen in late season (fall).

VARIETIES OF NOTE

AROMATNAYA Russian variety that is reportedly sweet enough to eat fresh, after it has ripened. It has a pineapple-like flavor and an aroma of citrus.

KARP'S SWEET Another variety that is sweet before cooking. Named in honor of fruit writer and "detective" extraordinaire David Karp, who stalks the globe looking for, sampling, and writing articulately about rare and exotic fruit and its origins. (And for this he gets paid!) Karp obtained scion wood of this cultivar from a paradisiacal valley in Peru, Valle de Majes, situated at an altitude of 650–2,600 feet in a climate that is warm year-round. And no doubt, the Andean condor flies overhead, too . . .

ORANGE The fruit is indeed orange. Sometimes it exceeds 1 pound. Early ripening.

PINEAPPLE Produces a vigorous tree with large fruit that is lemon colored. While the exotic fragrance is alluring, the physical appearance is not particularly attractive.

SMYRNA Large tree, large fruit. Aromatic even on the tree. Very sweet when cooked.

Varietal Recommendations: Stone Fruits

I took money and bought flowering trees
And planted them out on the bank to the east of the Keep.
I simply bought whatever had most blooms,
Not caring whether peach, apricot, or plum.
A hundred fruits, all mixed up together;
A thousand branches, flowering in due rotation.
Each has its season coming early or late;
But to all alike the fertile soil is kind.
The red flowers hang like a heavy mist;
The white flowers gleam like a fall of snow.

—PO CHU (China, 846–772 BCE), from "Planting Flowers on the Eastern Embankment," translated by Arthur Waley, 1918

Prunus is a large, diverse genus in the Rosaceae family, commonly referred to as stone fruits. Principal commercial crops in this genus include peaches, nectarines, plums, pluots, apriums, apricots, cherries, and almonds.

The name *stone fruit* comes from the stonelike pit encasing the seed. It is the soft, flavorful, juicy, aromatic (at full ripeness), mouth-watering combination of sugars and acids in fleeting succession that intrigues us as gardeners.

For the most part, stone fruits are nonclimacteric fruits. Non-climacteric fruits ripen gradually, and don't store sugar as starch but instead depend on their continued connection—via the conductive vascular tissue of the stem—to the parent (the tree) for continued sweetening. The fruits get no sweeter off the tree, though enzymes may promote their softening. Thus the quality of the fruit is dependent on the ripening that takes place on the tree. In fact, cold storage (colder than 50°F) retards natural pectin breakdown, causing stone fruits to become dry and mealy.

Indian Blood peach, historically grown by members of the Cherokee Nation

PEACHES AND NECTARINES

Prunus persica and *Prunus persica* var. *nectarin*

Peaches and nectarines hail from Xian in central China, at the beginning of the Silk Road. The species name *persica* (Persia) is a misnomer, probably attributed to its spread via trade caravans from China into Iraq and Iran and eventually to Europe. The fruit came to the Americas (Mexico and Florida) with the Spanish colonialists in the sixteenth century on their invasively ill-begotten conquering expeditions. It was then spread across North America by Native Americans. The nectarine is genetically identical to the peach but with a recessive gene for pubescence (or as on-the-ground gardeners say, the nectarine is simply a peach missing the "fuzz" gene). The nectarine is as old as the peach, with records of cultivation dating back to 2000 BCE. It is either a chance seedling or a whole tree mutation. Nectarines are generally less cold hardy than most peaches.

Commercially, peaches and nectarines are grown at latitudes between 25 and 45 degrees north and south of the equator. Major peach-growing regions include Chile, China, Northern Italy, Spain, Turkey, California, southeastern United States, New York, Pennsylvania, and Michigan. They can be grown closer to the equator than any other species of temperate-zone deciduous fruits because of their tolerance for heat and humidity, and their low-chill requirements for breaking dormancy.

The peach ranks only behind the apple in worldwide production and economic worth. Their sweet flavor, aroma, and nectar set the bar very high (along with apricots) for sun-warmed tree-ripe perfection that evokes the essence of summer. Peaches are the shortest lived of all deciduous fruit trees, with an average life expectancy of only 20–40 years (apples and pears live more than 80–100 years).

Peaches and nectarines have two basic flesh types—clingstone and freestone. Clingstones exhibit a firm-textured flesh that cannot be pulled off the stone (pit) and must be cut away with a knife. Because they hold their shape when halved or sliced, they are versatile candidates for canning, drying, or eating fresh. Freestones are softer-fleshed varieties with higher juice and sugar content, and separate easily from the pit. They lend themselves to eating fresh.

In general, white-fleshed peach varieties are sweeter than the aromatic, yellow-fleshed varieties, which have a greater sugar-acid balance.

Peaches such as Donut, Saturn, Peento, and Bagel are in a separate category. They are petite, sweet, melting-fleshed peaches native to China. They are small (2–3 inches across and 1 inch thick), and roughly shaped like many of their names imply—squat and round with a dimple in the center. They have a very short season and bruise more easily than any other type of peach.

Almost all peach and nectarine varieties are self-fruitful, that is, they accept pollen from their own flowers and do not need pollen from another variety to set fruit. Notable exceptions are Elberta types and Hale cultivars.

In choosing peaches, keep an eye out for resistance to peach leaf curl (*Taphrina deformans*), a leaf fungus that afflicts almost all peach and nectarine varieties in almost all growing regions. It is especially devastating in cool, coastal climates where trees can be completely defoliated in June during a bad year. Varieties resistant to peach leaf curl include Frost, Avalon Pride, Mary Jane, Red Haven, Indian Blood, and Q1-8. Extremely susceptible but great-tasting varieties include Babcock, Elberta, and the

Saturn types. (Peach leaf curl can be controlled with one to three applications of copper spray between leaf drop and bud break.)

Old School Versus New School

Peach tastes can be linked to flesh color and varieties, which I generally categorize as "old school" versus "new school" varieties. Old school varieties don't color evenly or have as bright a sheen to their skin. They have a more balanced sugar-acid ratio, which contributes to a fuller "old-timey" peach flavor—more of a well-rounded balance between sugar and acidity, less of a full-on sugar rush. They have a very limited shelf life, must be tree ripened to have full flavor, and bruise easily, giving rise to that old farmers' market adage, "Real peaches don't stack." They don't store, either.

Old school peach varieties are ripe when the background color has no tinge of green and is expressing full yellow or white coloring. The foreground color of red and/or golden yellow may be more a function of varietal characteristics than ripeness. Tree-ripe peaches that have achieved full sweetness should be extremely, sublimely aromatic and yield slightly to the touch.

Because old school varieties are more difficult to grow, they're considered all but obsolete in today's commercial produce world. And because the fruit deteriorates rapidly and becomes mealy in cold storage, the older varieties are a mere remembrance fading in the rear-view mirror—a tribute to a time when there was a fierce loyalty to varietal brand names. Old school varieties include your classic name-brand peaches like Suncrest, Elberta, Babcock, J. H. Hale, Red Haven, Le Grand, Rio Oso, Sun Grand, and Baby Crawford.

New school peach and nectarine varieties are all sugar and sweetness with very little acid. They have a rich pink-red hue to their skin, are firm fleshed and larger on average than the old varieties, and continue to ripen off the tree under refrigeration. They have a sublime, delicate flavor that is less peachy and more sugary. New school varieties include Arctic Supreme, Arctic Glo, White Lady, Sugar Lady, Snow Giant, and Arctic Jay. New school peach varieties all equal or surpass the superlatives good, better, best. These varieties break almost all the rules—they ripen before background color comes up, can be picked firm, will have high sugar content, and can be refrigerated and shipped long distances.

All peaches and nectarines are self-pollinated; they do not require another variety to produce fruit. One peach or nectarine tree of any variety will produce for you.

OLD SCHOOL PEACH VARIETIES OF NOTE

AVALON PRIDE (300–400 chill hours/midseason ripening) High flavor, yellow flesh, semifreestone. Extremely resistant to peach leaf curl.

BABCOCK and **GIANT BABCOCK** (250–300 chill hours/midseason ripening) Two different varieties with significant similarities. Medium and large fruit, skin mostly red, freestone. White flesh, sweet, juicy. Consistently heavy yields.

BABY CRAWFORD (800 chill hours/midseason ripening) Small, intensely flavored sweet freestone peach. Yellow flesh.

DONUT (400–500 chill hours/early-season ripening) So named because of its shape. Sometimes called Saturn peach. White meated and exquisitely sweet, this flat peach originated in China. Clingstone. Not particularly resistant to peach leaf curl.

ELBERTA, **FANTASTIC ELBERTA**, **LATE ELBERTA**, and **FAY ELBERTA** (700–800 chill hours/midseason ripening) These similar varieties all have firm, yellow, juicy fruit with golden hue and red blush. Freestone. Sweet and holds reasonably well off the tree.

LORING (750 chill hours/midseason ripening) Large yellow fruit with a striking red blush. High flavor, good eating quality, also for canning. Clingstone.

MARY JANE (600 chill hours/late-season ripening) Red skin, yellow flesh, sweet taste. Clingstone. Peach leaf curl resistant. Sets fruit under adverse weather conditions.

RED HAVEN and **EARLY RED HAVEN** (800 chill hours/midseason ripening) These two similar varieties are the standard for assessing all mid-season varieties. Firm yellow flesh, pleasing smooth texture, red-golden skin, clingstone. Good for fresh eating and canning. Peach leaf curl resistant.

RIO OSO GEM (500 chill hours/mid- to late-season ripening) Heavy bearer of large, firm freestone fruit. Red skin, great taste, late maturation. Small tree. One of the best tasting varieties ever.

SUNCREST (700 chill hours/mid- to late-season ripening) Classic California peach as lauded in *Epitaph for a Peach*, by David Mas Masumoto. Large, round fruit, highly aromatic, flavorful balance between acid and sugar—old-timey flavor. Skin is two-thirds red, one-third yellow, colors unevenly, bruises easily. Clingstone.

SWEET BAGEL (250–300 chill hours/midseason ripening) Round shape, melting sugary flesh, small fruit, clingstone. Not particularly resistant to plain leaf curl. Yellow-fleshed fruit. Bigger than Donut.

NEW SCHOOL PEACH VARIETIES OF NOTE

ARCTIC SUPREME (700 chill hours/midseason ripening) White-meated peaches with the lightest, sweetest flavors. Freestone. Red over creamy white skin.

FROST (700 chill hours/midseason the ripening) Late-blooming, sweet, flavorful variety with yellow flesh. Clingstone. Extremely peach leaf curl resistant.

MP1 (600–700 chill hours/midseason ripening) Chance seedling from Washington State. Yellow flesh, semifreestone, highly flavored. Use for fresh eating, canning, or cooking.

Q1-8 (600–800 chill hours/late-season ripening) Also called Salish Summer. Latest-blooming, sweet, flavorful white-meated freestone. Peach leaf curl resistant.

STARFIRE FREESTONE (850 chill hours/midseason ripening) Staggered ripening over 2–3 weeks. Rich flavor, yellow flesh, freestone. Good in cool summer areas.

WHITE LADY (800 chill hours/midseason ripening) Low acid, high sugar, melting white flesh. Medium to large, red skin, firm flesh, freestone.

NECTARINE VARIETIES OF NOTE

ARCTIC GLO (400–500 chill hours/midseason ripening) White-meated, new school freestone, sprightly sweet flavor with firm flesh.

FANTASIA (500 chill hours/midseason ripening) Large yellow freestone, old school. Sweet with rich flavor when fully ripe.

HEAVENLY WHITE (650 chill hours/midseason ripening) Very large, white-meated new school freestone. Good blend of sugar and acid with a complex flavor.

PLUMS

While nearly all the landmasses of the northern temperate zones
(latitude 25–45 degrees north) have native species of plums, the
cultivated plums can be divided into four species—European, Asian,
Damson, and the elusive greengage.

European Plums

Prunus domestica

These are the plums of choice throughout Europe, more widely planted
than apples and pears. In the Slavic countries, European plums exceed
50 percent of all acreage planted to fruit trees. There is evidence of
European plums being grown in Europe prior to 2,000 years ago.

In common parlance, the terms *European plums*, *domestica plums*,
and *prune plums* are often used interchangeably. European plums
consist of sweet, fresh eating types and those that can also be dried as
prunes. European plums offer a more diverse spectrum of colors, shapes,
sizes, tastes, and uses than any other fruit. The fruit is small and oval-
oblong—almost egg shaped. Skin colors are in the blue-purple range for
prune types to yellow, orange, and red for dessert types. They thrive in
areas with moderate summers (75°F–100°F), low humidity, and moderate winter chill. Major production areas worldwide include western
United States, New York State, Italy, Chile, Turkey, Romania, the Balkan
States of former Yugoslavia, France, Austria, and Germany.

The trees of European plums are upright and vigorous when young (much like the peach) and develop a pendant-weeping form and weak vigor when established. At 50–80 years, they are fairly long lived. They tend to be a shorter tree than Asian plums (10–15 feet). European plums also have a higher chill requirement to bloom and set fruit (500–900 hours); they bloom later than their Asian counterparts (*P. salicina*) and hence in some years avoid the pollination problems caused by erratic spring weather and rain.

European plums are smaller and firmer, with less juice, than Asian plums. They are also freestone (separating easily from the pit). Because of their high sugar content, they dry readily as prune plums. Fresh off the tree, European plums are a high-quality dessert fruit and, because of their low juice content and freestone nature, are excellent candidates for cooking in tarts and other recipes.

All European plums are cross-pollinated, and they can be finicky. They need to be near a different variety of European plum that blooms at the same time in order to produce fruit. Luckily, most plums bloom close together; the Asian plum varieties Santa Rosa and Wickson are universal pollinators and can also be used. All the following varieties require approximately 600–800 chill hours.

VARIETIES OF NOTE

ITALIAN PRUNE (mid- to late-season ripening) Large, purple, heavy-setting plum with a sweet fruit with yellow-green flesh.

SCHOOLHOUSE (mid- to late-season ripening) Large oval yellow plum. Found seedling from Port Townsend, Washington.

SENECA (late-season ripening) Large, sweet, red-skinned fruit with yellow flesh. An upright vigorous tree.

VALOR (midseason ripening) Similar to Italian prune but with much larger fruit. Fruit has purple skin, yellow flesh. Sweet with great flavor.

Asian Plums

Prunus salicina

Also known as Japanese plums, this species originated in China 2,000 years ago, was introduced to Japan in the 1600s, and subsequently was brought to the United States by horticulturists John Kelsey and Luther Burbank.

Burbank used this stock to breed the Satsuma plum, the Santa Rosa plum, and countless other varieties that launched the California plum industry. The fruit is large and heart shaped to conical. The skin color can range from golden yellow, orange-red, or blood red to purple and black. Flesh color usually reflects a variation on the skin color. The taste is slightly acid over sweet and the flesh is juicy. They are best eaten fresh. Unlike European plums, Asian Plums are not freestone. Two notable exceptions are Satsuma and its improvement, Mariposa. These two varieties also feature less acidity and thus can be dried, à la prune plums.

Asian plums bloom abundantly early in the season (late January through early March), and thus fruit earlier than European plums (late June through early August). They generally produce heavy crops; if even 1–2 percent of the blooms set fruit, thinning is required. They tolerate milder winters; that is to say they bloom and set fruit with fewer chill hours than European plums. The trees tend to be vigorous, rambunctious growers, often approaching 10 feet a year on standard rootstocks. They are very upright growers, with the exception of the Satsuma and Mariposa varieties, which develop a weeping growth habit later in life, like that of European plums. Their pollination needs are similar to European plums.

All Asian plums are cross-pollinated; they need to be near a different variety of Asian plum that blooms at the same time in order to produce fruit. Most Asian plums bloom around the same time; Santa Rosa and Wickson plums are universal pollinators and can also be used.

BEAUTY (250 chill hours/very early-season ripening) Better adapted and more productive in cool, wet, rainy springs than Santa Rosa. Flesh is red streaked. Skin is red over yellow. Sweet and full of flavor.

CATALINA (400 chill hours/early- to midseason ripening) Large, black-skinned fruit with sweet, firm flesh that is a treat when eaten out of hand.

ELEPHANT HEART (500–600 chill hours/late-season ripening) Old-time favorite with a big, heart-shaped fruit. The sweet, rich flesh is firm textured and dark red. Notorious for setting a shy or light crop almost annually.

EMERALD BEAUT (600–700 chill hours/very late-season ripening) It's a real "beaut." Intensely sweet, strikingly green-yellow flesh, free-stone. Fruit hangs and sweetens on the tree. Crisp and crunchy, too.

HIROMI RED (600–800 chill hours/midseason ripening) Relatively new variety bred by Floyd Zaiger. Purple-red skin and flesh. Sweet juicy flavor.

LARODA (400–500 chill hours/midseason ripening) Dark purple-skinned fruit with rich, juicy flavor and a red-amber flesh. Extended harvest, lasting 5–6 weeks after Santa Rosa plums.

Santa Rosa plum

SANTA ROSA (300 chill hours/early-season ripening) Bred by Luther Burbank. Fruity bouquet aroma (on the tree!). Complex set of flavors—tart near skin, sweet with an intense, almost overpowering perfume in center, and slightly tart again at pit. Rapidly fading as California's leading cultivar—40 percent of crop in 1960s, 4 percent now. Has been lamentably superseded by firm (almost rubbery) black-skinned varieties more suited to the racquet ball or squash court. Good universal pollinator for plums.

SATSUMA and **MARIPOSA** (300 chill hours/midseason ripening [Satsuma] and late-season ripening [Mariposa]) Two more Luther Burbank originals. Meaty, firm flesh. Blood red, low juice content, almost freestone. The only Asian types that can be halved and dried. Moderate vigor trees. Small pit. Mariposa is an improved Satsuma.

SHIRO (600 chill hours/midseason ripening) Midsized, yellow fruit with a sweet, mild flavor. Thought to be somewhat self-fruitful, unlike most plums, but your safest best is to pair it with a pollinator.

Damson Plums

Prunus insititia

Damson plums, which are both common to and beloved in the United Kingdom, are small spreading trees with small, oval, blue-skinned fruits and amber flesh. While some texts describe the taste as acid spicy/tart, the reality is they are wickedly phenolic and acrid fresh. However, when made into jam or preserves, they sweeten measurably. Their high pectin content gives the jams a creamy, spreadable texture. These trees need little pruning and no thinning. Generally, Damsons are referred to by their species name, without varieties singled out. Two exceptions are Shropshire and a newer addition, Blues Jam.

> The Damson plum is self-pollinated; it does not require another variety nearby in order to produce fruit. All Damsons need 800 chill hours and are late-season ripening. All the following varieties require approximately 800 chill hours.

VARIETIES OF NOTE

BLUES JAM (late-season ripening) A 2005 Cornell release with a cute name. Can be cooked, but it has no astringency and can also be eaten fresh off the tree. Purple skin and yellow flesh; makes a dark purple jam.

SHROPSHIRE (mid- to late-season ripening) From Shropshire, England, where the natives say it's the best of the Damsons. Compact habit of growth. Black-blue skin, yellow flesh that turns red when cooked. Sugary but acid taste fresh off the tree. Best used for preserves and canning.

Greengage Plums
Prunus italica

This species, also known as gage plums, originated in Turkey and was brought to Mediterranean Europe by the Romans. The plums all but disappeared (as did much of intellectual and artistic value) during the Dark Ages of medieval Europe and were rediscovered in France in the 1700s. Sir William Gage introduced the gages to England in the 1720s and oh so modestly eliminated varietal labels, which resulted in all greengages being named after him. The trees are weak to moderate in vigor and extremely narrow and upright. At their tree-ripe perfection, the gages feature a green, yellow, or golden skin and a sugary sweet taste with slight tangy undertones. The greengage is arguably the most intensely rich-tasting fruit on the planet. True greengage plums are hard to find in stores but worth the search.

> Greengage plums are cross-pollinated; they need to be near another variety of greengage that blooms at the same time in order to produce fruit. Greengage plums are notoriously finicky when it comes to pollination, making it difficult to produce a heavy crop. But the rich years make the shy years worth it.

VARIETIES OF NOTE

BAVAY'S (700 chill hours/late-season ripening) Yellow dotted skin. Larger than most gage types. Holds on the tree well. Flavor is rich, juicy, and candy-drop sweet, as are all the gages.

CAMBRIDGE (700–900 chill hours/mid- to late-season ripening) Yellow skin with a distinct red blush. Tree has a very compact form, good for the small garden. Rich, sweet, dense flesh. Good pollenizer for other greengage plums.

COE'S GOLDEN DROP (700–900 chill hours/very late-season ripening) Oblong, egg shaped. Golden green fruit with golden flesh. Seriously sweet, with undertones of apricot. Vigorous growing tree. Ripens late, thus extending the plum season.

EARLY LAXTON (700–900 chill hours/early-season ripening) Pink-orange oblong plum with yellow, firm flesh. Great for cooking. Abundant bearer and one of the first plums to bloom and crop each year. Good texture but not the sweetest of the gages. Introduced in England in 1916.

KIRKE'S BLUE (700–900 chill hours/early-season ripening) Challenging variety to fruit consistently, but dividends include an unusually large round fruit for a gage plum, superior flavor, and juicy yellow flesh dripping with sugary juice. Introduced in London in 1930.

Blenheim apricots

APRICOTS

Prunus armeniaca

The species name is a misnomer; it's not from Armenia but from western China. While apricots are delicious, in truth they're very hard to grow successfully. Commercially, they have a limited climatic range—mostly California, Turkey, and southwest Colorado. That said, in terms of sweetness and sheer pleasure in eating, they set a very high bar, one virtually unobtainable by any other species.

Apricots are self-pollinated; they do not require another variety nearby to produce fruit.

VARIETIES OF NOTE

AUTUMN (500 chill hours/late-season ripening) Also sold as Autumn Royal. The latest of all 'cots, in fact the only reliable late 'cot. Similar high flavor as Blenheim (of course, nothing really compares). While Royal has larger fruit than Blenheim, it is an intermittent cropper.

BLENHEIM (400 chill hours/early-season ripening) There's really only one variety to grow, and it's Blenheim. All others, though big and impressive, taste like the box they came in. I've tried every one I could, and none is as good as Blenheim. Blenheim is small and lumpy and funny looking, and has its problems, but it's the best. While not as outstanding as Blenheim, Moorpark and Autumn may be worth your consideration.

MOORPARK (500 chill hours/late-season ripening) An old variety dating to the 1600s in Europe. Tree is hardy (for an apricot) and an attractive specimen in the landscape in each and every season. Rich flavor and strong aroma. Reliably productive (again, for an apricot).

PLUOTS AND APRIUMS

These interspecific fruit hybrids, developed by Floyd Zaiger of Dave Wilson Nursery in California's Central Valley in the 1990s, are without a doubt the most significant fruit introduction of our lifetimes. In addition to being a monumental genetic breakthrough in breeding, pluots and apriums are hands down the sweetest fruits on the planet. They've revolutionized the whole plum industry to the point where consumers demand them and even ask for specific varieties.

Pluots are 75 percent Asian plum, 25 percent apricot. They are oval, egg-shaped fruits with a candy-sweet flavor. Unlike Asian plums, they are freestone (the stone separates easily from the flesh), and the flesh has firm texture. The tree resembles the Asian plums, with vigorous, upright growth. Pluots have moderate to low chill hour requirements and bloom slightly later than Asian plums.

Apriums are 75 percent apricot and 25 percent plum, and are Zaiger's improvement on Luther Burbank's plumcots. Around the turn of the twentieth century, Burbank made the initial breakthrough in the category by trying to produce an apricot-like fruit that would bear along the wet, cool coast of California. He developed the Burbank plumcot, a cross between a plum and an apricot. Many decades later, Zaiger managed to take it further and bred the even more reliable and delicious aprium. Both the fruit and the tree of the aprium resemble the apricot in shape and habit, except the tree is a natural semidwarf growing to 8–10 feet.

Burbank's plumcot

All pluots are cross-pollinated; they need to be near a different variety of pluot or a universal pollenizer (Wickson or Santa Rosa plum) that blooms at the same time in order to produce fruit. Most varieties, however, bloom around the same time.

PLUOT VARIETIES OF NOTE

DAPPLE DANDY (400–500 chill hours/late-season ripening) Freestone, creamy red-white flesh with a rich plum-apricot sweetness and flavor. Skin matures to a maroon-yellow dappled color.

FLAVOR GRENADE (300–500 chill hours/midseason ripening) Yes, the flavor explodes in the mouth. Insanely sweet while still having a somewhat firm and crunchy texture. Sets a very reliable heavy crop year in and year out.

FLAVOR KING (400–500 chill hours/very late-season ripening) Sweet, spicy flavor, purple-red skin, crimson flesh.

FLAVOR QUEEN (400–500 chill hours/midseason ripening) Unique yellow skin with amber-orange flesh. Long harvest period.

FLAVOR SUPREME (700–800 chill hours/midseason ripening) Rich-flavored red flesh with firm texture, green-maroon dappled skin. Early harvest.

All apriums are self-pollinated; they do not require another variety nearby to produce fruit. Only two aprium varieties are commonly available, and they're both good. They both require approximately 200–300 chill hours.

APRIUM VARIETIES OF NOTE

COT'N CANDY (late-season ripening) A white-meated aprium as good as a Blenheim apricot and way sweeter.

FLAVOR DELIGHT (early-season ripening) Oblong, rough skinned, with apricot color and flavor. Self-fruitful but will set better crops with another apricot as a pollinator.

SWEET CHERRIES

Prunus avium

Avium in Latin means "bird." And so it goes with cherries: cherries are the most apically dominant of all deciduous tree species; in other words, they are extremely tall. Even when the trees are on size-controlling rootstocks, it is difficult to keep them under 15–20 feet. Most check in at 25–35 feet. Ergo, tall cherries are for the birds—no, really, you will have to net the fruits or the birds will get them all, if the weather doesn't get them first. Even in the limited climates where cherries will succeed, there is the peril of rain (or, even worse, hail) as you approach harvest.

Accordingly, though they are marvelous specimens—a beautiful natural form with exquisite bark colored a sheeny silver gray with striated markings that seems to sparkle in the sunlight—cherries are both challenging and impractical.

However, some varieties offer possible remedies to the height problem. And there are some training systems that effectively keep cherries pedestrian, most notably the KGB and UFO systems. I kid you not. There is no conspiracy, no collusion—KGB stands for Kym Green Bush and UFO for upright fruiting offshoots. Again, there is no conspiracy here, just research-based trial and error that looks like it might succeed.

A relatively new rootstock, Root-1, dwarfs cherries. It was developed by Floyd Zaiger and purportedly keeps cherries at 8–12 feet. Zaiger is the genius who brought us pluots and apriums. A revered, wizened octogenarian who eschews the computer, Zaiger takes no notes and has no background in genetics and yet he is the most amazing tree breeder of our times. His kids follow him around with laptops and transcribe his brilliant insights and "databank" before it fades into the sunset.

The cherry varieties I recommend here are all self-pollinated, which is not the norm for cherries.

VARIETIES OF NOTE

CRAIG'S CRIMSON (800 chill hours/mid- to late-season ripening) A Bing look-alike. Naturally dwarf, very productive.

LAPINS (500 chill hours/late-season ripening) Another Bing type. Great taste and a firm, meaty texture. A tall tree.

STELLA (400 chill hours/early- to mid-season ripening) Somewhat natural dwarf that can be kept at around 15 feet regardless of rootstock. Fruit is a dead ringer for Bing.

III

Sourcing and Planting Bare Root Fruit Trees

You've found the perfect, sunny spot. You've assessed your soil and embarked on a soil improvement regimen. You've planned your irrigation and joyously picked out your varieties, including compatible pollenizers. Now you're ready to buy the tree, and *then* you'll be ready to plant the darn tree.

Time of Planting

Ideally, deciduous fruit trees are planted as dormant, bare root stock at the outset of the planting season. The window for planting is wide and regionally dependent: late winter to early spring. Consult your local nursery or neighbors to find out the norm in your area. Fruit tree roots begin to grow—and therefore can take up water and nutrients and distribute stored carbohydrates—about 3–5 weeks before any aboveground activity is visible. Thus, the earlier the tree is planted, the quicker it will begin to grow and the greater the first year's growth. The difference between an early planting and a late planting can be as radical as 2–3 feet of growth. Keep in mind that temperate-zone, deciduous fruit tree roots can and do start to grow at much lower soil temperatures (low 40s) than vegetable and flower crops (low to mid-50s).

While trees can be obtained in containers later in the season, container-grown specimens are more expensive and nurseries offer a limited selection of varieties and rootstocks. More importantly, container-grown trees do not respond well to the root restriction of pots, and it is extremely dicey to successfully transplant them during the active growing season.

With that in mind, I recommend sticking with bare root trees. If you are ordering online, many nurseries take orders for dormant, bare root trees 6–12 months in advance of planting. If buying retail and local, hustle on down to your local garden center ASAP upon the seasonal arrival of bare root stock (usually January through March). Every catalog or nursery will tell you its shipping and arrival dates, and many have strict cutoffs. Nurseries sell the higher-quality trees first, so place your order on time.

Sourcing a Quality Tree

There are four primary sources of trees: graft or bud your own; buy at local retail nurseries; try mail-order nurseries; or inherit trees by buying land or a house with trees already in place. Here I'll address the retail and mail-order options, which are the most accessible to new growers.

Unless you are buying fruit trees in quantity or looking for rare heirloom varieties or unusual scion and rootstock combinations, buying retail has some advantages over mail order. Retail shopping allows you to inspect and accept or reject individual trees. Quite often, retail prices are on a par with or even cheaper than mail-order costs.

Many mail-order tree nurseries sell direct to home growers, no matter how many trees. Mail-order tree nurseries generally fall into two categories: large-scale conventional nurseries and small- or medium-scale nurseries, only some of which sell organic trees (see Resources, page 266). Don't worry: it's perfectly okay to buy a tree from a conventional nursery. Do what you need to do. The moment you get it home, it'll become organic for the rest of its life.

Larger-scale nurseries offer good economies of scale, with hundreds of thousands of trees. Bigger nurseries have a good range of size-controlling rootstocks available for each species of fruit. The price is usually reasonable, and the tree quality superlative. On the flip side, large nurseries often carry a limited varietal selection—usually the varieties are those currently in vogue for large-scale commercial production and include very few, if any, heirlooms.

In contrast, small- to medium-scale nurseries usually offer a diversity of varieties and a wealth of heirlooms. However, they usually have an extremely limited selection of rootstock types. Tree quality is variable from nursery to nursery, species to species, and year to year. The prices usually make you say "ouch!" With no volume discount, expect to pay double what you would at a larger nursery.

BARE ROOT TREE FORMS

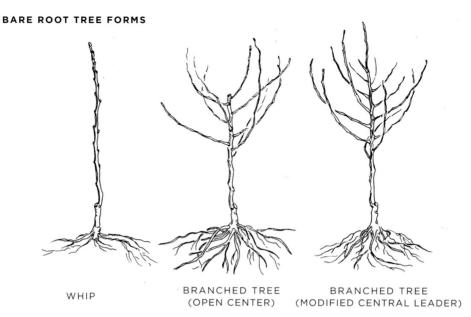

WHIP

BRANCHED TREE
(OPEN CENTER)

BRANCHED TREE
(MODIFIED CENTRAL LEADER)

(See page 178 for an explanation of tree forms.)

Selecting Quality Trees

A primary tenet of success is to plant a large, quality tree and then to grow it aggressively. A bigger tree has greater leaf surface, thus more photosynthetic grow power, and will establish more quickly than a smaller tree. The old adage was, plant a whip (an unbranched tree), not a branched tree, but no more—plant a big, branched tree. It'll get you out of the chute and down the road quicker.

When choosing a tree, things to select for include the following:

- A root system proportional to the branch system. When you are buying retail, a good way to gauge proportions is to look at more than one bare root tree and compare them. Keep in mind that to the novice, good proportions might have the appearance of being way out of balance (in favor of branches).

- A good number of branches (five to nine) and a good length of branches (more than 2 feet).

- A tall tree (4–7 feet).

- Good branch distribution—both vertically and horizontally.

- Branches with a minimum of 5- to 6-inch vertical spacing are ideal. Such spacing achieves sufficient sunlight distribution within the tree canopy in the early years and especially at maturity. If two or more branches emanate from the same vertical point on the trunk, one tends to be strong and one weak. You're looking to avoid weakness.

- Ideally, you want equidistant horizontal branch spacing—like spokes on a wheel—although you can easily move or train a young branch up to 180 degrees. Good spacing of branches, coupled with moderately wide crotch angles (see illustration, page 173), yields mechanically strong, vigorously growing branches.

- Look at the angle of the branch where it's attached to the trunk at the crotch. The branch should be about 30–60 degrees (above horizontal). Narrow crotch angles beget overly vigorous growth at the expense of fruit and have a tendency to snap and break at maturity. Conversely, flat-angled branches tend to be weak and become serious saggers that crowd and shade branches below.

- A thick-caliper trunk of $\frac{1}{2}$–$\frac{7}{8}$ inch. (Caliper is the industry-standard measurement for the base of a tree trunk.) While a tree of this size may cost slightly more at purchase time, the cost difference is soon recouped via earlier and more efficient cropping. With a tree caliper more than $\frac{7}{8}$ inch, the law of diminishing returns kicks in—that is, there's nothing wrong with it; it just doesn't pay the dividend of more fruit sooner.

Preparing the Planting Hole

The old gardening quip, "Don't put a $5 tree in a 50 cent hole," needs to be adjusted for inflation: "Don't put a $20 tree in a $2 hole." Use common sense; activate your horticultural sensibilities. Ask and answer the question, Should I be planting fruit trees in this ground now? Properly preparing your planting hole will make a world of difference in the early years of your fruit tree's growth and aid you in quick establishment of the tree.

If you haven't assessed your soil yet, do so (see page 21) and engage in a rigorous soil-building program. But if you *must* plant now, the multiyear hole which follows should speed the process, provided you continue improving your soil in subsequent years.

I recommend prepping the planting hole the previous summer before planting, which nets the advantage of easy, quick planting once bare root trees arrive, especially if the soil is wet, as it often is endlessly into the spring. If you don't dig your hole beforehand, it's okay, but try to plant when the soil is not too wet. Soil moisture should be between 50 percent and 80 percent of field capacity; see "Estimating Soil Moisture by Feel," page 157.

If your soil is moderately fertile (as determined by your soil assessment), the hole may not need to be augmented with compost or fertilizer. If this is the case, simply digging a hole slightly wider and deeper than the root system (2–3 feet by 2–3 feet) should suffice. Then, after you've planted the tree, feed it as you normally would (see "Seasonal Feeding," page 154).

A slightly more aggressive approach would be to dig the same size hole and supplement the soil excavated from the hole with no more than 25–30 percent (by volume) compost. The fill soil and compost should be thoroughly mixed prior to refilling the hole. This approach will both improve soil structure and boost growth in years one and two.

Conventional wisdom (these days) is that you should do nothing to enrich the soil in the planting hole. As general advice, this is not bad. However, I often find that, in general, life is specific. That is to say, most of those studies were done on ornamental trees planted in the Southeast. With fruit trees, one of the tenets of success is to rapidly (within 3–5 years) establish the height and spread of the tree. An enriched planting hole, coupled with aggressive annual growth goals, achieves this aim. The goal is to double or even triple the canopy of the tree in each of the first 3 years. Sunshine, water, and fertilizer are your tools. It's pedal to the metal, judiciously of course.

THE MULTIYEAR HOLE

An even more aggressive or radical approach to hole preparation is something I call the multiyear hole. It is time, labor, and materials consumptive but has proved to work quite well over the years at the Chadwick Garden.

The multiyear hole is for the impatient, salivating-to-plant-right-now crowd. It is, in essence, a shortcut. A multiyear hole provides a way to take unimproved soil, plant trees today (or tomorrow, depending on your digging strength and stamina), and simultaneously start using intensive techniques to improve the soil outside the planting hole.

The multiyear hole should be, at minimum, 3 feet wide and 2 feet deep. Assume a tree's roots will extend 1 foot per year beyond a 3-foot planting hole. Assume you have some sense of your soil's fertility, because even though you're impatient, you've assessed your soil (see page 21). If your soil needs improvement, enlarge the width of the hole 1 or 2 additional feet, depending on how much improvement you think your soil needs (poorer soil equals bigger hole). If your soil is in bad shape, it might take 2 years to upgrade the native soil, so you'd dig a 5-foot-wide hole. I wouldn't go bigger, in most circumstances. As far as depth, it makes little sense to dig any hole deeper than 2–3 feet, as most deciduous fruit trees have a high percentage of their effective feeding roots in the top 1–2 feet of the soil. To dig the multiyear hole:

- Dig a hole 2–3 feet deep and 3–5 feet wide depending on the quality of your soil. As you dig, separate the topsoil and the subsoil into two piles. The topsoil is closer to the surface and is usually darker, more open, and crumbly, and has less clay (even if it's a clay). As you dig downward, the subsoil often becomes lighter in color, has a higher clay content (sticky), and is more compacted.

- Discard 40 percent of the poor-quality subsoil and blend the remaining 60 percent with good garden (not potting) soil (20 percent) and compost (20 percent).

- Blend compost into the topsoil to achieve 60–70 percent native soil and 30–40 percent compost (premixed).

- Plant the tree (see page 112), filling the hole with the improved subsoil, then top it off with the improved topsoil.

- Apply compost and fertilizer as instructed on pages 154–156.

- Now your hole is a truly hospitable place for a tree to grow. But you should immediately start to improve the soil outside the hole, so that by the time the roots reach the hole's perimeter, the outer soil is sufficiently fertile (see chapter V, How You Grow a Tree). Your ultimate goal is to diminish the differential between the improved hole soil and the unimproved native soil around it by the time the tree roots "arrive."

Tutorial: Planting the Tree

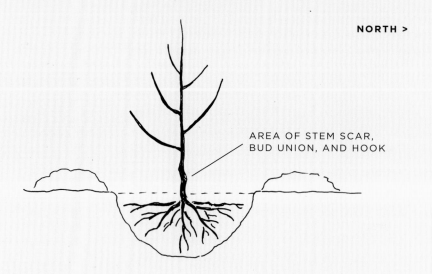

NORTH >

AREA OF STEM SCAR,
BUD UNION, AND HOOK

Now that you've dug the hole, it's finally time to plant the darn tree.

SOAK THE ROOTS If the tree roots are dry, soak them in water for 2–6 hours, no longer.

FIND A FRIEND Grab a buddy to help out. Person one will hold the tree in place while person two fills the hole.

GET A PLANTING BOARD OR STICK Any old piece of wood—a two-by-four, pool cue, hockey stick, or bamboo—will do. It should be about 4–5 feet long. Place the planting stick across the top of the hole, so that you can see where true ground level is at all times. This is important because the bud union (the swollen portion of the trunk at the base of the tree where the scion was attached to the rootstock) should be planted 2–4 inches above the true soil level. (For cold winter climates, having the bud union just at or above soil level is recommended.) The bud union is the weakest, most vulnerable portion of the tree. If the bud union is buried, there is a propensity for the trunk to rot. Or, the buried portion of the trunk above the bud union may sprout adventitious roots that can be vigorous enough to produce an unwanted additional tree 20–30 feet tall. Don't bury your bud union!

PREP THE HOLE Use a digging fork to fracture the soil at the bottom and on the sides of the hole just a bit, to improve both drainage and root penetration. This is particularly advisable if you have a clay soil.

SPRINKLE THE ROOTS I recommend sprinkling a hearty helping of mycorrhizal powder, a fungi that help the tree roots take up nutrients and water, on the dampened roots before planting.

POSITION THE TREE The tree should be placed in such a way that its vulnerable parts are protected from sun and wind. Look at the lower portion and find the stem scar, where the trunk of the rootstock was lopped off after the bud or graft took. Position the bud union with the stem scar facing north to protect it from sunscald. You should also try to position the hook, or curve, on the trunk into the prevailing wind, although protecting the stem scar from sunburn takes precedence. Often people whitewash the trunks with a water-based indoor or exterior latex paint that is diluted 50 percent with water to protect against sunburn, but this is critical only if you live in a high light-level, hot, interior climate. And even then, only do it for the first couple of years; after 2–3 years, the shade afforded to the trunk by the canopy should obviate the need to whitewash. Much of the above minutiae falls into a category Elliot Coleman (New England farmer, systems thinker, farm tool fashioner) refers to as "1 percent solutions," or things that don't really matter. My take on this: "A whole lot of *doesn't matters* . . . do."

PLANT THE TREE Person one holds the tree with the trunk perpendicular to the ground at the proper planting depth, with the bud union 2–4 inches above true soil depth (refer to the planting stick!). Person two slowly fills the hole with the excavated backfill soil (improved or not). Fill the hole about one-third full, then pause and gently tamp down the soil with your foot. At this point the tree should stand straight unaided. Then, repeat the process twice more. Recheck the depth of planting (bud union) and appropriately adjust by adding more soil or pulling the tree up a bit.

WATER IT IN As always in gardening, planting is immediately followed by watering in. This is an axiom—ironclad. When watering in fruit trees, you can channel your inner kid and mud it up. It's not like a delicate trickling in around the roots of a young delphinium or lettuce seedling. A thorough soaking of the entire root zone will "get the tree off" and remove any undue air pockets. Good soil and root contact is essential for transplanting success.

PRUNE You needn't do it the same day you plant, but newly planted trees should be pruned soon, before they break dormancy and sprout new leaves or buds. The goal with initial pruning is to firmly establish the tree's form. See chapter VI for pruning instructions.

IV

How
a Tree
Grows

"The physiology of
fruit trees is complex.
Deciduous fruit trees
are perennial, woody
plants that are taxed
every year to produce
large fruit crops. Often
as much as 70 percent of
the tree's carbohydrates
are harvested as fruit;
yet the tree must have
sufficient carbohydrate
stores to maintain basic
life processes, to form
and grow new flower
buds for the next season
and survive the cold
stress of winter."

—MIKLOS FAUST,
*Physiology of
Temperate Zone
Fruit Trees*, 1989

So much of fruit tree growing is about a tree's patterns of growth: *this* is what the tree does; thus, *this* is what you do to the tree. If you want to grow trees successfully, you need to learn to recognize, understand, assist, and direct the tree's patterns throughout its annual cycle of growth. First and primarily, it's about the tree. Then it's about you. And, ultimately, the confluence of the two. Knowing the *how*—how a tree actually grows, and hence how you care for the tree—leads to good care, informed care, optimal growth, and annual abundance. You can pair the seasonal information in this section with "Seasonal Feeding," page 154, to fully synchronize your care with the tree's needs.

Deciduous trees are long lived; apples can easily live 75–100 years. There are pears in the hills of Tuscany that are probably in excess of 200 years old. But the yearly seasonal growth of trees is another matter. It's a madcap scramble, a sprint—*all-out, now!* And you need to be *all-in,* right now.

Inside the tree, the trunk and branches contain a superhighway of conductive vessels or tubes (*xylem* and *phloem*, if you want to get technical, and you do). These tubes run from "stem to stern"—from shoot tips to root tips—and vice versa. The xylem pumps water, nutrients, and growth hormones up from the soil and throughout the tree. The phloem flows the other way, moving sugars, starches, and growth hormones from leaves to all portions of the tree, along with the signals that tell the different parts of the tree when to grow.

In spring, you look at the orchard and the process is apparent: trees are blooming, bursting, burgeoning with life. There are flowers, fruit, leaves, and extending shoots. It seems the tree is exhibiting all modes and manner of growth, all at once. This isn't really true. The tree and its components grow in patterns and sequence. Growth is also partitioned, punctuated; it's even syncopated.

It's a nice rhythm: First, the roots grow. Then flowers unfurl. The flowers get pollinated, fertilized, and (hopefully) set fruit. The fruit begins to enlarge. At the same time, internally, undifferentiated cells are differentiating into next year's fruit buds. On the heels of flowering, leaves unfurl, branches extend up and out toward the light, and fruit continues to enlarge.

Or, as Pete Seeger poignantly sang—a verse from the "good" book, originally—*to everything there is a season.* A time to reap? Think of good fruit years. A time to build up: that's fertilizing. And when it's time to break

down, we're talking about compost and green manures. Most importantly, don't forget *a time of love and a time of peace*. Those are evergreen.

Your mission, should you choose to accept it, is to synchronize the components of your tree care with the tree's cycle of needs. In short, become a servant of the seasons and the morning's early light, as well as an intergenerational soil steward—one generation passing the torch to the next, on down the line.

When you get down to feeding your trees throughout the seasons, your two primary tools will be compost and cover crops, with selected inputs of fertilizers (see chapter V, How You Grow a Tree). The former represent major chords; the latter, minor chords. And isn't music a little more lush if different notes are blended together? With coordinated tree care, a sweet harmony.

And what key are you playing in? We only have four: spring, summer, fall, and winter. Familiarize yourself with what happens in each.

Strong suggestion: You might be advised to dog-ear the chart on the facing page. As you read this chapter, and as you go about tending your trees, you would do well to keep referencing these charts. They are, in a nutshell, what the tree does and when, and hence what you do to the tree and when.

Fruit Tree Growth

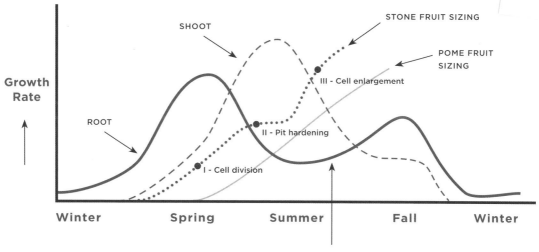

Growth Rate

SHOOT

STONE FRUIT SIZING

POME FRUIT SIZING

III - Cell enlargement

ROOT

II - Pit hardening

I - Cell division

Winter   **Spring**   **Summer**   **Fall**   **Winter**

Dormancy of summer often indicated by terminal (fruit) bud set on branches *

Carbohydrate Reserves in Tree

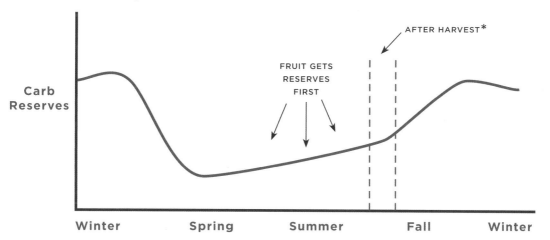

Carb Reserves

AFTER HARVEST *

FRUIT GETS RESERVES FIRST

Winter   **Spring**   **Summer**   **Fall**   **Winter**

Spring through early summer equals "grand period of growth":

—Roots are actively growing, especially in the early portion of this period.

—Shoots (branches) make almost all their yearly growth in this period.

—Flowering, fruit set, and initial fruit development and enlargement.

—Internally: undifferentiated cells are (hopefully) differentiating into next year's fruit buds.

All this is happening at once, in a compressed time period.

* These are critical times to provision for water and nutrients. They are often coincident with a second root upsurge.

Spring in the Orchard

Spring is the most dynamic time of the year in the orchard. But as poetic, pastoral, and even inspiring as the above quote is, with fruit trees, leaves are akin to the tip of the iceberg. Much of what fruit trees do annually is compressed into a narrow window from the spring equinox to just past the summer solstice. This time of year sees maximum root and shoot growth followed by flowering and fruit set and sizing (enlarging), plus the beginnings of next year's fruit buds.

There is a considerable lag between a tree's spring growth needs and the uptake of nutrients from the soil, as well as the production of carbohydrates from the leaves. So the roots, with their carb and nutrient reserves, act as a bit of a sourdough starter for spring and early summer growth. They kick-start the annual cycle of tree growth.

THE GRAND PERIOD OF GROWTH

Pomologists of the late nineteenth and early twentieth centuries often referred to the "grand period of growth"—the tumult of activities compressed into a specific short period of intense growth during spring into early summer. This is when that syncopation really gets going—roots, flowers, fruits, leaves, and shoots are growing actively and exhausting the tree's stored reserves, and next year's flowers and fruit buds are getting started inside the branches.

The first wave of root growth occurs a few weeks prior to any visible bud swell, leaf, or shoot growth. Fruit trees have radial root systems that are somewhat asymmetrical. With the exception of a taproot that serves primarily to anchor the tree, most of a fruit tree's roots are shallow, superficial, and fibrous or branching. They generally extend out to or beyond the drip line—the imaginary circle around the circumference of the tree canopy where rain or irrigation water drips off the leaves and onto the ground. Roots can grow at cooler soil temperatures than the aerial portions of the tree, and so they do. Fruit tree roots start growing in the low 40s, as compared with most vegetable and flower crops, which make little or no growth with soil temperatures below 55°F. These conditions are sometimes referred to as biological zero. In the early spring, roots become active to fuel the aerial components of the tree. The curve of growth is essentially straight up (see Fruit Tree Growth chart, page 119), peaking in midspring and tapering

"None of the wonders of our technological age can match the miraculous awakening of a tree from winter sleep; to put on its spring attire of rich green foliage—a spectacle of regenerative power that only nature is capable of performing."

—BRUCE CAPON, *Botany for Gardeners*, 1990

off by the summer solstice or shortly thereafter. The noun *surge* would be an apropos description of this first wave.

With stone fruits, especially apricots and peaches, the initial rate of fruit sizing is impressive, even alarming. You might even think you've gone through the looking glass with Alice, or you've fallen into the pages of *James and the Giant Peach*. But usually 6–8 weeks in, sizing virtually stops. At this juncture, the pit with its embryo is enlarging and hardening. After this lag period, growth in size and increase in weight continue until harvest. With apples and pears, sizing is more consistent, slow, and steady.

Toward the end of spring, root growth slows down and shoot growth reaches its peak. In a slow, relentless manner, fruit is enlarging, moving toward harvest.

Summer in the Orchard

In midsummer, fruit takes over and garners the lion's share of resources. Root growth slows down, shoot growth subsides, and carbohydrates have been depleted.

This ebb is the reason W. H. Chandler, a senior statesman of American horticulturalists whose 1951 book *Deciduous Orchards* is still considered an authoritative tome on the topic, coined "dormancy of summer," to describe the quiescence of fruit trees in the summer. In these hot months, as much as 70 percent of a tree's annual carbohydrate reserve goes into fruit production. More than any and all activities in fruit trees, fruit production is a huge nutrient sink. You could even say fruit is a corporate robber baron—grabbing a disproportionate percentage of the resources available. It's your job to play Robin Hood. You can redistribute the wealth through adequate fertilization in spring and summer and by beginning your cover crops in late summer (see page 144).

Come around to late summer, approaching the autumnal equinox, there is a second significant, if less explosive, wave of root growth. Then root growth slows again and reaches a yearly low, as the tree loses its leaves and enters dormancy. This is an important time to be attentive to watering and weed control.

Fall in the Orchard

In fall, the trees are one moment ablaze with color and the next, bare and exposing their lovely architecture. The trees go deciduous, dropping their leaves, but their roots continue to grow at a slow rate, storing carbohydrates and nutrients for spring growth. As the days grow shorter and temperatures drop, dormancy proceeds apace. The colder the temperatures, the quicker dormancy sets in.

UNDERSTANDING DORMANCY

Dormancy is an adaptive feature of deciduous trees to prevent cold injury and death to tender buds and leaves. It's simply a life insurance policy, not unlike hibernation in animals, with the added benefit of being an antifreeze. In dormancy, all growth and activity slow down. While dormancy begins in mid- to late summer with the cessation of branch growth, it accelerates well before the obvious leaf drop of autumn. Shortening days (fewer than 12 hours of daylight) and lower temperatures (below 45°F) increase the rate of dormancy. The colder it is, the quicker leaf drop and dormancy happen.

The word *dormancy* itself is a misnomer. Although trees appear winter dormant, with the cessation of growth and the shedding of both fruit and leaves, there is still some metabolic activity even in the dead of winter. Roots rarely go totally dormant, insulated as they are by the soil, and while shoot growth ceases, internally trees are continuing the formation of next year's fruit buds that were initiated in spring and early summer.

The first visible sign of the long descent into dormancy is the cessation of shoot extension, which you usually see in midsummer. This is heralded by terminal bud set on the ends of branches. This tip bud is pronounced and swollen; with pome fruits, it's often a fruit bud. At this point, the tree will no longer make further extension growth, even if aggressively watered and fertilized. Instead, it will absorb nutrients, translocate carbohydrates, and store them in the trunk, inner bark, and roots for quick mobilization during next year's grand period of growth.

Before the leaves drop, they pull nutrients, especially nitrogen, back into the tree. Around this time, trees also develop bud scales. Bud scales are leaflike appendages but are tougher than leaves. They envelop and protect buds from cold injury. Think of them as bud blankets. The buds appear to swell and take on a fuzzy gray hue.

This can sometimes be alarming, because the buds look as if they are going to break from dormancy and grow right now. Five letters can fix this: R-E-L-A-X. Remember, it ain't necessarily so. During dormancy, a tree cannot be forced into growth until its chill-hour requirements have been satisfied.

Finally, the tree drops its leaves. Full dormancy lasts from leaf drop (fall) to bud swell (spring).

Internally, dormancy is largely controlled by a plant hormone called abscisic acid (ABA), which is produced in the bud scales (blankets!) that protect buds from cold injury. During early dormancy, abscisic acid accumulates in bud scales and moves down the branch by gravity. This hormone sends a message to the tree (as anthropomorphic as it sounds, it's accurate): *Don't grow yet. Rest! Wait for spring!*

The accumulation of abscisic acid in buds keeps them from breaking dormancy during false spring thaws, thus providing an evolutionary safety net. Over time during the winter, cold temperatures and UV sunlight degrade the abscisic acid in the bud scales. Dormancy is finished when the abscisic acid accumulated in the bud scales is exhausted and no longer controls the inner workings of the tree. The tree will break from dormancy and grow anew when it warms up.

Winter in the Orchard

In winter, the trees are seemingly dormant, but in reality they are only quiescent. There is no apparent growth, but internally flower buds are slowly developing, with spring waiting in the wings. Roots, although hidden from view, exhibit some activity in all but the coldest climates. It seems that winter is just about long enough to make you forget about summer, and summer long enough to make you forget about winter.

A philosopher's perspective: "In the depths of winter I finally learned that within me lay an invincible summer."

—ALBERT CAMUS, *Lyrical and Critical Essays*, 1968

A grower's perspective: "Winter is a time of promise because there is so little to do— or because you can now and then permit yourselves the luxury of thinking so."

—STANLEY CRAWFORD, *A Garlic Testament: Seasons on a New Mexico Farm*, 1998

V

How You Grow a Tree

Now that you understand the tree's patterns of growth, we'll look at some of the things you can do to facilitate a healthy, vigorous, productive tree. We'll start by understanding the French intensive approach to soil management through cultivation, compost, and cover crops. I'll offer suggestions for seasonal feeding of your trees; how to know when to water; and how to minimize harm from pests and diseases by providing a biodiverse habitat for beneficial plants and critters. Let's get into it.

The French Intensive Approach to Organic Gardening

In Europe, organic growers are referred to as *biological* growers, which is probably a more appropriate and descriptive term than *organic*. The system of biological gardening we use at the UCSC Farm & Garden has many names: Biodynamic French Intensive, French intensive, raised bed gardening, deep bed system, wide bed system, Chinese intensive, and Biointensive gardening (as popularized by John Jeavons). This method of raised bed, intensive gardening was pioneered at UCSC by English master gardener Alan Chadwick in 1967. At the time, raised bed gardening and even organics (let alone an entire organic food industry) were virtually unknown in the United States. Now these techniques are commonplace, even to the point of the mechanized, tractor-pulled spader, which simulates single and double digging on a field scale.

Chadwick's unique method was an amalgam of his own horticultural experiences in European market gardens and the remarkable phenomenon of the French market gardeners prevalent around Paris from the 1700s through the early 1900s. At that time, there was a scarcity of open land and an overabundance of horse manure (horses being the primary mode of transportation). The ingenious *maraîchers* (market gardeners) devised their system in order to produce early and out-of-season crops at times of year when they would bring a high price at the marketplace. By the mid-1800s, about 1,500 acres were devoted to intensive garden cultivation in Paris, distributed among approximately 1,100 growers—a little more than an acre per garden. Growers often produced eight or nine crops a year at four or five times the normal yield per acre, and they

Raised bed intercropping
in the alleys between
Flavor Grenade pluot trees

marketed more than $1 million worth of produce a year. No mean feat in Paris, which sits at the same latitude as the US-Canadian border.

The Parisian market gardeners put a premium on deep digging and fortifying the soil with insane amounts of composted horse manure. In essence, they were growing in almost pure compost. Additionally, they often dug the soil out 3 feet deep, layered in 1 foot or more of piping hot horse manure, and then replaced the top 2 feet of topsoil. The heat generated by the buried manure was trapped by cold frames (glass-topped boxes placed above the beds during cold weather). In this way, the maraîchers were able to generate air and soil temperatures much more *genial* than the outside environment and grow crops out of season.

Chadwick also drew from the literature and historical records of ancient cultures—Egypt, Mesopotamia, China, and particularly the Greeks and Romans—in their various intensive cultivation techniques. He dubbed his hybrid gardening system the "Biodynamic French Intensive" method.

By any name, this system is both ingenious and elegant, as well as complex and highly productive. Its most commonly recognized feature is wide, deeply dug, permanent raised beds, which are copiously infused with ample amounts of compost that is incorporated, along with green manures, at depths of 1–2 feet in the soil profile. Other notable components of the French system are intercropping, close spacing of plantings, and use of transplants (rather than direct seeding).

In nature, it can take 1,000–2,000 years for 1 inch of topsoil to form. By using the French intensive raised bed system (in conjunction with cover crops and compost), it is possible to simulate the creation of as much as 2 feet of topsoil in a mere 1–3 years. What takes centuries of time to achieve in nature can be speeded up to a few short seasons by the ingenious and sensitive cooperation of humankind—that's us, the dirt gardeners!

Soil Basics

Before you begin to improve your soil, it helps to know exactly what it's made of. Soil is made up of biotic (living, or that which was once alive) and abiotic (nonliving) components, or building blocks, that function together to form a stable system. The biotic components consist largely of living plants, living organisms (macro and micro), and organic matter (plant and animal residues), which can be fresh, partially decomposed, or fully stabilized (that's called humus, and it does *not* taste good with pita chips). The abiotic elements of soil are minerals, air, and water.

Remember when we did the soil feel test in "Site Selection"? (See page 10.) When you pick up a handful of soil, only half of that volume is solid material (minerals and organic matter). The other half should be pore space occupied by air and water. To the extent that your soil practices are good, you will improve the structure of your soil and increase the volume of pore space in it. Thus, your soil will hold more water and air.

Here's a breakdown of the components of an ideal soil, by volume:

MINERAL (45 percent) Rocks that have been ground down over geologic time as a result of physical, chemical, and biological actions. Think of it as rock or stone "flour."

ORGANIC MATTER (5 percent) A wide range of organic (carbon-containing) substances, including living organisms, plant biomass, and the carbonaceous remains of organisms and plants. Some soil microorganisms break down the remains of plants, animals, and other microorganisms; others synthesize new substances.

AIR (25 percent) Soil air occupies the interstitial spaces between soil particles. Its primary role is to provide oxygen to microorganisms and plant roots.

WATER (25 percent) Soil water, often called the soil solution, is the vehicle for dissolved nutrients to "flow" into plants and, along with the products of photosynthesis, grow the plant.

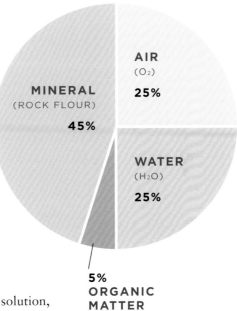

MINERAL (ROCK FLOUR) 45%

AIR (O_2) 25%

WATER (H_2O) 25%

5% ORGANIC MATTER

ORGANIC MATTER: ALMOST A PANACEA

Organic matter is the keystone of fertile soil. Although it makes up only 3–5 percent of the soil, organic matter has a pronounced positive influence on all the soil's properties—physical, chemical, and biological. When added to soil as compost or green manure, it yields the following:

- Nutrients for immediate use by microbes and plant roots. It also holds and releases nutrients over time. This is especially true of nitrogen, the most volatile and motile (movable) of all nutrients, and the one needed by plants in the largest quantity.

- An open, permeable soil surface that allows air and gas exchange to replenish the soil's oxygen content, and makes it easy for water to enter, percolate through, and drain out of the root zone.

- A feedstock and habitat for microbes.

- A low population of soil-borne plant diseases and pathogens.

- A high population of beneficial soil microorganisms.

- Improved soil structure, tilth, and workability.

On a monograined, structureless sandy soil, organic matter creates better aggregation (ability to clump) and aids with moisture and nutrient retention, building the "body" of a soil. On a wicked sticky clay, it adds more continuous macropores from the surface to the subsoil, allowing for easy root growth. Organic matter increases the oxygen content of clay soils, thus facilitating better root growth and a flourishing biological community. Organic matter is also a good indicator of nitrogen content, and vice versa.

Although I'll stop short of calling it a panacea, whatever the problem with soils, the answer is almost always to add organic matter in the form of compost and/or green manures from cover crops.

SOIL'S THREE PROPERTIES

When seeking to improve your soil, it helps to understand that soil possesses three distinct types of properties: physical, chemical, and biological.

Physical properties of soil include its *texture* and *structure*:

- Soil texture is a physical measurement of the percentage of sand, silt, and clay particles in a soil (as determined by grain size, with sandy soils being the largest and clay the smallest). It is a given and cannot be altered.

- Soil structure refers to the arrangement of individual soil particles (sand, silt, clay) into aggregates or clumps; ideally, it takes the form of a granular or crumb structure with a mix of small, intermediate, and large stable aggregates. An apt analogy might be the profile view of a sliced loaf of whole wheat bread, with its marbled and pebbled crumb structure.

Chemical properties of soil relate to its nutrient-carrying capacity and pH (acidity). When you did your soil test, the test looked at the chemical properties of your soil to determine the results. If you have chemical deficiencies you will have to add nutrients in the form of fertilizers (see page 152).

Biological properties of soil refer to the community of creatures that live in and off the soil, forming it in the process. These critters are principally bacteria, fungi, and actinomycetes (microorganisms that are especially effective in breaking down hard-to-decompose compounds). As farmers and gardeners, we continually find ourselves in both perpetual service to and reverence of that community.

While the three properties of soil are discrete, they are also synergistically interactive. For example, by using compost and green manures, you provide a feedstock for microbial populations (a biological property). These microbes break down organic matter with their "enzymatic jaws" so that it can be dissolved in soil water and taken up as nutrients by the plant (a chemical property). The microbes, in turn, die and contribute their own organic matter back to the content of the soil. Thus, you improve the chemical properties of your soil by promoting its biological properties.

Similarly, by adding organic matter at least once a year (see "Seasonal Feeding," page 154) and using timely, skilled cultivation techniques (see page 132), you create good soil aggregation and improve soil structure (a physical property). This creates large, continuous pore spaces in the soil; with their balance of air and water, these pore spaces create a favorable habitat for the microbes and plant roots that live and grow there. Thus, you harness

SYNERGISTIC INTERACTION

PHYSICAL PROPERTIES

BIOLOGICAL PROPERTIES

CHEMICAL PROPERTIES

the physical properties of a soil to create and maintain hospitable conditions for soil organisms and plants (a biological property). The interactive possibilities are endless.

The Three Cs: Cultivation, Compost, and Cover Crops

The main pillars of the French intensive (or any sound) approach to soil management are what I refer to as the three Cs: cultivation, compost, and cover crops. By applying these methods to your soil in a regular, intentional way, you can vastly improve the health and vigor of anything you plant, including fruit trees.

CULTIVATION

Cultivation (a word often used interchangeably with *tillage*) is the process of working the soil, whether by hand or with a tractor. In a Chadwickian sense, soil cultivation is a purposefully broader concept than simply digging or tilling the soil; it's a process that leads to optimum fertility. I like the double meaning of the verb *cultivate*—to till or improve soil—and its lesser-used connotation—to cherish, to seek the acquaintance or goodwill of something. Your goal is to do all of the above for your soil.

The main techniques used in the French intensive system are single digging (12–15 inches deep) and double digging (24–30 inches deep). This deep digging develops the physical properties of the soil by rapidly improving soil structure and fertility, which as we now know can also positively influence the soil's biological and chemical properties. The main idea is to create a well-drained, well-aerated, fertile soil structure by placing nutrients evenly throughout the top 1–2 feet. This enables plant roots to probe and penetrate throughout the bed with ease, especially in a downward direction. Cultivation allows for a continuous system of large and intermediate pores from the surface to the subsoil, which in turn allows plants to meet their water, air, and nutrient needs.

Aside from the distinctive look of the raised bed, one of its main attributes is its permanent nature. Permanent beds, be they raised or flat, foster an ideal soil structure and substantially reduce soil compaction. The bed becomes a zone of maximum fertility, while the paths between beds absorb most of the degradation and compaction resulting from foot traffic.

A word of caution about cultivation from Alan Chadwick: "The skin of the Earth must be approached with great sensibility. It is alive and it contains a spirit. It is easily bruised or damaged. In some respects, it is even more delicate than the bloom on the surface of a plum. Approach it without sensitivity, or at the wrong time, and you will damage it." Ill-timed (too wet or too dry) or poorly executed digging techniques (including overworking the soil) lead to frustration, the creation of soil clods, surface puddling, runoff, breakdown of soil structure, and, most importantly, poor plant performance. This is especially true in either very clayey or very sandy soils. Again, assess your soil once a year. It'll tell you what's up.

Tutorial: Digging a Raised Bed Prior to Planting

Deep or double digging once or twice during the year prior to planting and/or immediately prior to planting can set the stage for good initial tree growth. Your tools of choice for this task are a D-handle spade, a tilthing fork (a.k.a. common garden fork), and a good bow rake.

1. Mark out the dimensions of your raised bed using string and wood stakes. For fruit trees, 6 feet wide and long should be sufficient for one tree, but the length is variable, depending on the number of trees to be planted and the spacing between them.

2. Assess and adjust soil moisture. Never work fully saturated soil, as this can damage the soil structure. The moisture level should be between 50 percent and 80 percent (see "Estimating Soil Moisture by Feel," page 157).

3. With a spade, skim off any vegetation on the bed and throw it in your compost pile (see page 141).

4. Apply compost evenly over the entire surface of the bed at a rate of about 10 cubic feet per 200 square feet (a standard contractor's wheelbarrow holds 5 cubic feet). The advantage of spreading compost prior to digging is that this material will be evenly distributed to the depth that you dig. It's more efficient than digging, then applying compost, then working the compost into the soil at depth. And as this is such a labor-intensive digging technique, shortcuts can pay a dividend.

5. Open up a trench across the width of one end of the bed. Make the trench about two spades wide (12 inches) and one spade deep (12–15 inches). The trench should have a distinctive U shape.

6. Take the soil from this first trench and put it in a wheelbarrow. It will fill the last trench you create, at the other end of the bed.

7. Lace two to three spadesful of compost evenly across the bottom of the trench.

8. Work the subsoil in the trench with a fork evenly across the trench. Thrust the fork into the soil in the bottom of the trench, thus penetrating another foot or so. With a rocking motion, pry the soil loose, but leave it in place. This will work the soil another foot deep. The compost will filter down into the holes made by the fork tines, further loosening up the deeper soil and providing nutrients to the tree's deeper roots. Working this second depth of soil is the "double" part of double digging; single digging omits this deeper penetration.

9. Standing on the undug portion of the bed, plunge the spade about 12 inches into the topsoil and slide or lever it forward to fill the open trench you have created. This action, sometimes called slide digging, creates a new trench next to the first (now filled) trench.

10. Work your way across the bed one spadeful at a time, repeating the process. As you move down the bed, you simultaneously fill each open trench and create a new trench. It is sometimes helpful to clean up each trench as you go. After creating each trench, apply compost across the bottom and fracture the second depth with a fork.

11. When you reach the end of the bed, use the soil from the first trench to fill the last trench. Congratulations, you have just rough dug a raised bed!

This is just a preliminary step, also known as primary cultivation. To finish the job, you must engage in secondary cultivation by tilthing the bed. This set of steps refines any rough clods unearthed by your digging and creates a smooth, particulate level soil surface.

Tilthing the Bed

This finishing technique is referred to as tilthing, derived from the word *tillage*. The tool used is a tilthing fork (common garden fork). Go ahead and tilth your bed! Be detailed and precise. And do it in style—with panache, even.

1. You are now going to work the top 6–8 inches of the soil with your fork thoroughly and evenly across the whole bed. The most efficient way to do this is to first position yourself on one side of the bed. Stand facing the bed (but not on the bed). Starting in the center of the bed and proceeding outward to the edge where you're standing, work half the bed's width. Then walk around to the other side and work the other half.

2. Thrust your fork into the soil 6–8 inches deep at about a 45-degree angle, then lift it upward. The lifting and twisting motion will bring all the large clods up to the surface. Break up the rough clods by swinging your fork from side to side with a gentle glancing motion. You don't want to smash straight down, as that may damage or compact your soil. The more you shake it up, the finer the tilth of the soil will be. Directly sown seeds or small transplants require a finer tilth. Not so much with fruit trees, so keep the soil slightly rough.

3. Use a bow rake to remove any remaining coarse particles of soil and to smooth the surface and shape the bed. Your ideal bed should be slightly raised and flat topped, with straight sides (perpendicular to the ground). Achieving this straight-sided look is referred to as berming the bed. Simply give the sides a gentle whack or two with your rake, methodically moving up and down the length.

Thus the raised bed becomes a nurturing ground, teeming (and teaming) with life and nutrients, possessed of all the necessities for the growth, flowering, and fruiting of the trees you will plant.

A raised bed,
prepared via tractor

COMPOST

Compost (the process and product) is another example of harnessing biology to assist us in promoting a healthy, robust soil that in turn grows quality crops. Compost is one of the easiest and most essential ways to increase your soil's organic matter content and brings with it all the structural, nutrient-holding, aeration, and hydration benefits of organic matter. It's also an environmentally sound way to reduce and recycle garden and kitchen waste.

Around where I live, a lot of bumper stickers read "Compost Happens" (a play on "Shit Happens"). Yeah, compost happens, but you may be able to make compost better (and certainly quicker) than nature can.

Composting is all about the decomposition and transformation of heterogeneous organic wastes (basically anything that was once alive) into a homogeneous, stable end product—organic matter/humus or, as we call it, compost. This decomposition is carried out by succeeding waves of micro- and macro-organisms. You could refer to a compost pile as a microbial layer cake. Quality compost is a uniform product—black in color, crumbly in texture, sweet smelling, and slightly greasy to the touch. It is a powerful reservoir of plant nutrients that are released slowly over time via further biological activity. Rather than think of a compost pile as a bunch of rotting organic materials, think of it as "black gold"—arguably the most precious substance on the planet.

How Composting Works

The composting process has three distinct phases:

1. Mesophilic (50°–113°F): Moderate temperatures, usually lasting under a week

2. Thermophilic (113°–150°F): High temperatures, usually lasting 3–4 weeks

3. Curing: Ambient temperatures, lasting more than 3 months

During the first, mesophilic phase of composting, waves of bacteria and fungi multiply rapidly and feed on the succulent plants in the pile, secreting enzymes and acids that break down the plant material. When the compost pile is properly constructed, the first 24–48 hours feature an explosive, exponential growth of these organisms (bacteria can double their populations every 20–60 minutes). Often, there is no recognizable plant material in the pile after even a few days, thanks to the biochemical decomposition taking place.

The next phase features thermophilic, or heat-loving, organisms—still some bacteria, but increasingly fungi. Small piles, made incrementally, will not get hot enough to reach this phase. Fungi act to decompose more complex carbon compounds.

As the pile cools and begins its curing process, a third microbial population comes to the fore—a type of actinobacteria often referred to as actinomycetes. These have the simple cell structure of bacteria, but more closely resemble fungi. Their enzymatic role is to degrade tough, resistant-to-rot woody stems and bark. Their gray-white filaments look cobwebby and have a pleasant, earthy smell. They can rot a redwood stake in the ground in 9–15 months.

When a pile has cooled and cured for 1–3 months, macroorganisms—"shredders and chewers"—move in to finish the job. These organisms, such as mites, springtails, centipedes, millipedes, sowbugs, ants, and earthworms, are physical (as opposed to chemical) decomposers. They use their mouthparts to chew, shred, and further break apart resistant materials, as well as feed on dead bacteria and fungi. In doing so, they also create a softer, more "open" substrate that can be recolonized by bacteria and fungi, which break the materials down further.

You can sometimes buy organic compost at nurseries or even by the truckload at some larger-scale landscape supply stores. The principal US organics certifying agency is the Organic Materials Research Institute (OMRI)—look for the label. But even when certified, not all composts are created equally. I highly recommend starting your own compost pile, which allows you to know exactly what's in your compost and has the added benefit of reducing your landfill footprint.

Tutorial: Starting a Compost Pile

In constructing a compost pile, you are setting the stage for the decomposition of bulky organic wastes and the recycling of nutrients and are creating a feedstock for those microbial populations and macro-organisms. In a sense, composting is a form of animal husbandry, and a compost pile is simply pasture for microbes. As with any successful husbandry effort, habitat, diet, clean air, and water are the keys to success.

CHOOSE A PILE SITE AND SIZE

You'll want the pile away from any scavenging critters, but not directly under, say, your bedroom window. A good site is under the shade of a deciduous tree, which affords shade in summer and sun in winter.

Conventional guidelines suggest a minimum ideal size of 5 by 5 by 5 feet, using the logic that a big pile has more internal mass and thus a more hospitable decomposition environment. But don't despair—one of the more successful (no muss, no fuss) compost piles I have ever built was during a community workshop. It was a scant 2 by 3 by 2 feet. It produced beautiful compost in 3–4 months. Size isn't everything.

Some recommendations regarding pile dimensions:

- Width should not exceed 6–8 feet so that the pile can get enough oxygen (oxygen does not permeate more than 3–4 feet into a pile without human assistance).

- It is impractical (involving too much heavy lifting) to build a pile more than 3½–4 feet in height.

- The pile can be any length—it simply depends on the volume of material you have on hand.

- A cube or rectangular shape is better than a pyramid or tapered haystack.

GATHER YOUR INGREDIENTS

Compost can be made of any organic materials, including manure. (But don't include poison oak or ivy, sumac, or other plants you don't want in your garden! Annual weeds are okay, as long as they haven't gone to seed.) What is most important is the carbon to nitrogen ratio (C:N). The ideal initial C:N ratio is 30–40:1. This means the pile has 30–40 times more carbon-rich material than nitrogen-rich material by weight.

This C:N ratio is the ideal proportion to fuel the diet of the pile's microbial decomposers. Microbes use the carbon-rich ingredients as structural building blocks and (as do we) for carbohydrates that fuel their work and help them to build the proteins, amino acids, and enzymes necessary for cell growth, function, and reproduction.

Enzymes are also key to the decomposition process; they act as biological catalysts, accelerating biochemical reactions and hastening the breakdown of organic matter. Interestingly, the enzymes produced by bacteria and fungi persist and function long after the producing organisms have died. These same enzymes contribute to the breakdown of the "microbial corpses" that produced them.

Materials high in carbon include dry "brown" materials such as straw, leaves, and wood chips. Materials high in nitrogen include animal manures and wet "greens" (fresh, lush plants) such as yard trimmings, cover crops, and kitchen scraps (no meat).

CHOP 'EM UP

The principle is the smaller the particle size (think chopping, shredding), the greater the surface area, the more the microbes can occupy the space, and thus the faster the rate of decomposition. Chopping plant material also breaks apart the rigid, often waxy outer cuticle of plants, making the succulent innards more accessible to the secretions of bacteria and fungi, thus speeding and contributing to more thorough decomposition. You can chop your materials on the ground before you add them, or chop them in place as you add layers to your pile.

LAYER 'EM IN

You can achieve the desired C:N ratio of 30–40:1 by combining comparative volumes of carbon-rich (brown) and nitrogen-rich (green) ingredients in layers. In creating the microbial layer cake, as with other layer cakes, thin, repeated layers work best. Start at the bottom:

- C: 2 inches straw/leaves/wood chips, etc. (Straw is a good absorptive material to use at the base of the pile.)
- N: 2 inches kitchen scraps
- C: 2 inches straw/leaves/wood chips, etc.
- N: 6 inches fresh horse manure
- C: 2 inches straw/leaves/wood chips, etc.
- N: 4 inches greens
- C: 2 inches straw

Repeat to height of 3–4 feet.

This pile features 40 percent carbon-based materials and 60 percent nitrogen-based materials by approximate volumes and, predictably, will do quite well.

Note that vegan or nonmanure piles work fine. The value of animal manures is that they are rich in both nitrogen and microbes—helpful in jump-starting a pile.

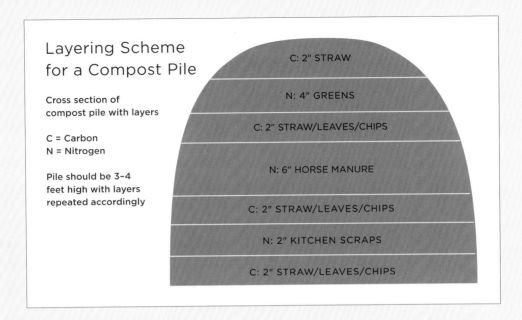

Layering Scheme for a Compost Pile

Cross section of compost pile with layers

C = Carbon
N = Nitrogen

Pile should be 3–4 feet high with layers repeated accordingly

C: 2" STRAW

N: 4" GREENS

C: 2" STRAW/LEAVES/CHIPS

N: 6" HORSE MANURE

C: 2" STRAW/LEAVES/CHIPS

N: 2" KITCHEN SCRAPS

C: 2" STRAW/LEAVES/CHIPS

DON'T FORGET TO MOISTURIZE

Compost pile ingredients should be about 40–60 percent moisture (by weight). This equates to the consistency of a wrung-out sponge. It is best to apply water (sprinkle spray, not drench) incrementally to each layer as you construct the pile. The moisture is for the microbes, but also softens the pile ingredients. A note: As water will trickle down from top to bottom, apply less water to the lower layers of the pile. And as plants are merely supported columns of water, more water will be released into the pile as decomposition progresses. Thus, be conservative with the initial water application.

AERATE

Composting is a highly aerobic process, as oxygen fuels the metabolism of the microbes that do the decomposing. Once the composting process is under way (1–3 weeks), a pile will settle, losing 30–50 percent of its volume as the materials are physically broken down. At that juncture, there is usually a sharp drop in temperature. As the pile settles, reducing pore and air space, and as microbial populations exhaust the oxygen supply, oxygen becomes a limiting factor. This is an opportune time to turn and reaerate a pile. Simply take your fork and turn over the compost so that the layers are rotated thoroughly, top to bottom and side to side. A spike in temperature is often associated with turning: as oxygen is resupplied, microbial populations boom. The heat generated is a by-product of their metabolism as they continue to break down materials in the pile.

The Home Gardener's Dilemma

Typically, home gardeners have small, incremental volumes of compost materials; little easy access to animal manures; an overabundance of wet, nitrogen-rich kitchen scraps; and a shortage of all other ingredients. You can still make reasonable compost (low heat, long term) by alternating thin layers of kitchen scraps (1–2 inches), with layers of straw or leaves (2–3 inches), and perhaps a little garden soil (1 inch). Moisten the dry ingredients as you go. Build the pile in a 3-by-3-foot area with layers over time until it is 3 feet high. With this incremental method, it may take a month or two to build the pile. Within this time period, turn the pile once or twice. Start the next pile adjacent to the first. In layering a pile, consider alternating wet and dry ingredients, as well as large or bulky and small-particle ingredients. Layering approximates the much harder job of mixing, shredding, and homogenizing.

Compost is a lot like democracy—the broader the constituency base, the greater and richer the end product. It's worth stockpiling a range of ingredients to use in the home garden pile:

- Bale of straw (not hay, as hay has seeds)

- Trash can full of leaves, wood chips, etc.

- Bagged chicken manure

- Garden greens and debris (covered with a tarp to protect them)

Introducing these ingredients into the layering system along with kitchen scraps will result in a better composting process and a more nutrient-rich end product. If flies or gnats are a problem, a light dusting of wood ash, lime, or soil helps.

Please, I implore you: you must make compost!

COVER CROPS AND GREEN MANURES

Cover crops (often used as green manures) and their positive, restorative effects on the soil come down to us through agricultural antiquity. Their ability to stimulate the growth of subsequent or "follow" crops is well documented in Chinese manuscripts from 3,000 years ago. Greek and Roman cultures also featured liberal reference to cover crops in technical treatises and poetry. The Roman poet Virgil's classic *Georgics* (*Earth Works*) is an epic poem of agriculture, culture, and animal husbandry laced with frequent and quite specific reference to the use of green manures and compost.

A cover crop is simply any plant used to protect (cover) the surface of the soil and prevent erosion. Bare soil is anathema (Greek for "an accursed thing") to good soil stewardship and is not often found in natural systems. A cover crop's foliage shields exposed soil from the explosive impact of rain, and its roots bind and hold the soil to prevent erosion. Cover crops can also be used as "trap crops" to catch nutrients and prevent them from leaching downward in the soil profile. *Green manure* is the term for a cover crop that is chopped up and turned into the soil as a form of fertilizer.

Overall, cover crops and green manures can improve the physical properties and structure of a soil, increase the organic matter content, protect the soil surface, improve water infiltration and retention, cycle and sequester nutrients, increase nitrogen levels, provide habitat and food for beneficial insects, suppress weeds, offer a rest or fallow period for soil, and reduce or eliminate the need for purchased fertilizer. Yes, they can do it all—a good elixir.

"Where no kind of manure is to be had, I think cultivation of lupines will be found the readiest and best substitute. If they are sown around the middle of September in poor soil, and then ploughed in, the following spring, they will answer as well as the best manure."

—COLUMELLA, *De Re Rustica,* first-century Rome

Buckwheat cover crop

Materials

Typically, annual grasses (such as oats, barley, and annual rye) and legumes (such as vetches, bell and fava beans, clovers, and field peas) are used in tandem. While they are neither legumes nor grasses, buckwheat and some brassicas are fast-growing utilitarian cover crops and can be used as well.

Annual grasses act as "nurse crops." They germinate quickly (within 3–5 days) and provide leaf cover for the soil surface and soil-holding action via the roots until the slower-emerging legumes get established (7–10 days). Grasses have a fibrous, shallow root system that "works" the surface soil to about 1 foot deep and has an ameliorating effect on soil structure. Grasses slough off dying roots on an almost daily basis and grow new roots, thus increasing the organic matter content of the soil even as they grow. Although grasses, buckwheat, and brassicas add organic matter, they do not fix nitrogen.

Legumes feature a deep taproot (bio-drill) that breaks up compaction at depth as well as shallower, fibrous root systems. Some legumes, notably vetches and bell beans, are prolific biomass producers, with as much as 6–8 feet of top growth. Legumes also fix nitrogen.

At plow-down time, when you incorporate the cover crop back into the soil, the combination of grasses and legumes contributes to a balance of carbonaceous material (grasses) and nitrogenous material (legumes). This results in an optimal formula for organic matter increase and immediate fertilizer effect.

In mild to moderate winter areas, and especially in Mediterranean climates, cover crops are best seeded from September to October and plowed into the soil in spring. If you are trying to improve your soil before planting fruit trees, I recommend a mixture of bell beans, vetch, peas, and an annual grass.

In cold winter areas, the aim is to establish both root and shoot growth before the arrival of killing frosts. Therefore, sow in late summer. Winter rye and vetch are the most cold-hardy crops; they will sprout and regrow briefly in the spring before being plowed down. The other species will die at frost, but leave a protective thatch. When turned in during the spring, they will add valuable organic matter to the soil. Oats sown

Cover crops, clockwise from upper left: Vetch, mustard, bell beans, BBVOP (bell beans, vetch, oats, and peas mix)

COVER CROP WINTER HARDINESS CHART

The following are the USDA Hardiness Zones recommended for different cover crops.

LEGUMES	
CLOVERS (GENUS *TRIFOLIUM*)	
Alsike	zone 4
Berseem	zone 7
Crimson	zone 5
Red	zone 4
White	zone 4
SWEET CLOVERS (GENUS *MELILOTUS*)	
Annual white	not frost tolerant
Biennial sweet clover	zone 4
Cowpeas	not frost tolerant
Bell or fava beans	zone 8
Hairy vetch	zone 4
Field peas	zone 7
GRASSES AND OTHER NON-LEGUMES	
BRASSICAS	
Foraged turnips	zones 6–8
Mustard	zones 6–8
Daikon	zones 6–8
Canola	zones 6–8
BARLEY	zones 3–9
BUCKWHEAT	not frost tolerant
CEREAL RYE (*SECALE CEREAL*; NOT BE CONFUSED WITH RYE GRASS, WHICH IS A PERENNIAL USED IN LAWNS)	zone 3
OATS	zone 8
SUDAN GRASS (BLACK SORGHUM)	not frost tolerant
TRITICALE (A "SUPERGRASS," HYBRID BETWEEN WHEAT AND RYE)	zone 3
WINTER WHEAT	zone 3

in mid- to late summer also yield a good amount of biomass by the time killing frosts occur, although they are the most cold sensitive of all these species.

If you're embarking on a soil-building regimen and wish to grow multiple cover crops per year, sow a quick-maturing cover crop like buckwheat (matures in 40 days) or mustard (90 days) multiple times a year. Simply sow, grow, and turn in. Rinse, repeat. Once fall comes, switch back to an overwintering cover crop.

In later years, when planting cover crops around established fruit trees, I prefer to use only bell beans. The reasoning is that vetch is an 8-foot vine and recognizes the tree as a trellis, wreaking all kinds of mayhem as it intertwines and shades flowers and leaves in the spring. And grasses are often hard to eradicate in handworked systems. In California, I have used bell beans as the sole source of fertilizer input for our established trees for 35 years. We simply chop them on the surface in the spring using a cheap machete, then mulch them over with 3–4 inches of wood chips. In the first 2 years after planting, I apply two to three shovels of compost and ½–1 pound of an organic granular fertilizer (see "Seasonal Feeding," page 154) in addition to the green manure crop, before applying mulch.

Soil Preparation and Seeding

Soil preparation can be as simple and easy as lightly skimming off any existing vegetation with your spade (throw the scraps in your compost pile!). In this process, the surface of the soil should become open and loose enough for seeds to penetrate. Irrigate, wait 3–5 days for it to dry down, then broadcast-scatter the seeds on the soil surface. Rake the seeds in with quick, short strokes using a bow rake (not a leaf rake), moving in one direction—either to or fro, but not both—to cover the seed. Mulch with straw, leaves, or wood chips, then water. Stand back, go write the Great American Novel, reappear periodically to check out the crop's progress, and plow down in early spring.

If you are improving your soil before any fruit trees are planted, as well as afterwards on ongoing basis, seeding to have 8–10 plants per square foot is adequate. As sort of an insurance policy, you usually seed at a slightly higher rate than you want, so I recommend 20–30 seeds per square foot. This is a light scattering of seeds. An admixture by weight (not volume) of 60–90 percent legume and 10–40 percent grass should suffice.

Green Manure: Plow-Down Methods

There are two general approaches to incorporate (plow down or turn in) cover crops into the soil as green manure. The first is to incorporate the crop at the succulent stage: for grasses, before flowering; for legumes, when 25–50 percent in bloom. This causes the cover crop to decompose quickly and to act primarily as a fertilizer for the next crop.

A second approach is to incorporate the crop back into the soil at a more mature stage, half to full bloom, so that it adds to the organic matter content of the soil and its nutrients are then stored in the reservoir of humus and released slowly over a number of years.

The first approach is generally used on established soils to fertilize crops, and the second on developing soils to build organic matter and improve structure—to build the "body" of the soil.

There are several techniques for plowing down cover crops:

- Chop them down with a spade or machete, chop them up on the surface a little bit, and mulch them with straw, leaves, or ramial wood chips (see page 153).

- Chop them down, chop them up quite a bit, flip them into the soil with a spade, and then mulch them.

- Skim off the cover crops at the base of the plants and combine them with a carbon source (straw and/or leaves) to make compost, and subsequently reapply a previously made compost to the soil. Note: When growing legumes, it is important to leave the roots and nitrogen-filled nodules in the soil (see below); take only the vegetative portion of the cover crop for compost construction.

Nitrogen Fixation

Nitrogen is the most expensive, mobile, motile, and thus precious of all nutrients. It is needed in greater amounts than any other nutrient. Look at the roots of your leguminous cover crop. Can you spot little pinkish white nodules on the roots? That's nitrogen. Through a biological and chemical process now called facultative-parasitic—formerly known by the more poetic term *symbiosis*—soil bacteria in the genus *Rhizobium* (root zone) associate with the roots of legumes, such as beans and peas, and fix atmospheric nitrogen in a form that plants' roots can assimilate. In other words, free nitrogen fertilizer! The rhizobial bacteria are attracted to the roots by chemical secretion and enter the roots via an infection thread, a tunnel-like ingrowth of the root hair. They then migrate farther inward into the root hair. Eventually the bacteria enter the main part of the root, rupture, and spew bacteria into root cells, which enlarge and form pink-colored nodules where the bacteria grab nitrogen from air in the soil and convert it into a form (ammonium) that plants can use. In return, the legume provides the bacteria with carbohydrates, protein, and oxygen.

When the cover crop is cut off or plowed under, the nodules slough off the roots in 3–7 days, spill out into the soil, and release their nitrogen, along with nitrogen from the foliage of the legume, which is then available for use by your fruit tree or other crops (or weeds— a cautionary note). This is a gardener's dividend from the coevolution of grazing animals and perennial legumes. The animal chews at and agitates the perennial legume, nodules slough off, and nitrogen is released into the soil to regrow the legume. You (and your spade or fork) are basically playing the role of the cow (or bison or zebra).

Bell bean roots with nitrogen nodules

"The best fertilizer is the footsteps of the farmer."

—ANCIENT PROVERB

Bagged Organic Fertilizers

You would be well advised to walk around your garden. Walk around frequently; daily is best. But at least twice a week. By putting yourself out in the garden, you will see what is or isn't happening. Thus you can be in touch and provide for your tree. Observation as a form of fertilizer.

In one sense, a gardener's skills are allied with those employed by naturalists—observing, asking and answering questions; drawing what you can from that; and then developing an action plan. In another sense, good garden management is similar to playing defense in basketball. You need to lock in, read, and react. The more keen your observational skills, the quicker your responses will be.

If you have moderate soil fertility, it is feasible to grow your fruit trees with only cover crops and/or compost as your fertilizers. But a little purchased fertilizer can help support optimum growth during the early years. These fertilizers should be organic, and I mean *certified* organic. Look for an OMRI (Organic Materials Research Institute) label.

A word of caution: There are no certifying standards for the use of the word *natural*—it means nothing. Similarly, although the practice is sketchy, any fertilizer manufacturer can use the word *organic* on the bag or bottle. If you are in doubt, contact your state's organic certifying agency.

For better or worse, using organic fertilizers is not an exact science. (Once we have 150 years of research on them, as we do with conventional fertilizers, we may be able to offer more exacting prescriptions. But for now . . .) Most bagged fertilizers will have rates of application listed on the package, as well as correct ratios for mixing a "tea" if you want to use it as a foliar feed (spray it on the underside of leaves). You should always coordinate the use of bagged fertilizers with the results of your lab soil test.

Fertilizers always denote their content ratio of the big three: nitrogen (N), phosphorous (P), and potassium (K). So a fertilizer labeled 8-2-4 contains 8 percent nitrogen, 2 percent phosphorus, and 4 percent potassium by weight. Unless your soil test indicates a deficiency for another nutrient, you'll usually only need to provide nitrogen for your trees.

In general, fruit trees need nitrogen throughout their lives. A nitrogen fertilizer's effectiveness has to do with how much of the nutrients are retrieved by the tree before the nitrogen is leached downward in the soil, out of roots' reach and potentially into the water table. Conventional growers often use nitrogen fertilizers containing as much as 40 percent nitrogen. While such an approach certainly yields vigorous tree growth, reliable research now indicates that as much as 40–90 percent of the nitrogen applied leaches downward through the soil profile, tainting the water table with nitrates. This distressing issue has become almost pandemic nationally; in many agricultural communities, you can no longer drink the local well water. High-nitrogen fertilizers like blood meal, bat guano, and feather meal are quick-acting and powerful tools to establish trees, but how sustainable environmentally and economically are they?

I recommend just a little high-nitrogen fertilizer at planting and in year two to quickly establish the tree (see "Seasonal Feeding," page 154). Thereafter, my choices for getting trees their requisite nitrogen are compost and/or leguminous cover crops used as a green manure.

Ramial Wood Chips: A Superior Mulch

Mulches are a great way to protect the surface of the soil and reduce water loss, and they make a good substrate for a host of soil fungi and actinomycetes. While straw, leaves, and wood chips are excellent mulch materials, I especially find ramial wood chips to be superior. The term "ramial" simply means the chips are from live, hardwood tree branches that are less than about 3 inches in diameter. As ramial wood chips decompose, they liberate nutrients for the tree and serve as a feedstock (carbon) for soil microbes. They also raise the organic matter content of the soil, creating a dynamic reservoir for nutrients, particularly nitrogen, phosphorus, and sulphur.

Over 30 years ago, I began applying ramial wood chips as a fruit tree mulch. I used what was available from the UCSC tree crew. In our area, we have few deciduous hardwood trees; we have mostly conifers, evergreen oaks, and (unfortunately) eucalyptus, our invasive pals from the land down under. The conventional wisdom dictates not to use conifers or eucalyptus for wood chips because their leaves contain tannins, resins, acids, and other exuded substances that could have a negative effect on tree growth. Well, I'm the type of gardener who, whenever I hear, *Don't do X*, I immediately run out and do X. I do it on a small, trial basis to see: *Is it true? What might be the consequences and repercussions of doing X?* I applied these chips to our orchards. I am here today to tell you that not only are there no negative effects, but, *au contraire*, the positive effects are phenomenal. I apply a layer in spring and fall.

You can get ramial wood chips from some nurseries, garden centers, or local tree services. If a store or tree service hasn't heard the term "ramial" or says they don't have them, then try to get chips from hardwood trees, preferably from smaller branches. At the end of the day, any wood chip mulch is better than none.

Seasonal Feeding

Let's look at how you might use compost and fertilizers in concert to feed your tree throughout the year. Now is the time to refer to your dog-eared Fruit Tree Growth chart (see page 119).

SPRING FERTILIZATION

Pomologists may call spring "the grand period of growth," but 1950s iconic rocker Jerry Lee Lewis, although not as educated or erudite as those people of letters, summed it up more pointedly: "whole lotta shaking going on" in those trees in the springtime. As the tree's nutrient reserves are tapped dramatically in the spring, you need to jump to it and tend your trees. The earlier in the spring you can get out into the orchard and fertilize, the better. However, working the soil when it is too wet rapidly destroys soil structure and works against good plant growth. An organic grower's pursuit is to improve soil structure and function. Don't be impatient and mess with wet soil.

The prescription below has worked well for me for 35 years.

For newly planted and 1- to 2-year-old trees, apply the following materials in early spring:

- Spread two or three spadesful of mature compost in a 2- to 3-foot circle around the trunk, staying 4 inches away from the trunk.

- On top of the compost, evenly spread *one* of the following organic fertilizers: ½ pound blood meal (12 percent nitrogen); ¾ pound Sustáne (8 percent nitrogen); or 1 pound Down to Earth Citrus Mix (6 percent nitrogen). (Citrus Mix works fine for other fruits as well.) Work these amendments into the top 4–6 inches of the soil with a garden fork.

- Mulch this entire "donut of fertility" with 4–6 inches of ramial wood chips (see page 152).

- Thoroughly water the circle; water activates fertilizers, particularly a dry fertilizer.

Consider supporting this early-season fertilization with additional inputs 6 weeks later and monthly through the first of August. This is especially important if the young tree has not made 12–18 inches of new shoot growth. Such inputs might include the following:

- For each tree, mix 4–5 ounces fish emulsion and ½–1 ounces liquid kelp into 2½ gallons water (half of a 5-gallon bucket).

- Gently bucket (i.e., pour) around the base of the tree in a 2- to 3-foot circle out from the trunk.

- Alternatively, apply this as a foliar feed (early or late in the cool parts of the day) by spraying it on the undersides of the leaves for rapid absorption.

For established trees that are growing well, apply the following materials in early spring:

- It is doubtful that you need to apply bagged fertilizer, provided you're sowing a fall cover crop and green manure.

- Apply a very thin surface scattering of compost up to 5 cubic feet (the capacity of a contractor's wheelbarrow) per large tree, or 5–10 tons per acre on a larger orchard scale in the spring. You might even consider applying compost every *other* year, if you see that branches are making greater than 8–10 inches of new growth and the quantity and quality of fruit is satisfactory. Apply compost in a circle around each tree (garden scale) or to the alleys between the trees (orchard scale).

- As always, a mulch of ramial wood chips (see page 152), straw, or leaves on top is good.

MID- TO LATE-SUMMER FERTILIZATION

Since trees have their second concentrated root growth spurt in mid- to late summer, the application of nutrients at this time serves the tree well for winter storage and mobilization in the following spring. This is especially valuable to organic growers with late, wet springs. In a wet spring, it can be difficult to impossible to fertilize early because the soil is wet and cold.

For newly planted and 1- to 2-year-old trees, apply the following materials in mid- to late summer:

- Spread two or three spadesful of mature compost in a 2- to 3-foot circle around the trunk, staying 4 inches away from the trunk.

For established trees, apply the following materials in mid- to late summer:

- Apply compost at a rate of 5 cubic feet (a contractor's wheelbarrow) per tree, or 5–10 tons per acre.

Be cautious about applying nitrogen-rich fertilizers too late in the season, for fear of stimulating lush leafy growth into the fall and delaying dormancy. Succulent growth in the fall is subject to cold injury, which can damage the tree. But you should be safe applying compost at this time of the year. Compost is a low-nitrogen product and slow releasing, primarily under the warm conditions of spring and summer. Check with local professional and amateur growers about the best times for applying compost in your specific region.

Watering

Water from the sky is a blessing for gardeners, generally. In some regions, rain is plentiful and watering is only minimally necessary. In other areas, a good watering regime supplements natural rainfall and begets optimal growth and fruiting. In semiarid and arid areas, fruit tree growing is not possible without a regular and ample supply of water. And as the textbooks say, photosynthesis only happens in an *aqueous solution*. This means abundant water must be in the leaves for the process to proceed. In almost all circumstances, you will need to water your trees.

When you water, you fill up all the pore spaces in the soil. This is your goal: *saturation*. After the soil reaches saturation, a short while later, when air and water reoccupy the soil pores equally, the soil is said to be at field capacity, or 100 percent of field capacity. This means the level of moisture in the soil is at its ideal threshold. Roots grow, microbes prosper, and life is good for a fruit grower.

A soil can't be at saturation at all times, nor should it be. As a soil water manager, you want a swing between wet and dry. When you water, you temporarily squeeze all the air out of the soil. The soil begins to dry out (often called dry-down) 24–72 hours after saturation, and air reenters the soil. When your soil is at 60–100 percent of field capacity, air and water are well balanced in the soil, and water is readily available to roots. But as the soil continues to dry down, water availability becomes restricted. The water is there, but it's held tightly in thin films on the

"Water is the pulse of the garden."

—CHRISTOF BERNAU, Garden Manager at the UCSC Farm

How Plants Take Up Nutrients

Good watering aids fertilization—good watering *is* good fertilization.

As you learned in "Soil Basics" (page 129), *soil solution* is the term for the water in the soil that occupies the pores or air spaces between the solid particles. In thinking about the soil solution, don't picture purity or Perrier water. The soil solution is dynamic, more like a viscous primordial ooze. It contains microbes, various dissolved gases, partially decomposed organic matter, and a host of acids, sugars, and more. It is murky but fecund. Most importantly, it contains dissolved nutrients from organic matter, fertilizers, and the solid mineral component of the soil (a.k.a. rock dust).

For nutrients from the soil to be available to plants, they first need to be broken down or decomposed. This is accomplished primarily by beneficial soil organisms, although weak acids in the soil water also help out. The decomposition process reduces particle size to the point where nutrients are easily dissolved in the soil solution. Picture a spoonful of sugar (or protein powder) stirred into a glass of water. It is at this point that the plant's roots are able to absorb the nutrients.

You could say the nutrients hitch a ride with the water.

Plants absorb nutrients through three different methods: root interception, mass flow, and diffusion.

Root interception is just what it sounds like: the plant's roots grow outward and come into physical contact with the nutrients in the soil, absorbing them. The better your soil structure, the more air and water it will hold, and the more easily roots will move through it.

Mass flow is a simple principle. As water constantly evaporates out of the stomata on the underside of the leaves, it creates a wicking or sucking action, drawing more water from the soil up into the plant and leaves, creating a pressure gradient. This is akin to sucking on a straw in a glass of water.

Diffusion is also a passive process. Gases and liquids move from areas of high concentration to areas of low concentration. As water and nutrients are exhausted at the root tip, more nearby water moves toward the roots, thus replenishing both the water and the nutrients. It's almost as if nature abhors a vacuum.

edges of the soil particles—virtually useless to the trees. In fact, a dry-down to even 50 percent is potentially dangerous, so water earlier, at 60 percent field capacity.

With watering, as with other orchard and garden skills, it is essential to develop interpretive skills—what I call a horticultural IQ. There's no set rule for watering your trees. You need to monitor your soil's moisture and respond accordingly.

ESTIMATING SOIL MOISTURE BY FEEL

To water appropriately, you must be able to properly assess soil moisture. Most large-scale farming operations assess soil moisture quantitatively using tensiometers, lysimeters, and such. But for home growers, there's a much more accessible, qualitative way to assess soil moisture—by picking up a handful of soil. This approach can be just as accurate as the high-tech one.

Here is a simple and effective field/feel test for evaluating soil moisture:

- Grab a handful of soil from about 6 inches deep.

- Hold the sample in the palm of your hand and firmly but gently squeeze it into a ball (don't squash it).

- Ask and answer one simple question: does it ball up and remain intact?

- If the answer is no, drop everything—water immediately. Don't let this happen again. You are probably below 50 percent of field capacity; if the soil continues to dry to less than 25 percent, you are approaching permanent wilting point. So sorry for your loss.

- If the ball holds together, and when you toss it lightly in your palm, it crumbles easily, you're at what an agronomist would call 60–80 percent field capacity, or what a gardener would call good growing moisture. No need to water yet. But get ready—you should water in a couple/few days.

- Kicking things up a notch, as chef Emeril Lagasse liked to intone back when the Food Network was both instructive and entertaining: If the soil moisture is such that the ball sticks together when tossed and leaves a slight oily stain on your palm, you are probably at 80–100 percent field capacity and won't need to water for quite a number of days.

- If your soil is much wetter than that, you are at full saturation. If you apply more water, it can't infiltrate the soil. It puddles and runs off. Stop.

I suggest checking soil moisture every 4–7 days and using 50–60 percent field capacity as your minimum threshold. Once you're at about 60 percent, it is time to water again and begin the oscillation between wet and dry.

If you want to learn more specifics about soil moisture assessment, I highly recommend the USDA National Resources Conservation Service website (see Resources, page 266), which has a treasure trove of accessible soil moisture information.

To fully enable photosynthesis, it's best to apply water early in the day, as it takes a few hours for that water to make its way to the leaves. And pay attention to the weather report—make sure your trees are well watered in advance of any heat wave.

As your trees grow, keep in mind that bigger trees require more water proportionally. Assume the root system extends slightly farther (a foot or more) than the drip line and water accordingly.

Fostering Biodiversity

Now, it's time to look at the environment you're creating for your tree. By fostering biodiversity in your orchard or garden, you'll be able to support successful pollination, prevent harm from unwanted pests, and support the larger health of the planet through organic systems.

Folk wisdom and science agree: the more diverse an agroecological system (your garden) is, the fewer crop pests there are. Until relatively recently in modern history, most gardens and even farms featured an eclectic planting of annuals, perennials, flowers, herbs, vegetables, and fruits. Growing a diversity of plants seasonally helps create a habitat that shelters and nourishes beneficial insects and pollinators. And growing plants of different heights, from ground level to treetops, creates a tiered canopy for beneficials to live and feed in. Flowers especially are an advertisement, a message saying to beneficial insects, *Yoo-hoo, if you come over here, you'll get a reward!* The reward is pollen and nectar—protein and carbs, the two basic building blocks of any diet.

Modern-day conventional agriculture has a simple mission: *get a good crop with high yields, a bumper crop, by any means necessary.* At first glance, this seems impressive, even admirable. Yet a preponderance of evidence indicates that we are destroying the planet and its peoples in the process. Pesticides, herbicides, irresponsible fertilizing practices, high carbon footprints, monocropping . . . the list is long. These are what we're trying to get away from with biological growing systems.

As organic gardeners, we care about the earth. We care *for* the earth, and as we care for it, we should engage in practices that create healthy, vibrant, resilient, managed ecosystems. Today's large-scale, energy-intensive, industrial farming efforts, though highly productive and seemingly efficient, are all too often exploitative of people, air, water, and soil systems. We need to do better. We need to be stewards of the planet and the people on it, not only of the soil.

Diverse cropping systems are much more balanced than monocrops: resilient, easier to manage, and in the end more productive, too. As a home grower, it's easy to welcome biodiverse plants and critters into your orchard. Not only will you be able to keep many harmful insects at bay and encourage beneficial pollinators, but you will have the pleasure of being in a virtual Garden of Eden. Just behave yourselves in the garden, and don't get too carried away . . .

The Four Ps

We would all do well to amend our gardens to provision for the Four Ps—pollinators (native and nonnative), predators, parasitoids (beneficial insects), and passerines (insectivorous songbirds). Beneficial predatory and parasitic insects and insect-eating birds can exert a huge control of detrimental insects such as aphids, thrips, mites, scale, mealy bugs, and caterpillars. Common members of the Four Ps include the following:

POLLINATORS European honeybees, bumblebees, solitary bees, syrphid flies, tachinid flies, and small nonstinging predatory wasps.

Two out of every three mouthfuls you eat are brought to you by the work of pollinating insects.

PREDATORS Minute pirate bugs, assassin bugs, soldier beetles, tachinid flies, ladybugs, and lacewings. Predators chew pests with their mandibles (jaws) or pierce them with tubelike mouthparts and suck out their innards. It's fun stuff.

PARASITOIDS Syrphid flies, tachinid flies, and many wasp species. Parasitoids typically lay their eggs nearby, on, or in pests. The larval stage is the parasite that kills the host pest by slowly eating first the nonessential organs, then the essential organs. This makes sense because the parasite wants to keep its host alive as long as possible. Some species serve variously as both predators (adult phase) and parasitoids (larval stage).

PASSERINES Common insectivorous garden songbirds include bushtits, chickadees, most warblers, vireos, hermit thrushes, flycatchers, wrens, bluebirds, and many more. These birds are voracious leaf and stem gleaners. One of my favorite fall and winter sights is when, on a chilly morning, walking the orchard, a gregarious flock of twenty to thirty bushtits swoops down on the apples and the birds blanket the trees, all the while devouring aphid eggs. Simultaneously, in the distance, a handful of chickadees is patrolling in a similar fashion.

Front yard pollinator habitat with yarrow

PLANTING FOR THE FOUR Ps

While we gardeners often stand in wonder and appreciation of the exquisite processes of nature, there are some things we can do that will aid and provision for the Four Ps. Members of certain plant families (some of which are also excellent as cut flowers) provide easily accessed food for beneficial and pollinating insects via pollen and nectar. You can attract beneficials to your yard and prevent harmful pests by planting a variety of the following:

Apiaceae family (carrot and dill family)

Angelica (*Angelica archangelica*): Probably the best flower to attract many species of predatory wasps.

Queen Anne's lace, Dara (*Daucus carota* and *Daucus carota* 'Dara')

White lace flower, bishop's lace (*Ammi majus*)

Asteraceae family (sunflower and daisy family)

Calliopsis (*Coreopsis tinctoria*)

Cornflower (*Centaurea cyanus*)

Cosmos (*Cosmos bipinnatus*)

Fleabane (*Erigeron speciosus*)

Goldenrod (*Solidago* spp.)

Lanceleaf tickseed (*Coreopsis lanceolata*)

Mexican sunflower (*Tithonia rotundifolia*)

Sunflower (*Helianthus annuus*)

Yarrow (*Achillea* spp.)

Brassicaceae family (cabbage family)

Sweet alyssum (*Lobularia maritima*): This is a powerhouse, attracting many parasitic wasp species.

Caryophyllaceae family (pink and carnation family)

Baby's breath (*Gypsophila elegans*, *G. paniculata*)

Clove pink, spice pink (*Dianthus plumarius*)

Florists' carnation (*Dianthus caryophyllus*)

Soapwort (*Saponaria vaccaria*): Tall, cutting types come in pink and white.

Sweet William (*Dianthus barbatus*)

Dipsacaceae family (teasel family)

Pincushion flower (*Scabiosa atropurpurea*, *S. caucasica*)

Fabaceae family (pea family)

Clovers (*Trifolium* spp., *Melilotus* spp., *Medicago* spp.)

Fava or bell beans (*Vicia faba*)

Lupines (*Lupinus* spp.)

Vetches (*Vicia* spp.)

Lamiaceae family (mint family)

Catmint (*Nepeta* x *faassenii*)

Lavenders (*Lavendula* spp.)

Mints (*Mentha* spp.)

Rosemary (*Rosmarinus officinalis*)

Sages (*Salvia* spp.)

Plumbaginaceae family (plumbago family)

Statice (*Limonium sinuatum, L. caspium, L. platyphyllum*
[formerly *L. latifolia*], *L. bellidifolium*)

Polygonaceae family (buckwheat family)

Annual buckwheat (*Fagopyrum esculentum*)

California native shrub buckwheat (*Eriogonum arborescens,
E. giganteum, E. fasciculatum*, and more)

Rosaceae family (rose family)

Roses (*Rosa* spp.): Particularly the single-flowered types.

Scrophulariaceae family (snapdragon and foxglove family)

Beard tongue or common florists' penstemon (*Penstemon* x
gloxinioides): Every state has a native penstemon species!

Foxglove (*Digitalis purpurea*)

Mullein (*Verbascum chaixii, V. phoeniceum, V. bombyciferum*)

Speedwell (*Veronica spicata*)

The Dawn Patrol

Our allies in the insect and avian world are particularly evident early and late in the day. Dawn and dusk. The crepuscular hours. As both poets and biologists tell us, these are times of heightened biological activity. Many varying demographics such as surfers, birders, naturalists, anglers, and hunters pursue their passions in the early light. Surfers refer to this as the dawn patrol.

One of the pleasures of my life is the almost daily, early-morning walkabout in our fields, gardens, and orchards. I find these to be synergistic times of both reflection and technical insight—a time of alchemy, inspiration, and profound humility that helps integrate science and spirit on a daily basis.

On a more practical basis, the dawn patrol is about honoring the dignity of our physical labor—noticing what needs to be done and then doing it in a timely manner. The dawn patrol is an ideal way to monitor and scout for problems. One of the keys to preventing harm from pests and disease is to recognize and detect problems early; then, whatever your chosen treatment, you can move on it pronto. What better way to do so than by a morning stroll augmented by the clear perspective of the dawn's light?

Many insectivorous birds are "birds of the bush"—that is, they like woodlands and shrubbery, not flat open spaces. By planting trees and shrubs, you will make them feel at home. At the UCSC garden, we have created a truly mixed mélange of everything you can grow in Santa Cruz. The garden is situated next to both chaparral and woodland. By planting trees, shrubs, flowers, and vegetables, we have virtually eliminated the demarcation between the garden and the surrounding wildlands. Consequently, eight to ten species of insect-eating birds grace us with their presence. Assisted as we are by these birds, we have traditionally had very low populations of harmful insects. We have never had to spray, with the exception for the rosy apple aphid and the voracious codling moth on apples.

I think Dr. Marla Spivak, professor of apiculture and social insects at the University of Minnesota and a 2010 MacArthur Fellow, eloquently sums up why it's so important to provide habitat and food for friendly pollinators:

> Improving habitat for native pollinators and beneficials is a step-by-step guide for changing our stewardship of the earth. It is a tangible way for people of all ages to make a difference. Active participation in this vital, grassroots revolution is easy: plant flowers! Sure, by creating floral and nesting habitat, bees, butterflies, and countless other wildlife species will prosper. But through this same simple effort, you will be ensuring abundance of locally grown nutritious fruits and vegetables. You will beautify our cities, roadways, and countryside. You will be helping to spread the word about the urgent need to reduce pesticide use, while at the same time creating habitat for beneficial insects that prey upon crop pests. You will be increasing crop diversity and ecological resistance through pollinator gardens, bee pastures, and flowering field borders that stabilize the soil, filter water runoff, and pack carbon into roots of native prairie plants. For many of our earth's current environmental ills, you will be part of the solution.

So I say, *vive la révolution*! The quiet revolution. Plant flowers!

Keeping Bees

While planting flowers will attract many pollinators, you can directly encourage bees by keeping them in your garden. If you want to set up your own beehives using the European honeybee, look for beekeeping associations and classes in your area. This is a fascinating pursuit that also yields the bonus of honey. For a large orchard, you'd need one or two hives per acre of trees; a robust beehive will have more than 30,000 bees. By having one or two hives in a small garden, you'll likely have yourself and your neighbors covered.

Or you could draft off of a local beekeeper near you. The honeybee has a range of 2–3 miles, and research suggests it may be as high as 7 miles. While honeybees prefer to operate closer to home, if someone in the vicinity keeps bees, you should be all right. Just remember to bring your neighbor some fruit at harvesttime.

Another, easier option is to raise mason bees. The mason bee, or the BOB (blue orchard bee), is among the most efficient of all orchard pollinators. Mason bees in numbers as low as two to three hundred can pollinate an entire acre of apples. They are solitary, nest in holes or in easily constructed bee hutches or hotels, and are self-sufficient. These bees eat

Mason bee hotel

fruit tree pollen almost exclusively. They are an industrious bee, flying and pollinating at temperatures as low as 50°F and under poor weather conditions, when it's wet and windy. Under good conditions, mason bees start flying and pollinating earlier in the day than honey bees and continue until sunset. Starter kits for mason bees can be purchased online.

Preventing Harm from Pests and Diseases

Despite your best efforts, you will experience both pests and diseases in your home orchard. It is inevitable. The only variables are how much pest and disease pressure you'll have, which pests and diseases, and when will they occur.

The dedicated organic grower has three approaches to limit pests and diseases: foster biodiversity to encourage beneficial insects and birds; use preventive strategies, like planting disease-resistant varieties such as

Pristine apples and Frost, Avalon Pride, and Mary Jane peaches; and employ arrestive strategies, mostly organic sprays. You should do all.

As in the real estate business, pest and disease occurrences are all about location, location, location! The incidence of pests and diseases is largely a function of your weather and climate. There is a great divide in this nation—not *the* Great Divide, nor the excellent song by The Band, but a more harmful division between East and West. Areas east of the longitudinal line that runs approximately from Fargo, North Dakota, south to Forth Worth, Texas, are generally wetter, warmer, and more humid during the growing season than areas to the west. Hence, the East has greater pest and disease pressure than the West. In all probability, one or many seasonal sprays may be required.

As with many aspects of organic horticulture, there is no one-size-fits-all remedy for harm. Each tree in each specific locale will have different risks. If you see something wrong with your trees, the best approach is to ask your local "authorities" at the nursery, community garden, or university agriculture extension. They will know, down to a cellular certainty, what pests and diseases occur in your locality. Bring a photo or sample of your troubled tree or leaves, and underscore that you're growing organically. They will recommend the right treatment and when and how to use it. They will probably do this for free or a reasonable fee.

BIORATIONAL SPRAYS

A spray program for your trees will likely include both pesticides and fungicides; in organic systems, herbicides are neither needed nor welcome. By sprays, I mean biorational, organically certified, non-GMO sprays. Biorational sprays will work effectively against the culprit disease or pest but will not be persistent in the environment, and they have few or no side effects. Most importantly, they are not harmful to humans.

In the world of organics, oil is your insecticide of choice—either vegetable oils such as soy and neem or light-viscosity petroleum oil. The mode of action is quite simple. If applied near the end of the dormant period, the oil covers and suffocates the eggs and emerging young of many soft-bodied insects, such as aphids, mites, and scale. Once it dries, it is no longer effective and not an issue in the environment.

For organic fungicides, your options are usually sulfur products, copper, or biological sprays. Sulfur and copper come in a number of formulations. With sulfur, it is important to get micronized products, which simply means those ground to a very fine powder. The powder is mixed with water and stays in solution in the spray tank. (You might do well to invest in a small 3-gallon backpack sprayer or a 1- to 2-gallon handheld one.) Micronized products cover the leaves and young fruits more completely than older formulations and are more effective at creating a physical shield to prevent fungal spores from getting a foothold and germinating.

Sulfur is effective against a range of fungal issues and yet benign, in a larger sense. Sulfur also stinks, and so will your garden for a week or two. There's no sugarcoating it. Warning: Do not use sulfur on apricots and apriums—it will kill the buds. Use copper.

Copper comes in a liquid form. Not only is it easier to work with, but it is often more effective at controlling a wide array of fungal diseases, such as scab, mildew, and peach leaf curl. Additionally, it doesn't smell!

A very viable third alternative for diseases is the use of biological sprays. These sprays contain beneficial bacteria that multiply exponentially when applied to leaves and young fruit and predate on harmful disease organisms. They also aggressively occupy space and simply outcompete the disease species. Two excellent products are Serenade and Sonata (don't you love the euphemistic brand names?), which provide protection against a broad array of common fungal and bacterial diseases such as blight, powdery mildew, leaf spot, rust, and scab. Although their effectiveness is not 100 percent (is anything?), they are good allies, especially when used with copper and or sulfur.

While sprays are sometimes a necessary part of orcharding, they're not a magic solution. Some organic gardeners rely far too heavily on sprays as a fix-all. If your trees get a pest or disease, by all means seek local help in choosing the appropriate organic, nontoxic spray. As you look to managing your fruit trees and controlling the inevitable outbreaks of pests and diseases, remember that you have a golden opportunity to adopt holistic strategies that promote biodiversity, to witness biology in action and harness it to assist you and your trees.

VI

Pruning and Training Pome and Stone Fruit Trees

When growing a fruit tree, you will undoubtedly spend more time pruning and training (manipulating the tree shape) than any other single activity. Arguably (but you won't get an argument from me), you will spend more time pruning and training than all other aspects of tree growing, cumulatively. It's no wonder that most pomology textbooks devote more than 15–25 percent of their content to these formidable underpinnings. On the other hand, many home gardening books are surprisingly lacking in depth when it comes to the topic. Although studies have proven that trees in the everyday environment have a calming effect on people, the average backyard gardener may feel anxious, overwhelmed, confused, even defeated by the seemingly daunting task of pruning.

There are really only a few basic concepts and some related strictures or dos and don'ts. Then, it's all repetitive practical application. By putting down roots on a piece of ground and starting to grow trees, it will only take two, maybe three years to get it and shortly after that, it will become second nature, almost intuitive.

With pruning and training, you're trying to do a number of things at once:

- Create a logical permanent branch structure on which fruit is borne.

- Create a form that allows sunlight into all portions of the tree, especially the lower and interior portions, and allows optimum exposure of the leaves to sunlight for photosynthesis.

- Create a branch structure that is mechanically sound and self-supporting to bear the collective weight of wood, fruit, leaf, and sap. Pruning strengthens branches.

- Allow human access for all aspects of operation, including observation, spraying, training, pruning, thinning, picking, and working on a ladder.

- Allow penetration of spray materials, as needed.

- Create a tree form and shape that is aesthetically pleasing.

- Remove the four Ds—diseased, dead, damaged, and disoriented branches.

- Keep the tree a manageable height (6–12 feet).

- Oh, and did I mention we want to grow good fruit?

Romantic gardeners might imagine pruning as a wholly intuitive process, a sort of improvised duet with the magic of nature. But pruning and training should be logical, linear, rational processes. Pruning is a regulatory activity, as are so many of the other procedures employed in fruit tree growing. Step by step, over the course of the early years, you create the tree. Initially, you stimulate it to grow with winter pruning. Once the tree is formed and mature, through the combination of winter and summer pruning you regulate, limit, and even eliminate growth, in favor of fruiting.

Pruning can be thought of as a conversation with a tree over time—a very long time. In a sense, it is akin to the call and response of America's classical music, jazz. First there is a "call" or directive from the lead musician, and then a measured response from the second instrumentalist. That response builds on the first (as Miles Davis to John Coltrane). With pruning, you make a cut (the call), and the tree responds. Depending on your intentions, you make a certain cut to elicit a certain response from the tree. Over time it gets rhythmic; a back and forth over the years. As with jazz, artistic license is at play here. Each pruner has a different style, but all cuts are based on certain fundamental principles. There is a flow to it, but also a logic.

Pruning Anatomy 101

Before pruning, it's necessary to understand the parts of the tree you'll be working with.

When it comes to a tree's branches, the terms *twig*, *shoot*, *branch*, and *limb* can be used interchangeably; however, twig and shoot usually refer to younger growth, whereas limb and branch refer to mature growth.

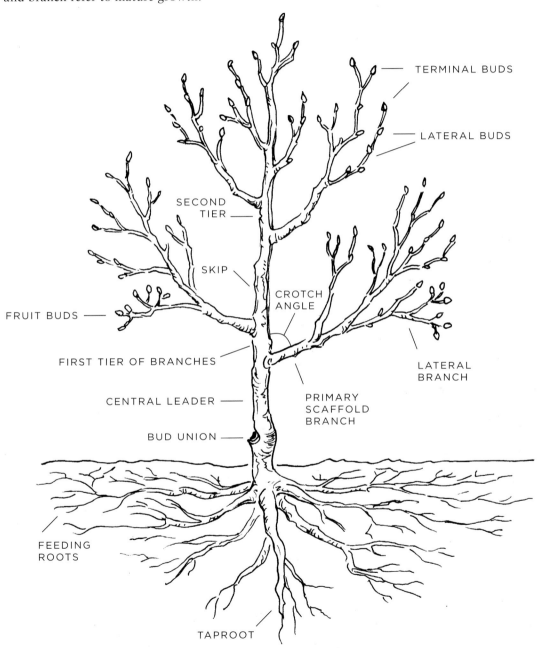

TERMINAL BUDS

LATERAL BUDS

SECOND TIER

SKIP

CROTCH ANGLE

FRUIT BUDS

FIRST TIER OF BRANCHES

CENTRAL LEADER

BUD UNION

PRIMARY SCAFFOLD BRANCH

LATERAL BRANCH

FEEDING ROOTS

TAPROOT

BUD TYPES

Buds are dynamic. They are growth points—undeveloped, embryonic shoots that appear as little bumps along the branches. Buds can go dormant in the fall, withstand the adversity of cold, even frigid winters, and then come busting out in spring and perform on demand.

A bud will produce leaves, branches (with leaves), or flowers (which when pollinated yield fruit). This depends on what type of bud it is.

All fruit trees have two basic bud types: vegetative and flower/ fruit buds.

Vegetative Buds

Vegetative buds produce leaves and branches with leaves. They are similar on pome fruit and stone fruit trees. Vegetative buds occur primarily on 1-year-old wood and also on older wood. One-year-old wood has *only* vegetative buds.

Vegetative buds are slender, pointed, and clasped tightly to the branch. During the summer, when the tree is leafed out, they are hidden by the leaves and difficult to identify. In winter, when the tree goes dormant, voilà, the buds are exposed. In dormancy, vegetative buds begin to fatten and become encased by bud scales (protective blankets) and take on a silver-gray hue.

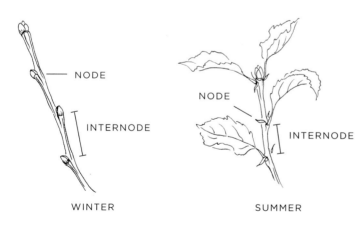

NODE

INTERNODE

WINTER

NODE

INTERNODE

SUMMER

Lateral vegetative buds
on a young pear

Flower/Fruit Buds

Flower/fruit buds produce flowers first, then fruit. They differ on pome (apples, pears) and stone fruit trees.

Apples and pears have compound or mixed buds composed of:

- Cluster of 2–6 flowers

- Surrounding circle of small supporting (subtending) leaves

- Short, weak shoot

Flower/fruit buds on **pome fruit** trees are plump and round, and protrude up from the branch. They occur primarily on lateral branches, but also on primaries, and only occur on 2-year-old and older wood.

Dormant apple branch
with swollen fruit buds

Apples in bloom

VARIOUS EXPRESSIONS OF YOUNG FRUIT
BUDS ON POME FRUIT (EARLY YEARS)

Flower/fruit buds on **stone fruit** trees are solitary, having a single flower and a single fruit. They occur almost exclusively on lateral branches—either on short, brushy shoots or on long, slender shoots. As with apples and pears, they only occur on 2-year-old and older wood.

APRICOT
FLOWER STAGES

Different species of fruit buds have different lifespans. Knowing the longevity of a fruit bud is important in pruning, as you may wish to renew them periodically.

Plum flower/fruit buds

LIFE SPAN OF FLOWER/FRUIT BUDS	
FRUIT	**LIFE SPAN**
Apples, pears	5–10 years
Apricots, apriums	3–5 years
Asian plums, pluots	4–5 years
Cherries	10–15 years
European plums	5–8 years
Peaches, nectarines	1 year
Quince	1 year

Tree Forms

The geometry and architecture of a tree are not, and should not be,
haphazard. Deciduous fruit trees are trained and pruned to articulated,
specific forms. Pruning and training should be used in tandem; they go
hand in glove. While deciduous trees can be grown to myriad specific
forms, one all-important factor unites them. They are simply geomet-
ric forms that facilitate the number one priority in fruit tree culture:
sunlight interception and infiltration, especially in the lower portion
of the tree.

Remember, fruit is largely produced from one source—the sun. You
can enhance a tree's interception of that energy by pruning and training
so the branches have good spacing, both vertically and horizontally.
Of the total direct sunlight that falls on a tree, you need 50–80 percent

of that light to strike all portions of the tree to produce and maintain quality fruit buds. In summer, when the tree is leafed out, this looks like what I call dappled sunlight—more sun than shade on the leaves. Sunlight does not naturally move (unaided) more than 3–4 feet into a tree canopy; at just 3 feet inside the canopy, light can be reduced as much as 60 percent. Thus, good interior light distribution relies on a tree form that allows alleys or shafts of light into the interior.

With pome fruit and stone fruit, by far the two most used forms are the open center (OC) and the modified central leader (MCL).

Of these two systems, the open center is much simpler in design and thus easier to master and teach. While somewhat more complex, the modified central leader has more fruit-bearing surface than the open center, and thus promotes higher yields per area.

The **open center form** mimics the geometry of a cone, with wide circular top and a relatively narrow base. Think of it as a sun cup: fill your cup with light; fill your life with fruit. A wide, open top with good horizontal spacing between primary branches creates alleys or shafts of light down into the core of the tree.

If you flip the cone or superimpose an equilateral or isosceles triangle on the tree, you get the basic form of the **modified central leader**. This form—narrow at the top and wide at the base—also achieves good sunlight interception and saturation into the tree's lower portions.

Now that you know the basic goals of pruning, we can get into different cuts, and when and how to employ them. At the end of the chapter, I'll detail how to create these two tree forms in a new tree.

Your Pruning Personality

Each grower has his or her own approach to the act of cutting branches off a tree. In my experience, there are two basic pruner personalities: whackers and haircutters. Whackers practice the age-old adage: *when in doubt, cut it out.* They don't think, just cut.

The haircutters, when confronted by a 30-foot apple tree, wonder if it's okay to snip a little *here* . . . and, after some gut-wrenching decision making, a *teeny* bit *there* as well. They tend to overthink.

I believe it was the Buddha, a fairly reputable source, who advised the middle way as a path of moderation, a.k.a. the path of wisdom, thus avoiding the extremes. Apply this precept to your pruning. Be neither a whacker nor a haircutter of fruit trees; seek the middle path.

If you can't find the middle path, don't stress—it's a process. Keep seeking balance, and keep in mind that it is generally better to underprune than overprune. If you take too much off the tree, you can't put it back on. The good thing about pruning is you can always do more at a later date.

In baseball, the greatest Zen sport, there are errors of commission (you dropped the ball—so be it, it happens) and errors of omission (you forgot to cover second base or back up home plate—no excuses). As coaches say, it is easier to accept the former than the latter. So it goes with pruning and training. You need to pay attention. Be vigilant. Be regular. No slacking. Prune a little annually; don't let a tree get away from you. Be stalwart, be informed, and learn to profit from your errors.

"Much of the pruning of a mature fruit tree is the correction of earlier errors and omissions."

—C. G. FORSHEY,
Cornell University
researcher

Types of Cuts and Their Responses

To prune well and purposefully, it is important to understand the different types of cuts, their expected effects, and when to employ them. There are two basic categories:

HEADING CUTS, in which a branch is cut back some portion of its length.

ELIMINATIVE CUTS, in which a branch is removed. In the daily parlance, almost everyone refers to these cuts generically as "thinning cuts."

HEADING CUTS

Under the broad umbrella of heading cuts, there are three subcategories:

- Standard heading cut
- Shortening cut
- Renewal cut

Standard Heading Cuts

The terms *heading cut* and *heading* refer to cutting back a branch to a portion of its previous season's growth (1-year-old wood). Heading cuts, done in winter pruning, stimulate branch growth in the following growing season but also delay fruiting for at least 2 years. However, when this branch does fruit, it will have more fruit than an unpruned branch. Another dividend of heading cuts is that they thicken and strengthen branches, enabling them to bear the weight of all that juicy fruit.

After you head a branch back using a standard heading cut, the top remaining bud mobilizes and regrows the branch. The next few buds down the branch will break from dormancy and grow as weak or moderate lateral branches (laterals). Almost all species of fruit trees bear almost all their fruit on laterals. On most species, these laterals will grow vegetatively the first year and begin to fruit the second or third year. Try *not* to prune laterals on apples and pears in winter, as this stimulates too much vegetative growth at the expense of fruit-bearing wood. That is, don't make a heading cut into 1-year-old wood on laterals. Remember, the function of laterals is to bear fruit. Laterals are our friends. (For more on how to treat pome fruit laterals, see "Summer Pruning and Its Effects," page 192.)

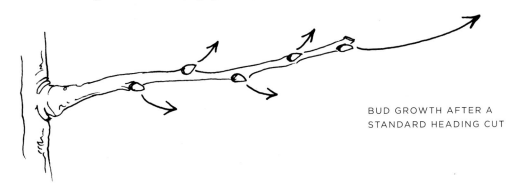

BUD GROWTH AFTER A
STANDARD HEADING CUT

As counterintuitive as it seems, *the more you want a branch to grow, the harder you cut it back.* When you head back a branch in winter, the magnitude of the growth response is directly proportional to the amount the branch is cut back. The harder the cut, the longer and stronger the response.

In a sense, there is only one operative question to ask (and answer) when looking at a branch: *Do I want it to grow more?* If the answer is yes, prune it in winter with a standard heading cut. If the growth goals are high, head it back a lot. If the growth goals are minimal, head it lightly. If the answer is no, leave it alone or train the branch down toward horizontal, or shorten it (see "Shortening Cuts," page 186).

A few examples:

GROWTH

- A tree branch left unpruned in the winter will grow minimally (often only inches) and set up fruit on the limb the following spring (this is okay).

CUT

GROWTH

- A light heading cut (less than 25 percent of the previous season's growth) will cause a weak regrowth of the top bud (less than 1 foot) and produce some laterals from the lower buds that will fruit in 2 years.

CUT

GROWTH

- A moderate heading cut (25–50 percent of the previous season's growth) begets a moderate growth response in the top bud (more than 1 foot) and produces even more laterals.

CUT

GROWTH

- A heavy heading cut (more than 50 percent of the previous season's growth) causes a strong regrowth of the top bud but little or no lateral formation.

How to Make a Heading Cut

Every cut on a plant induces a wound, even a good pruning cut. As with humans, wounds expose plants to disease and pests (bacteria, fungi) when they are open and unhealed. Your primary aim when pruning is to make a clean cut—one that facilitates a quick healing process.

First, find the bud you want to grow and extend the branch. Make sure it's a vegetative bud (see page 174). Buds are like directional arrows: the direction in which the bud points will be the direction the branch will grow. Think of a tree as an energy superhighway, with energy moving from the soil into the roots and out through the tips of the branches and buds. The energy of growth will continue to shoot upward with vigor in the direction the buds are growing. Generally, you will cut to an outward-facing bud, that is, facing or pointing toward the outside of the tree rather than a bud facing in toward the center of the tree.

TYPES OF WINTER PRUNING CUTS

HEADING
(1-YEAR-OLD
WOOD)

SHORTENING
(SLIGHTLY INTO
2-YEAR-OLD
WOOD)

RENEWAL

THINNING (LEAVE
COLLAR INTACT)

Make your cut into 1-year-old wood. To determine where the previous year's growth is, if a branch is pruned, you'll see the pruning stub from the previous year. If the branch wasn't pruned, you'll see a set of concentric rings on the branch demarcating where new growth begins. Using sharp, quality bypass hand pruners, prune ¼–½ inch above the desired bud. Leave a short stub above the bud. Make the cut at a 45-degree angle sloping away from the bud, so that water sheds away from the bud, not into the bud. This prevents the bud from rotting.

PROPER PRUNING CUT

45-DEGREE ANGLE

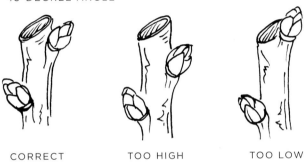

CORRECT   TOO HIGH   TOO LOW

Cutting to a lateral bud is a form of training, in that you redirect growth. For example, if two branches are too close together but you like and otherwise need them, you can cut each to an opposing lateral bud and they will grow apart, creating greater space and thus sunlight infiltration between both branches.

Apical Dominance

With heading cuts, it's essential to understand the concept of apical dominance. This hormonal response to sunlight in the tallest branch(es) of a tree says "grow!" to the top bud on a branch. The top bud produces a suppressing hormone, called auxin, that moves down the branch by gravity and suppresses branch growth of the lateral buds. When a branch is pruned and the apically dominant top bud is removed, the suppressing of lateral buds is suspended (for a few months until the lead or top bud grows and produces more auxin). During this time while apical dominance is in hiatus, lateral buds can and usually do grow branches. You can induce lateral branch formation (either on a leader or on a primary scaffold branch) by heading branches in the dormant winter season. These laterals will be your fruit-bearing laterals.

Terminal fruit bud on a young apple branch

Quintessential example
of a shortening cut

Shortening Cuts

A shortening cut is another type of heading cut. Shortening cuts involve cutting back an established branch (more than 5 years old) into older wood by cutting to a fruit bud instead of a vegetative bud. Cutting to a fruit bud tends to stop further extension growth. It is used when a branch has filled its allotted space and you don't want it to grow any longer.

Renewal Cuts

Another type of heading cut, this involves radically cutting back a mature branch (more than 7–8 years old) to a stub (4–6 inches long). It is used when a branch is too long and is shading other branches. This extreme cut regrows the branch, albeit in a weaker manner over the course of 4–5 years. Renewal cuts are mostly used in the top of the tree to prevent shading below. They should be employed sparingly.

A very important note: Shortening cuts apply mainly to pome fruits (apples and pears). You *can* make shortening cuts on stone fruit trees, but it can be dangerous to shorten main branches that are very vigorous, as the branches may grow back even stronger.

ELIMINATIVE (THINNING) CUTS

After heading cuts, eliminative thinning cuts are one of the most commonly used. Thinning cuts are used to eliminate the four Ds—dead, damaged, diseased, or disoriented (misplaced) branches—as well as overly vigorous, exceedingly weak, or shading branches. There should be no regrowth. Thinning cuts induce moderate, well-distributed growth evenly throughout the rest of the tree, but no specific growth at the wound site (theoretically, usually, hopefully . . .). If unexpected new shoots appear, thin them immediately.

A standard thinning cut completely removes an entire branch at its point of origin. There are also "redirective" thinning cuts, which remove a major portion of a branch but not the entire branch.

Redirective Cuts: Cutting to Weakness or Leader Replacement

Commonly used on mature trees, this type of thinning cut brings down the height of a tree or opens the interior to light. The leader referred to here is the main extension growth of a branch, be it the central leader on an MCL tree, the multiple leaders on an OC tree, or a primary scaffold or lateral branch. With a redirective cut, you simply thin a branch at a point where there is a slightly weaker fork and thus establish a new lead to the branch.

If the primary branches at the top of a tree extend too high, look down the primary branch and choose a suitable lateral branch replacement. The suitable replacement should be the following:

- Lower than the top of the branch (now).

- Snake or hook slightly to the outside of the tree to keep the center open to light.

- At a slightly flatter angle (45–70 degrees). Flat-angled branches grow less vigorously than upright branches and tend toward fruitfulness. However, the angle of the replacement portion of the branch can't be too flat or the flattened portion will throw vigorous, unfruitful sprouts called water sprouts.

- Less vigorous looking—a smaller, thinner branch.

- Already expressing fruit buds or fruit along its length, which ensures a step down in vigor.

LEADER REPLACEMENT

Make a thinning cut that removes the primary extension of the branch, replacing the lead of the branch with the shorter, weaker choice. This is also known as *leader replacement*, a term that can also gives rise to numerous political jokes during pruning workshops.

One clarifying thought regarding cutting to weakness: The height reduction needs to be a reasonable step down. That is, you can't make a 20-foot tree into an 8-foot tree. If the pruning is overdone, the tree will sprout many rambunctious, exuberant growths that ramble skyward. But it is realistic to make a 20-foot tree into a well-behaved, accessible 12- to 15-foot tree. Everything about cutting to weakness needs to be in moderation.

How to Make a Thinning Cut

To remove a whole branch, cut it off flush with the collar (the slightly raised area on the main branch or trunk at the point of attachment). Don't cut into the collar. Do not cut flush with the trunk or remaining primary branch. If the branch is larger (more than 2 inches in diameter), use a saw. However, with larger branches, if you simply cut the branch flush to the collar you can rip the bark, which is injurious to the tree. So use a two-step process. First, cut off most of the weight of the branch and leave a 1-foot stub. Second, remove the stub by making a final cut just beyond the branch collar. After you've made your cut, do not apply paint, sealer, or emulsions to the cut wound. It might make you feel better, the tree not so much. The collar has cells that help produce callus tissue, which will seal over and heal the wound. By using a sealant, you many induce rot, as you are enclosing detritus inside a deep, dark, dank place—it is not a pretty picture.

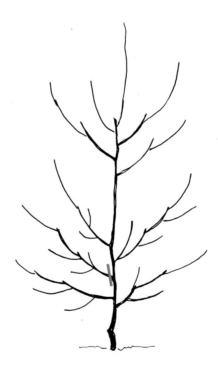

THINNING CUT

When to Prune

It is critically important you prune with great regularity at the two principal times of year, winter (dormancy) and summer. Beyond the two main seasons, pruning is generally an ongoing activity. You are always making some adjustive cuts as the need arises.

SEASONAL PRUNING: WINTER VERSUS SUMMER

In the winter, pruning via heading cuts is used to stimulate branch growth the following spring and summer. Conversely, summer pruning uses heading cuts to stop or slow down growth, delay extension growth, and induce flower bud formation. Winter pruning with heading cuts builds, extends, increases; summer pruning limits, shortens, decreases, eliminates. Winter pruning is analogous to pouring the foundation and framing the house: it creates the tree's structure, form, and extent. Summer pruning is all about finish work: trim, tiles, cabinetry. It refines form and keeps the interior of the tree open to sunlight, which is vital to fruit production.

WINTER PRUNING AND ITS EFFECTS

Winter pruning is your primary tool to establish the form and extent of the tree. As fruit only forms on branches 2 years and older, winter pruning can also delay fruiting. That's okay. You need to do it if you want your tree to grow a good fruit-bearing branch framework.

Winter pruning involves cuts, usually heading cuts, made into 1-year-old wood (the previous season's growth). When you make a cut, the top bud (vegetative bud) below the cut is stimulated to grow.

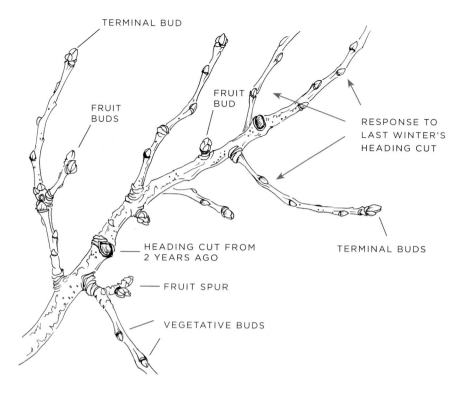

TERMINAL BUD

FRUIT BUDS

FRUIT BUD

RESPONSE TO LAST WINTER'S HEADING CUT

TERMINAL BUDS

HEADING CUT FROM 2 YEARS AGO

FRUIT SPUR

VEGETATIVE BUDS

The next two to five buds will generally break from dormancy and show moderate or weak vegetative growth. The harder the pruning cut (the greater the amount of the previous season's growth removed), the stronger the growth response.

Winter pruning invigorates because the stored supplies of sugars and starches (carbohydrates) in the roots are distributed through fewer outlets. Remember, a tree only has a certain amount of sugar to use. If a branch with twenty vegetative buds is cut back by half, leaving ten buds, there is essentially more flow through fewer outlets (buds), thus resulting in more branch extension growth (and bigger, sweeter fruit).

After winter pruning, the new leaves on the pruned branch are bigger, flatter, and thicker, and there is greater internodal distance (the distance between buds). All of this facilitates more efficient photosynthesis longer into the summer season. The leaves are thicker and tougher and thus are degraded more slowly by environmental conditions including wind, rain, or UV rays from the sun.

What if you don't prune? If a tree is left unpruned, the growth response is weak (a few inches).

The general winter pruning outlook throughout a tree's life goes something like:

EARLY YEARS (1–5) Using heading cuts, establish permanent framework and form.

MIDDLE YEARS (5–15) Still using limited heading cuts, but mostly shortening and selected thinning cuts, keep the tree within its allotted space and open to sunlight. Recognize and nip problems in the bud.

LATER YEARS (15–20 OR LONGER) Paramount emphasis is on sunlight distribution within the tree. Thinning cuts are the tool of choice. Rejuvenate and renew framework (selectively). Bring down height of tree. Use thinning cuts, the "cut to weakness" principle, and renewal cuts.

Timing of Winter Pruning

Winter pruning is usually done between leaf drop (in fall) and bud swell (in spring). The timing will depend on your region, but winter pruning usually happens late in the dormant season.

Goals of Winter Pruning Cuts

Via Standard Heading Cuts

- Create form and structure of tree to form primary scaffolds and laterals

- Thicken branches

- Stimulate vegetative growth

- Induce lateral branching

Via Shortening Cuts (pome fruits)

- Stop a branch when it has filled its allotted space

Via Renewal Cuts

- Renew overly vigorous branches in upper portion of tree

Via Thinning Cuts

- Open up a tree to more sunlight (light distribution) and to reduce tree height

- Remove dead, diseased, damaged, disoriented wood

Remember, with young trees you are trying to stimulate growth and create the form and extent of the tree. With older trees, you are trying to limit height and spread, and avoid crowding and shading. Thus, you tend to make mostly stimulating heading cuts on young trees and primarily shortening and thinning cuts on older trees. For bigger, older trees, it is paramount to limit growth and ensure sunlight penetration into the tree's core.

Do not prune pome fruit laterals in winter, unless you want them to grow vigorously and branch, which leads to crowding and shading, thus reducing both quality and quantity of fruit. You prune them in summer. Laterals on stone fruit trees may be pruned in summer or winter. They are more compliant. They grow a little and fruit, too. No worries.

SUMMER PRUNING AND ITS EFFECTS

In summer, you prune to control growth, not to stimulate it. A tree's response to summer pruning is frequently to form fruit buds very quickly, often within the season. Summer pruning reduces, limits, eliminates, and induces:

REDUCES Summer pruning reduces overall tree height and the number of shoots and branches, creating alleys of light that allow more sunlight into the interior of the canopy. This keeps the most easily accessed portion of the tree lively and fruitful and gets you to that all-important minimum of 50 percent sunlight. While thinning cuts can be made in summer or winter, the dividend of summer thinning is immediately seeing the increase of light into the tree's interior. This can be dramatic as branches fall to the ground and sunlight tumbles down. Give it a shot next time you want to impress an audience.

LIMITS After summer pruning, the regrowth of branches is minimal, often inches compared to feet following winter pruning. Therefore you can use summer pruning to shape the tree without creating unintended new growth.

ELIMINATES Summer pruning thins out excessive branches, both in number and in length.

INDUCES Under optimal conditions, summer pruning, especially on a pome fruit's lateral branches, induces rapid formation of the fruit buds that will become next year's fruit crop. These are perennial organs,

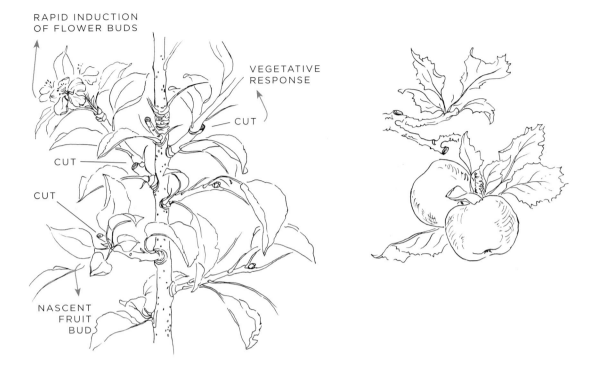

RAPID INDUCTION
OF FLOWER BUDS

VEGETATIVE
RESPONSE

CUT

CUT

CUT

NASCENT
FRUIT
BUD

bearing fruit for a number of years. Normally, a lateral branch will form and grow in year one. In years two and three, it forms fruit buds, eventually fruiting in years three and four. With well-timed summer pruning, sometimes the first year's lateral shoots form fruit buds and even flower and fruit that summer. Although the fruit won't mature that late in the season, you have formed a perennial fruit-bearing organ that will be productive for a number of years. At the very least, 1-year-old laterals can be induced to form fruit buds that will bear by the following summer, or the one after that.

Why does summer pruning work? As you now know, when you prune a branch using a standard heading cut, the branch responds by trying to regrow what was cut off. Whether a branch is headed back in winter or summer, the pattern of the response is identical. However, the magnitude of the growth response is radically different.

In summer, leaves engage in photosynthesis and produce carbohydrates. The tree translocates those carbohydrates throughout to grow roots, shoots, leaves, flowers, and fruit. By removing leaves during summer pruning, you remove a resource point and thus reduce energy for overall tree growth or regrowth. Remember, in the internal battle for resources, fruit usually acts as a strong resource sink: it can sequester more than 70–80 percent of a tree's resources annually.

Thus, by late summer, when summer pruning occurs, the tree has already allocated most of its reserves to existing branches, roots, and fruit; it is essentially tapped out, with inadequate resources (or enough summer season) left to add more than a few inches of regrowth on a pruned branch.

In addition, summer pruning of laterals on pome fruits releases ethylene gas at the site of the pruning cut. Ethylene is a gaseous hormone and growth stimulant. This released ethylene gas saturates the tree canopy, particularly the summer-pruned laterals. And although the causative mechanism is still unknown, it is thought that flooding the tree canopy with ethylene stimulates fruit bud formation, rather than vegetative branch extension.

What if you don't prune? Left unpruned, buds on laterals can take 2–3 years or longer to transition from vegetative buds to fruit buds. A midsummer pruning session often gives rise to a mini-spring effect—the trees flower within 4–6 weeks of a July pruning. And while you have no use for the untimely forming of fruit in early fall (these fruits should be removed ASAP), the fact that you have created fruit buds that will live on and bear fruit for a number of years is a huge victory.

Timing of Summer Pruning

Like winter pruning, summer pruning timing varies from region to region. Summer pruning is generally done in late July through early September. You should prune when the majority of the primary branches have set a fat terminal bud (often the beginning of a fruit bud) at the tip of the branch and have stopped actively growing for the season. When branches are still actively growing, their tips will feature a vegetative bud that continues to produce leaves and lengthen. This is visible— you see new leaves forming at the tip of a branch. In areas with harsh winters, please check with your local experts, as pruning too late stimulates succulent growth that then can be subject to winter cold injury.

Summer pruning of an apple's lateral branch using a shortening cut, before…

…and after

Goals of Summer Pruning

Via Thinning Cuts and Cutting to Weakness

- Tree height reduction and more sunlight (via thinning cuts) in interior of the canopy, which promotes fruit growth and ripening

Via Heading of Laterals

- Rapid induction of fruit buds, especially on pome fruits

Via All Types of Cuts

- Minimal regrowth of pruned branches (and thus the size of the tree is controlled)

In any season, any type of cut thickens and strengthens the pruned laterals, making them better able to bear fruit without breaking.

How to Treat Lateral Branches

Summertime lateral pruning applies primarily to pome fruits. Stone fruit laterals can be pruned in summer or winter. The pruning of laterals on stone fruit trees is not a stimulating activity; they just don't grow as much as pome fruits.

First, approach the tree and look at the laterals. They should be thinned so they are spaced approximately 7–9 inches apart on a primary branch.

When deciding which laterals to thin, start by looking for vigorous laterals that are growing upright (vertical). Overly vigorous laterals tend to grow too long and shade adjacent branches. Their hormonal impulse is to be nonfruitful. The best policy for vertical laterals is to

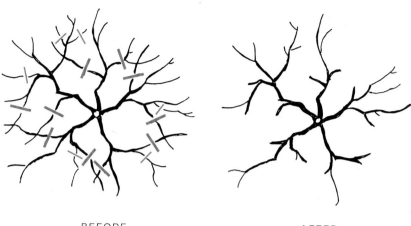

——— THINNING CUT
——— HEADING CUT

BEFORE

AFTER

completely remove them. Or you can prune them down to one fruit bud. Sometimes this causes the bud to grow a fruit, and the lateral becomes a little fruit hanger.

Keep the laterals of moderate or weak vigor (yes, a seeming oxymoron). Weaker laterals grow at an angle approaching horizontal, and do one or more of the following:

- If they are shorter than 8–10 inches and at 45 degrees above horizontal or flatter, leave them alone. They will probably stop growing and start fruiting of their own accord. I refer to them as self-managing laterals. Life would be a lot sweeter (literally as well as figuratively) if all laterals were of this nature and if one occurred every 7–9 inches on main limbs.

- If they are longer than 8–10 inches, summer prune them using the three-bud system or the general approach below.

- If they are not positioned at an angle of 45 degrees to horizontal and yet are perpendicular (90 degrees) to the primary branch, train them downward (see page 214).

Three-Bud System Versus General Approach

The three-bud system is based on the methodology of Louis Lorette, a French orchardist and nurseryman of the early twentieth century. In midsummer, after trees have set a terminal bud and stopped growing for the season, identify the current season's growth on laterals, then prune the laterals back to three buds of new growth. Ideally, the top bud will resume growth and extend, but minimally so. The next two buds may initiate fruit buds and bear within a year. Sometimes (startlingly) they'll initiate flowers and fruit immediately, in early fall. You don't want or need a small crop of fall fruits, so merely pluck the young fruit off and go about your fall and winter orchard tasks knowing that there will be a new flower (and fruit) on each bud come spring.

A more general approach to summer pruning of laterals is nonspecific: simply cut back laterals to three, four, or five buds, or to a sensible length (less than 10–12 inches long) that supports the weight of fruit, doesn't shade adjacent branches, and fits between primary branches.

Whereas some researchers "throw shade" and claim that the three-bud technique is erratic and ineffective, many veteran practitioners swear by it. Having practiced the three-bud technique successfully for decades, I find myself in the latter camp. However, over the years, I have had, variously, great and sometimes only moderate success in any given year. I suspect that the cause has to do with tree physiology and the progression of biological events within the tree. The time of year when the tree is responsive to summer pruning can vary by as much as a month from year to year. Some years, you are in sync with tree physiology and biology; other years, not so much. Thus, calendar dates are not a good cue as to when to summer prune. You need to tune into your trees. I recommend keeping a summer pruning journal and noting growth and terminal bud set so you can learn the optimal summer pruning window in your garden.

When you have success with summer pruning, you feel like a genius. When you are unsuccessful, you feel a fool. The truth, no doubt, is lurking in the middle. Good luck, keep in touch, do your best . . .

Approaching the Tree and Setting Pruning Goals

Prior to pruning, you should run down your mental checklist of the following:

- Have you assembled all the tools you need and sharpened them?

- What type of tree is it (species and variety) and what is its natural growth habit (upright, wide, strong, or weak)?

- How old is the tree, approximately?

- What tree form is it?

- How is it doing?

Assess the pruning needs for each component of the tree form (you will learn more about creating the forms on pages 204–212). Assess them in this order: the central leader on a modified central leader form; the multiple leaders on an open center form; the primary scaffold branches on a multiple central leader; and the secondary forking branches on an open center.

Then, decide your goals for pruning and training. It is best to limit goals to a modest number, no more than two or three.

For example, your goals might be the following:

- The tree is not showing adequate growth, so I'm going to stimulate it with heading cuts in winter.

- The tree is too tall, so I want to bring down the height by cutting to weakness and also thin a few branches to allow more light into the tree's interior (in the summer or winter).

Developing a set of goals also goes beyond simply pruning and extends to growth and care.

For example:

- Next season, I want to stay on top of fertility, irrigation, and weed control this next summer, to support the heading cuts I made in winter and stimulate more primary branch growth.

Once you have your goals set, you're ready to begin pruning. Usually, it is best to start at the top of the tree and work downward. Be both thorough and consistent.

Resuscitating or Reclaiming an Older, Out-of-Control Tree

A tree does not get out of control in a year; it takes a number of years of neglect. As it doesn't take a year to get out of hand, you won't bring it back in a year. Doing so is a process. You should be realistic. Is it worth it? Sometimes the solution to a tree that resembles Medusa's hairdo is to prune it with a spade. That's growers' lingo for dig it out. Then begin again, stay after it, get it right. But say you think it's worth it. How to proceed?

- Spend time with your tree. Try to visualize the tree you want. With trees of this nature, you will never have a perfect form. This is an instance where good enough will have to suffice.

- Tie some colored flagging tape around the primary branches you wish to retain (at about 8–10 feet high).

- Begin to prune the tree with only thinning cuts. Try to remove the most wood with the least number of cuts. You will almost exclusively be using a saw, maybe a small chainsaw!

- Whatever the total volume of wood you want to take out of the tree, take no more than 25 percent in any one pruning session. Above a certain number of cuts (of any kind) in an individual pruning session, all bets are off. The tree will behave badly and go bonkers.

- Because you are only making thinning cuts, which do not stimulate new growth, you can prune in both summer and winter.

- Remember, you are simply thinning unwanted branches, the ones you didn't flag.

- Double up:

  Pruning session #1—first winter

  Pruning session #2—first summer

  Pruning session #3—second winter

  Pruning session #4—second summer, the final one

In subsequent years you can do refined, detailed pruning, but not initially. In my experience, you come away from these types of pruning sessions chastened. Reformed, even. And you will vow never to let your trees get away from you again.

Additional Pruning Considerations for Quince

Although quinces are botanically allied with their pome partners, apples and pears, they are in truth outliers (or mavericks, if you will). The quince is not really a tree, but more of a shrub reaching 8 by 12 feet, often as wide as it is tall. It resents being pruned or trained into classic forms. It prefers to ramble a bit, in a natural, slightly ungainly manner. It has a casual if not unkempt countenance. Despite all this, or maybe because of it, the quince is a fetching specimen in the landscape. Along with the persimmon, it is one of the few deciduous fruits that does not bear its fruits on wood 2 years and older and does not express its flowers prior to leafing out.

In the spring, the tree leafs out with soft, downy, hirsute leaves and then makes a few inches of succulent shoot growth. Subsequently, the very tip of each branch will bear a solitary flower. And what a flower! It is inordinately large, usually white or white infused with soft pink. A sight to behold, a dream to smell.

The flower is followed by a solitary fruit. In general, quinces differ from other pomes in that they don't have compound fruit buds on older wood and clusters of flowers and fruit that needs to be thinned. If they overset, they self-thin. A very considerate fruit.

In pruning quince, managed neglect is the way to go: shape gently to a loose open-center form in early, nonbearing years. Once a quince is established, it is a mistake to do much, if any, pruning other than a little cleanup—thinning broken or wayward branches. Quinces bear fruit on the current season's growth, so if you make heading cuts, you cut off the fruit wood—never a good idea. The upshot is that they give you a lot for not much input.

Additional Pruning Considerations for Stone Fruits

All stone fruits are best pruned and trained to the open center form.

PEACHES AND NECTARINES

The peach is a vigorous (5–8 feet of extension growth per year) upright grower in the early years after planting. As the tree matures, it morphs to a more naturally spreading form with moderate to weak vigor. Peach leaves cast dense shade, so it is important to train trees to allow sunlight to penetrate into the center of the tree. Remember, sunlight translates to color and emphatically to high sugar content.

The largest, best-quality peaches are produced on lateral 2-year-old branches that hang on young, actively growing main scaffold branches (3–5 years old). With peaches, what you grew last year is what you're eating this year. During the first year, a lateral branch will grow while producing fruit buds internally. In year two, these branches bear fruit. They should be shortened to 12–18 inches (in summer or winter).

In the third year, the lateral shoot will die out (or start to) and not bear any fruit. Or it will grow new wood that bears the following year, but is too far away from the main branch for either good mechanical support or continued flow of nutrients for size and taste.

In any given winter pruning session, approximately half of the laterals should be cut down to one to three buds, or 1–3 inches, to renew growth and bear again in two summers. Similarly, after laterals have fruited, they should be cut back to renew the cycle.

Since new growth is prioritized on peaches and nectarines, primary branches are pruned hard annually in the winter to encourage good extension growth and the induction of laterals. As a result, it is not unusual to prune 40–60 percent of the previous year's total growth off a peach or nectarine (in contrast, pome fruits are pruned by 20–25 percent annually).

Additionally, once the tree is established and fruiting, the primary scaffold branches on an open center peach tree can be rescaffolded. The process of rescaffolding, also known as renewal, involves a major reduction of the tree canopy. Using renewal cuts, each primary scaffold branch is cut back severely by a majority percentage of its growth (for example, a 10-foot branch might be cut back about 8 feet). The net result of rescaffolding is to quickly regrow the tree canopy, which results more accessible fruit (height-wise) and higher fruit productivity. Rescaffolding is a reset. It's major surgery, with major results. With mature peaches, consider rescaffolding as often as every 5–7 years. This can be done incrementally—a few branches a year—or all at once.

PLUMS, APRICOTS, AND CHERRIES

All plums, apricots, and cherries should be pruned hard early in life to stimulate vegetative growth. With these fruits, as with peaches, when a branch goes flat, it weakens and produces smaller and smaller fruit. Prune to an inward- or upward-facing bud to redirect growth upward. European plums are inherently weak growers, so you will continue to prune them hard throughout their lives.

With Asian plums, apricots, and cherries, once they are established they should rarely be stimulated via heading cuts. Pruning at maturation devolves to the occasional thinning cut on major branches and renewal cuts on the brushy lateral fruit-bearing growth. In any given pruning session, 20 percent (one in five) of these laterals should be cut

back to one to three buds and regrown. They will fruit in the second year after renewal.

With cherries, be cautious about making cuts of more than 2–3 inches in diameter at maturity, as they can be an entry point for bacterial diseases that could bring down the whole tree. And lateral fruiting branches rarely need any treatment. The best policy for cherries is to more or less leave them alone once they're mature.

As with peaches, mature plums and apricots can be rescaffolded periodically (every 8–10 years). Do this if they are getting too tall or if the fruit wood is migrating up the tree, as it tends to do with age.

A Science and an Art

Pruning and training a tree need to be logical, thought-out, rational processes. With trees, form (morphology or shape) drives function (physiology). But there is a third component: aesthetics. You can and should learn to be a good technical pruner, a technician. But you should also get a feel for shaping trees in a graceful and pleasing manner.

Gardening is both a science and an art. Science is to be understood, mastered, respected, and applied, as you do when tending your tree. But art, or aesthetics (the philosophy of the beautiful), informs and enhances our existence. Just as the fruit of a tree is food for the body, the grace and beauty of a tree are food for the soul.

I am reminded here of something Alan Chadwick once said: "The reason for all of it is simply that I love beauty . . . I adore beauty and I detest ugliness." Alan was an aesthete as well as a skilled, technical horticulturalist. Along with understanding the principles and practices of horticulture, he had a strong personal infatuation with the arts, a particular attention to detail and beauty. As an aesthete, he possessed a sensitivity to all that was beautiful and a disdain for that which was ugly and dehumanizing.

May we all invoke his ethic as we grow our fruit trees and tend our gardens and fields.

Winter pruning scraps, a.k.a. future barbecue kindling

Tutorial: Forming the Open Center Tree Form

The open center (OC) form mimics the geometry of a cone, with a wide circular top and a relatively narrow base. For the open center form, think big sun cup. Fill the cup with sunshine and fill your life with fruit.

In general, this form is a looser training system than leader forms, such as the modified central leader (see page 208). It is more about filling space appropriately than adhering to a strict, sculpted form. With open center trees, often more primary branches are retained early in a tree's life and subsequently are thinned out as a response to light infiltration within the canopy. Light does not penetrate more than 3–4 feet into the canopy, so shafts of light need to be created via pruning and training.

The open center form is usually the form of choice for stone fruits (peaches, apricots, plums) and can be used with pome fruits (apples and pears) along with the various leader forms. While easy to understand and execute, the open center form has less fruit-bearing surface compared with leader forms. At maturation, the tree tends to "umbrella out," the result being shading of the bottom of the tree, shading of neighboring trees, and loss of vigor in the top of the tree.

A well-formed open center tree consists of three to five primary branches (multiple leaders) arising from the trunk 18–30 inches above the ground. These primaries should grow or be trained up and outward at an angle of 60–75 degrees above horizontal. They should be of equal vigor and be spaced evenly, radially around the trunk. They may feature Ys or forks to increase bearing surface.

The last component is the lateral, fruit-bearing branch structure. Laterals, or fruit hangers as peach growers call them, should be short (6–15 inches), stout and strong (mechanically), moderately weak (as pertaining to vegetative vigor). They should be perpendicular to the primary branch and spaced 6–10 inches apart, vertically.

Two-year-old plums in the
open center form

Forming an Open Center

━━ THINNING CUT
━━ HEADING CUT

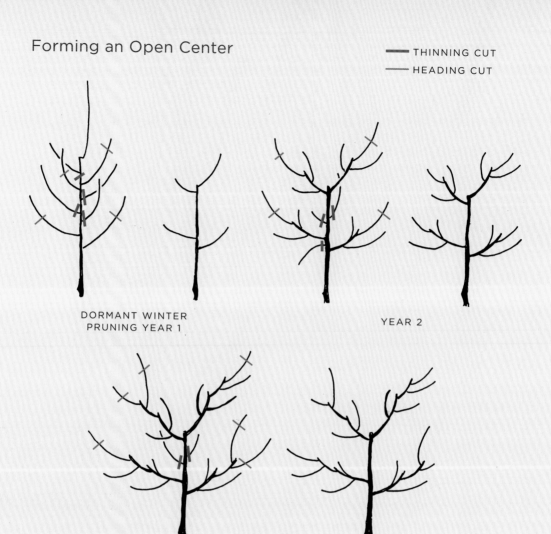

DORMANT WINTER
PRUNING YEAR 1

YEAR 2

YEAR 3

CREATING THE FORM

Select a thick (½–⅞ inch) caliper tree, either a whip or a branched tree. (A whip is a dormant, bare root tree with just the central trunk, no branches yet.) If using a branched tree, it should have a number of vigorous primary branches coming off the trunk.

If using a whip, after planting, head the whip at 18–30 inches above the soil level. A number of buds below the cut should develop into branches. Select three to five of these and proceed as per the branched tree (below). The primary difference between a whip and a good branched tree is generally 1–2 years' worth of growth.

The more developed the tree is at planting, the sooner it will become established and start fruiting.

If using a branched tree to create an open center, thin out the leader. Then select three to five of the strongest branches as your primaries, thinning all other branches. The primaries should be equally distributed around the 360 degrees of the trunk. If they are not, train them into place using nylon string and a well-driven stake or spreaders (see page 217). The branches should grow up and outward at an angle of 60–75 degrees above horizontal.

It is critical that the multiple leaders of an open center tree be of the same vigor and positioned at the same angle. Cut these branches back a quarter to half of their length to an outward- or under-facing bud. Think of the top bud on the branch as a directional arrow; the branch will grow in the direction the bud is pointing.

During the first growing season, micromanage these multileaders by training them slightly up, down, or sideways. Check them monthly. The goal is to manage for equal growth and a branch angle of 60–75 degrees from horizontal. That's the sweet spot.

At the end of the first growing season (winter dormant pruning), head back the three to five primary scaffold branches about 50 percent of their season's growth. This should be done proportionally to vigor; the weakest branches are cut back the most and vice versa.

These primaries can be cut back to two opposing buds. As they grow into branches in the second year, they will form a Y or fork. Do not allow any other adjacent buds to form additional strong branches; if they do, thin them. This forking can be repeated in years two to four. The net result of forking is to increase the fruit-bearing surface of a tree. This must not be done at the expense of excluding light from the lower portions of the tree. The Ys need not be patterned or symmetrical; you can choose to form them on only a few of the primary branches.

The training and winter heading cuts are repeated in subsequent years until the tree has reached the size allotted for it. At that juncture, heading cuts cease, and shortening cuts are employed, stopping upward growth.

Select lateral fruit-bearing branches that are perpendicular to the primary branches from which they grow. These laterals should then be trained down toward a horizontal position. Pome fruit lateral branches are not winter pruned, but rather summer pruned to 8–12 inches to limit growth. On stone fruits, lateral branches can be summer or winter pruned.

Tutorial: Forming the Modified Central Leader Tree Form

The modified central leader (MCL) form, also called the "head and spread" system, has been the standard training system in the United States for the past 40–50 years. This system results in relatively large, freestanding trees with a dominant central leader, from which radiate whorls of horizontal branches at two or three levels along the length of the leader (see illustration). The aim of this system is to create two or three whorls, or tiers, of horizontal scaffold branches over the 12–14 feet vertical run of the trunk, or one continuous whorl over that same run. The positioning of the tiers should be five to seven branches at 2–4 feet above the ground; a second whorl of three to five branches at 6–8 feet; and a third whorl of two or three branches at 10–12 feet. Or you can simply have two tiers, which will result in a shorter tree.

The lower limbs are positioned at 45–60 degrees above horizontal and are headed back annually in dormant season by a quarter to half of the previous season's growth. This approach strikes a balance between forcing lateral fruit-bearing branches and continued vegetative extension growth. When these limbs have filled their allotted space (3–5 years), they are pruned back to a weak lateral with a shortening cut into 2-year-old wood.

For them to develop fruit wood, the lateral branches that develop on the horizontal primary scaffold branches must be managed for control of excessive vigor. This can be done by:

- Thinning out any upright, overly vigorous shoots.

- Training or tying down moderately vigorous shoots. Bending a limb from vertical to horizontal causes growth to weaken and fruit buds to form early—especially toward the base of the shoot.

- Lightly heading or tipping (20–25 percent) weak or moderate lateral shoots in winter. This causes a moderate resumption of growth and weak lateral branching and development of fruit buds.

- Summer pruning.

- Leaving shoots alone in winter (or tying them down) to deinvigorate them and cause fruit bud development.

TREATMENT OF THE CENTRAL LEADER

Each winter, the tip of the central leader is headed back 2–3 feet above the previous season's whorl of branches. This causes it to branch and begin to form another whorl of branches, and to resume upward extension growth.

MCL trees can take up to 5–6 years to establish the entire tree framework. They involve a lot of pruning and limb positioning, with numerous heading cuts to develop and stiffen large permanent scaffold limbs. The extensive pruning and low tree density delay cropping, but when the tree does crop, it will have a high fruit load potential.

Excessive vigor in the top of the tree is inevitable, especially with vigorous rootstocks such as MM111. Failure to incrementally control this top vigor usually leads to excessive shading in the lower portions of the tree and poor fruit and fruit-wood quality. This requires extensive major limb removal, which in turn throws the tree out of balance and begets excessive (in number), overly vigorous shoot growth that is almost impossible to manage at the expense of fruit production.

LEAVING A SKIP

Having a skip on the leader between the tiers is a good way to allow sunlight into the lower portions of the tree. A skip is simply an area on the trunk of a central leader between the lower and upper tiers that has no branches. The skip should be 2–3 feet long. If any branches try to form on the skip, thin them out immediately. The skip is "nothing"—just a gap, really—but it's something, something big.

A young Golden Russett apple in the modified central leader form being trained with spreaders

CREATING THE FORM

From a whip:

- Select a tall (ideally 5-7 feet) whip.

- Plant it in late January through March (as early as advisable).

- Make a heading cut on the leader at or slightly above the height you want your first tier of primary scaffold branches to begin. Branches are fixed in place vertically for the life of a tree, although they increase in both girth and length. The standard height to make a heading cut on a semidwarf tree is 18–30 inches above the ground. Remember, the lower the tree begins to branch, the shorter the tree will be at maturity. Also, extremely low branches are difficult to work under for weeding, fertilizing, and other tasks.

- In spring, the top or lead bud will assume apical dominance (see page 184) and regrow that which was pruned off and then some. The goal is to grow the leader 2–4 feet or more in the first growing season. It should be absolutely ramrod straight. Driving a 6- to 8-foot T-post into the ground and tying the leader vertical aids in extension growth. Somewhat simultaneously, the next two to five buds down the trunk or leader will break from dormancy and grow branches. These branches will comprise all or a portion of the primary scaffold branches in the tree's first tier. Usually five to nine primary scaffold branches are desired, but four will suffice. These branches should have good spacing between them, both vertically and horizontally. The vertical spacing is pretty much a given, but branches can (and should) be trained horizontally so that they are spread equally around the 360 degrees of the trunk.

- These primary scaffold branches should be trained at 45–60 degrees above horizontal. The weaker ones should be trained upward to 60–70 degrees, and the stronger ones positioned at 45 degrees.

- In the early years, the goal is to maximize branch extension, but having equal vigor in all primary branches is also important. Thus it is not uncommon to micromanage branches up and down during the first season to assure equal vigor (see "Training," page 214).

GROWTH GOALS FOR YEAR ONE:

- Leader (lead or top bud on a trunk) extends 2–4 feet.

- Vegetative buds (two to five) below lead bud grow as primary scaffold branches 1–3 feet long.

- Thereafter, prune as you would a modified central leader.

From a branched tree:

- Plant a tree with five to nine primary branches that are 18–36 inches long. The tree should be 5–7 feet tall and at least ½ inch in caliper.

- Select 5-7 primary branches. Criteria for selection:

  Crotch angle (see illustration, page 173) is moderately wide at the point of attachment

  Strong and long branches, greater than ¼ inch caliper, 15–18 inches in length

  Growing at angle of 45–60 degrees (in relation to horizontal) or trained to that angle

- Thin unwanted and excessive branches.

- Head the keeper branches back by half their length, cutting to an outward or under-facing bud.

- Train primary scaffold branches as per above and for equidistant spacing (left to right) around the trunk.

- Head the leader 18–24 inches above the top primary scaffold branch.

Forming a Modified Central Leader

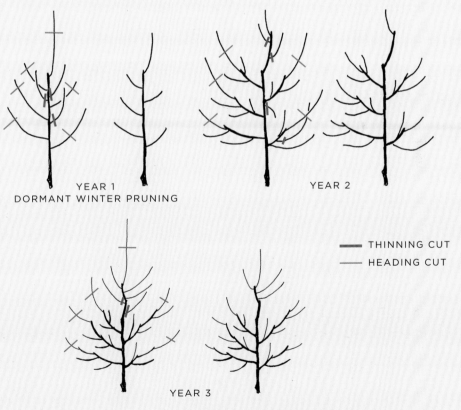

YEAR 1
DORMANT WINTER PRUNING

YEAR 2

YEAR 3

— THINNING CUT
— HEADING CUT

FIRST WINTER DORMANT PRUNING

- Cut (head) back all primary branches in the lower tier a third to half of the previous season's growth, to an outward- or under-facing bud. This continues growth in an outward direction, keeping the center of the tree open to sunlight.

- Make a heading cut on the leader 2–3 feet above the top branches in the first tier. The growth response should be that the leader extends upward 2–4 feet, and the next two to five buds below the lead bud grow primary branches in the second tier. The leader must always be positioned higher than the surrounding primary scaffold branches. (In midsummer, thin any unwanted branches that grow from winter pruning.)

- Aid subsequent training of the leader straight with a stake if necessary.

- Make microadjustments of primary branches left and right (horizontally) and vertically (45–60 degrees) to achieve equal vigor and growth in all branches and equidistant horizontal spacing for sunlight infiltration.

GROWTH GOALS FOR YEAR TWO

- Extend the leader another 2–5 feet.

- Extend primary branches 2–4 feet.

- Lateral branches form behind heading cuts on the primary scaffold branches. These laterals will bear most of the fruit load in subsequent years.

SUBSEQUENT YEARS

In subsequent years, you continue to head back the central leader in the modified central leader form and the multiple leaders in the open center form in winter, initially (years three to seven) by about a quarter to a third of their previous season's growth. Last winter's pruning wound stub should help you identify where the previous season's growth began.

The pruning of well-kept, annually pruned mature trees generally falls into the category of maintenance pruning. You are simply trying to clarify tree form with your annual pruning sessions—no major surgery! Thinning cuts become your cuts of choice: thin unwanted, unnecessary branches; make occasional thinning cuts at the top of the tree to keep the lower portions open to sunlight. You can also think about slightly reducing the tree height.

Pruning Tools

Pruners are often as passionate about their tools as they are about their trees. It's not just knowing how and where to cut (prune); how *well* you cut matters. Decisive, correct, clean pruning cuts enable a tree to heal and heal quickly—that is, to develop callus tissue that seals the wounds and prevents the entry of disease. Sharp, quality tools facilitate all of the above. In addition to protecting your reputation as an astute pruner, using good tools protects you with less wear and tear on your muscles and joints. And always use the right-sized tool for the job. How do you know to switch from pruners, to loppers, to a saw? When you grimace or strain while making a cut.

Good tools also facilitate faster, more efficient work. And there is something to be said for a tool that fits, feels right in your hand. Granted, one tool has a better feel than another in any given gardener's hand, but there is the best and the rest. You're aiming for best. A quality, sharp pair of bypass hand pruners, loppers, and long-reach pruners, and a handsaw make orchard work a joy, impart speed and ease, and fit ergonomically like a glove. Preferably a pair of kidskin gloves. When you hold a pruner, ask yourself, Does it pass the feel test? The French call them *secateurs*. There is a bit of grace and elegance to the way that word resonates.

The basic tools you need are:

- Bypass hand pruner: Use for precise cuts ⅝ inch in diameter and smaller.

- Bypass lopper: Use for cuts 1½ inches in diameter and smaller. This gives the hands a rest.

- Long-reach pruner: If there is one tool I never head out to the orchard without, it's my 4-foot ARS pruner. It also comes in 6-foot and extendable versions. Use for cuts ¾ inch in diameter and smaller.

- Handsaw: Use for cutting big branches.

- Saw for deadwood: Nothing dulls your blade like cutting through deadwood. Use an old saw or buy a cheap one for cutting deadwood.

For pruners and loppers, you usually have a choice of bypass or anvil. I recommend bypass pruners, which have two curved, thin blades that, well, bypass each other as you squeeze, or "pull the trigger." They make a clean, precise cut, a bit more elegant than an anvil cut.

With tools, you get what you pay for. Expect to pay about $75–$85 for hand pruners; more than $75–$85 for loppers; more than $100 for long-reach pruners (4 or 6 feet); and $60–$80 for quality saws.

In terms of brands, my nominees for best pruning tools in a supporting role are ARS and Felco. From there, it's a slippery and steep downward slope.

Remember, your trees will bear your mark and your brand for decades, as in, *This tree is pruned by* _____. In a sense, your choices—what to cut, to cut or not, where to cut, how much to cut— as well as how well you cut, will identify you as a pruner. Make good choices: Acquire and maintain good tools. Keep them clean and keep them sharp. They are your allies.

Training

As a fruit tree manager, you control and regulate branches by winter pruning, which stimulates growth, or by training branches flat, which encourages fruiting. Training is simply the manipulation or bending of a branch. The branch may be moved up or down, left or right. In essence, you are always tinkering with the tree throughout its life.

An upright branch is vigorous and makes extension growth. A flat branch stops growing and fruits. When you train a branch lower, toward horizontal, you trigger hormones that encourage fruiting.

You also use training in the early years to spread branches horizontally so that they are distributed evenly (360 degrees) around the trunk, like spokes on a wheel. This allows alleys and shafts of light into the core of the tree, enabling better sunlight distribution.

Alternately, but less commonly, a branch might be elevated (trained upward vertical). This has a slight invigorating effect if done early in the growing season. Overall, the invigorating effect of elevating a branch is less pronounced than the deinvigorating effect of lowering a branch.

Your goal with training is to balance growth with fruiting, to tone down vigor so that the tree's resources are redirected toward fruit. The perfect balance between vigor and fruiting is achieved by training primary branches to a 45-degree angle on modified central leader trees and to 60–70 degrees on open center trees, and by pruning lightly.

Training in action

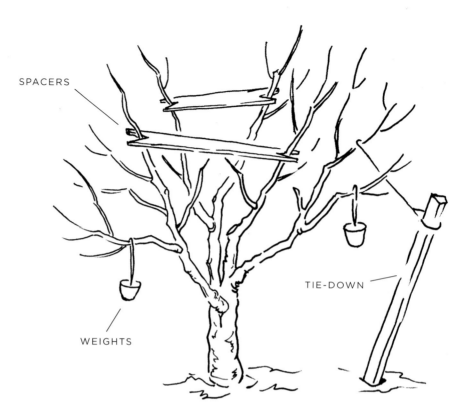

SPACERS

TIE-DOWN

WEIGHTS

BASIC TRAINING TECHNIQUES AND TOOLS

Look at your tree and think about the direction in which the branches
are growing. Are there branches that might be slightly adjusted side
to side to improve the distribution of branches around the trunk? Are
there branches that are growing toward upright that might be brought
closer to horizontal in order to increase fruit production? It's a bit
of a try-and-see skill, but whenever you manipulate a tree's branch,
it's important not to push it beyond its flexibility, or you'll break the
branch. Branches younger than 12–18 months are more supple than
older branches (especially if older branches are pruned—they stiffen).

Once you've identified which direction you want to train which
branches (from vertical to horizontal or from side to side), choose
your tools:

TIE-DOWNS You can use a stake to prop up a branch that is growing downward or tie down a branch with string and a stake to train it
toward horizontal growth. Drive the stake into the ground at an angle
(30–45 degrees), with the top slanted away from the tree. You can also
use a stake that's roughly parallel to the trunk. The stake needs to be

driven 18–24 inches deep to secure the branch. Attach the branch to it with string, thereby pulling the branch downward.

When using tie-downs, it is important not to tie a slipknot around a branch, as it will girdle it. Use nylon or synthetic string; don't use jute or other natural fibers, as they won't hold the tension. It is also important to keep a branch straight as you train it. If you bend the branch downward, buds at top of the curve will take off and grow vigorously. The best angle for a balance between growth and fruiting is 45–60 degrees.

SPREADERS Spreaders can be made from a piece of redwood lath wood with a V-notch cut in each end or with a two-penny (2d) finishing nail in each end. Spreaders can be inserted between branches horizontally and at low angles, to encourage them to grow in an evenly distributed pattern.

Frequently spreaders can be used between branches or between the branch and the trunk to widen or adjust the crotch angle (see illlustration, page 173). When branches are young (first few months of the first season), you can also use a clothespin or toothpicks to widen the crotch angle and begin to position a branch.

WEIGHTS Sometimes a weight will do the job better than a stake. You can make your own weights easily and inexpensively. Pour Sakrete (or any other quick concrete mix) into seedling six-packs. Place a U-shaped fencing staple into the wet concrete. Once it dries, you have a weight with a built-in attachment loop. Next, attach the weight to a branch with a loop of string and a clothespin (see photo, below).

For example, this is how you might train a branch from upright to horizontal: Using a notched wooden spreader, insert one end against the trunk and one end at the middle of the branch to be trained down. Lower the branch to a 45-degree angle. The spreader should keep the branch in place at the new angle. You will probably have to finesse it a bit to get it perfect. Depending on the branch, you might use a hanging weight to bring it lower.

DIY weights

Flavor Grenade pluots, well thinned with good branch spacing

Flavor Grenade pluots, well thinned with good branch spacing

Thinning

In their natural state, fruit trees are all about scrambling for sunlight, flowering, getting pollinated, producing a large quantity of fruit containing seeds, putting those seeds on the ground, and germinating a new generation of genetically diverse individual trees. These new specimens of seedling fruit trees carry many of the traits of both parents. This is desirable in terms of increasing biodiversity and the richness of the gene pool, but only occasionally will these trees be useful, reliable, productive, and attractive to the human palate. The tree's goal of producing many fruits and seeds runs counter to your goals as a human: to produce a moderate amount of good-sized, good-tasting, nutritious, attractive-looking fruit on an annual basis. For pome and stone fruits, one of the tools to make the tree adhere to your goal is fruit thinning (except quince, which are self-thinning).

Fruit thinning is a regulatory activity that has a narrow window of effectiveness. You are attempting to regulate the leaf-to-fruit ratio of the tree. In the good years, fruit trees set more fruit than they can carry into the fall. On standard-size trees, it takes thirty to forty leaves or 100 square inches of leaf surface to produce one good-sized fruit. As counterintuitive as it may seem, trees on semidwarfing or dwarfing rootstocks require only a third to a half of the leaf surface to produce a quality fruit. It's how they partition their resources: fruit over wood.

"Persons complain that the thinning of fruit is expensive and laborious, and this is true; but it is a fair question whether there is anything worth the having of which the same may not be said."

—LIBERTY HYDE BAILEY, *The Principles of Fruit Growing*, 1897

As always, fruit growing is about the balance of resource distribution. Remember, as much as 70 percent of a tree's annual reserves are exhausted by fruit. One reason for thinning and reducing the number of fruits is to liberate nutrients for all the other physiological needs of the tree. Most commonly, fruit thinning is regarded as a tool to improve fruit quality and improve the health of the tree.

Thinned or unthinned, a tree will produce about the same poundage of fruit. The question is, Do you want 120 apples or peaches that are 10 ounces each, for instance, or 400 fruits that are 3 ounces each and have large seed cavities or pits and minimal flesh? Again, think about your resource allocation. More is not always better.

Thinning also puts more sunlight on all portions of a fruit. Sunlight on fruit increases color, especially red. Believe it or not, fruit can photosynthesize (slightly) and manufacture its own sugars and starches. Additionally, thinning encourages fruit to achieve optimal size and shape. Optimal flow of sugars and starches from leaves to fruit enhances all aspects of nutrition, flavor, and taste. Good spacing and one fruit per cluster (on pome fruits) aid in these regards.

Another reason to thin your fruit trees is to reduce alternate bearing. Most fruit species are alternate bearing: carrying a large crop in one year and a very light crop in the following year. Apples are a notorious species in this regard. The fruit grower's goal is to bear a moderate (pretty good) crop every year, good weather willing. Once a tree enters into an alternate-bearing cycle, it tends to stay mired there. Don't go there with apples. As fruits form seeds, a plant growth regulator, gibberellin, develops within the seed. Generally, gibberellins (there are approximately 28 different types) control cell elongation. It's a good thing for fruit development and sizing (enlarging). However, gibberellic acid moves from the seeds back down into the fruit bud and suppresses the internal development of next year's flower buds, thus inducing alternate bearing. Incidentally, the rapid development of many seeds in an apple bodes well for its staying on the tree and sizing well and quickly, once thinned. Apples with a low seed count tend to be small and drop. So there is considerable importance to thinning fruit early and aggressively in years when the tree sets heavily. Growers refer to the annual setting of a sizable crop as a rebloom, as in "good rebloom," year to year.

TIMING OF THINNING

As with so many aspects of existence, timing is everything. Thinning must be carried out as soon as possible to have a significant effect on the size of this year's fruit.

Apples begin to differentiate new flower buds shortly after petal drop in the spring. Accordingly, thinning should occur within 35 days of full bloom, before there is much seed or gibberellin development. Thinning within 35 days should produce 100 percent effective results (100 percent rebloom the next year). If thinning occurs at 60 days, effectiveness drops to 60 percent, and at 95 days to 0 percent. With pears, the timing is not as critical for rebloom. But thinning in pears promotes fruit size. Stone fruits are similar to pears.

The critical time for thinning stone fruit is in phase one (see Fruit Tree Growth chart, page 119), by 30–40 days post bloom, when they are about ¾–1 inch in diameter. As a rule, you thin early and aggressively in heavy fruit years, moderately in average years, and minimally in light years.

With young trees, it is important to thin *all* fruit for the first 2–3 years, so that the tree can establish itself before fruiting.

An apple fruit cluster that needs to be thinned to one fruit

Fruit is generally thinned at about pinkie-fingernail size (how's that for precision and instrumentation?). At this point, it is easier to grab, hold, and flick the fruit off. You can move quickly flower to flower, branch to branch, tree to tree, row to row, anon . . . It is also easier to move quickly and efficiently without injuring or breaking off fruit buds.

WHAT TO LEAVE, WHAT TO PUT ON THE GROUND

Thin for size—leave the biggest fruit, thin the smallest. Small fruit will remain small. You might say that small fruit gets smaller as the season progresses. This statement is not literal. It's just that small fruit does not size proportionally to large fruit; it falls even further behind. Also thin any disease- or pest-damaged fruit.

Pome fruits generally set in clusters of two to six fruits. Thin to one fruit per cluster, with 6- to 8-inch spacing along the branch. Generally the most central flower in the cluster (the king bloom) has the most pollen and sets and sizes the biggest fruit. Leave it: long live the King! Sometimes a lateral fruit in the cluster will be bigger. Leave the biggest fruit. If you can't tell which is biggest, it doesn't matter too much, so just leave one and move on.

With apples, small varieties need good spacing to ensure maximum size (McIntosh types, Cox's Orange Pippin, Golden Delicious, Yellow Newtown Pippin, and the oh so grower-unfriendly Gala). However, with some large cultivars (Mutsu, Jonagold, Spigold, Spitzenburg, Chehalis), it is permissible to leave 20–25 percent of the fruit in clusters of two and still produce a good-sized fruit. In these cases, you keep two opposing apples to allow maximum space between the two fruits.

Stone fruits are easier to thin than pome fruits. Because stone fruit buds contain only a solitary flower, they set a single fruit and (unlike pome fruits) don't need cluster thinning. So it's simply about spacing on the branch. Small-sized stone fruits—European plums, apricots, apriums, and greengage plums—can be thinned to one fruit every 3–5 inches on the branch. Larger stone fruits—Asian plums and pluots—should be thinned to 5–6 inches. Peaches and nectarines should be thinned to 6–8 inches. Proper thinning equals proper size and is especially critical on small-fruited varieties of peaches like Saturn types and Baby Crawford, and all nectarines (which tend to be smaller than peaches).

APPROACHING THE TREE FOR THINNING

With apples and pears, grab the base of the fruit bud with one hand and flick the unwanted fruit in the clusters down and outward or away with the other hand.

With stone fruits, there are no clusters. Hold the base of the fruit bud with one hand, grab the fruit with the thumb and forefinger of the opposite hand, and remove the fruit with a simple circular flick o' the wrist. All fruit buds are produced at great expense to both tree and grower: handle with care. A bold, definitive, and quick motion is the most effective.

When thinning, as well as with so many other orchard tasks, you quickly become an advocate for semidwarf and dwarfing rootstocks—toward ladderless pedestrian orchards.

In a commercial organic orchard, hand thinning can account for as much as 70–80 percent of yearly labor costs, one of a number of reasons for the premium price of organic fruit versus conventional fruit. Conventional growers use caustic contact sprays to thin fruit with 70–100 percent effectiveness. While pesticides and chemical thinning sprays are effective and extremely labor saving, they are toxic to honeybees and other pollinating insects as well as to a host of beneficial insect species present in the orchard at spray time. Their effect on nontarget species, including humans, is dubious at best. Dr. Curt Rom at the University of Arkansas has developed and is conducting trials on organically certified thinning sprays that consist of diluted concentrations of fish oil and emulsified lime sulfur.

But for now, the organic grower makes the labor-intensive commitment to hand thinning.

VII

Selecting and Growing Citrus, Pomegranate, Fig, and Persimmon Trees

Although stone and pome fruits are most widely grown throughout the United States, many other, less common but equally valuable fruit trees are worth growing in your garden. While some are limited to gardeners blessed with warmer climates (citrus, persimmons), others have a surprisingly wide range (figs, pomegranates).

Citrus: Year-Round Options

The genus *Citrus* is undoubtedly the premier genus in the Rutaceae (rue) family. This family features 150 genera and 1,600 species and consists largely of evergreen shrubs and trees. Home gardeners willing to cultivate an appreciation for a wider range of citrus tastes beyond sweet oranges, acid lemons, and grapefruits can have a succession of citrus fruits on almost every day of the year.

CLIMATE

Citrus is native to the tropics of Asia. Citrus-growing regions include Mediterranean, subtropical, semitropical, and tropic zones within the approximate boundaries of latitude 40 degrees north and south of equator. The area encompasses parts of the United States, Spain, Italy, Turkey, Iran, India, South China, Southeast Asia, southern Japan, Argentina, Brazil, South Africa, Australia (east and south coast), and the northern island of New Zealand. In the United States, the best citrus regions are at latitude 20–40 degrees north: central Florida; California's central and interior valleys and south coasts; low desert areas such as the lower Rio Grande Valley in Texas and southwest Arizona; and all along the Gulf Coast states.

While citrus grows well in the tropics, the highest-quality fruit is produced in subtropical, semitropical, and Mediterranean areas. In the tropics, citrus skin stays green, and trees have a constant flowering-fruiting cycle, thus making it difficult to distinguish mature fruit from immature fruit. Also, tropical fruit does not hold well on the tree. In semitropical climates such as Florida and the Gulf Coast, with their hot, humid summers and mild winters, citrus will develop the largest and sweetest fruit and a high juice quality and content— in fact, it can be overly sweet. Acid fruits such as lemons tend to be undesirably sweet and lower in acid taste in semitropical climates.

Meyer lemons

Subtropical and Mediterranean climates, like those found in parts of California, central Chile, Australia, the western Cape of South Africa, and, of course, the Mediterranean basin, feature seasonal changes in day length plus some considerable day to night temperature fluctuations. These climate factors produce citrus with the brightest fruit color, smooth skin, and an optimal blend of sweetness and acidity, giving it the richest, fullest flavor for fresh eating. The main disadvantage of citrus grown in these conditions is the danger of cold and frost. In cool coastal climates, sweet citrus (oranges, mandarins, and grapefruits) may have a lower sugar content than desirable. The farther north citrus is grown, the more gardeners fear the specter of frost. These areas will probably experience severe frost (25°F–30°F) every 10 years.

Cold Hardiness

A citrus species' cold hardiness corresponds to the climate of its place of origin. The chart that follows lists the most prominent citrus species and their places of origin, from least cold hardy to most cold hardy. The temperatures listed here are the approximate temperature at which frost damage begins to occur; flowers are the most cold sensitive, followed by fruit, leaves, and wood. Generally it is safe to grow citrus in USDA zones 8–10. Some species, such as kumquats and Meyer lemons, can survive in zone 7.

CITRUS COLD HARDINESS			
TEMPERATURE	**SPECIES**	**PLACE OF ORIGIN**	**COMMON NAME(S)**
32°F	*Citrus medica*	India	citron, etrog, Buddha's hand
32°F	*C. aurantifolia*	India, Southeast Asia	limes: Mexican, Bearss, key, Tahitian
28°F	*C. limon* or *limonia*	Southeast Asia	lemons
26°F	*C. paradisi* (natural hybrid of lemon and pomelo)	Caribbean	grapefruit
24°F	*C. maxima* or *grandis*	Malaysian Peninsula	pomelo
24°F	*C. paradisi* (grapefruit) *x reticulata* (mandarin)	N/A	tangelo
24°F	*C. sinensis*	Southeast China, Vietnam	oranges: sweet, sour, blood
24°F	*C. nobilis reticulata x sinensis*	N/A	Florida oranges: temple, sweet
22°F	*C. reticulata*	Southeast Asia	mandarins, tangerines
22°F	*C. limon* cv. (orange x lemon)	N/A	improved Meyer lemon
20°F	*C. mitis*	Philippines	calamondin
18°F	*Fortunella margarita* and hybrids	Southeast China	kumquat, limequat, orangequat, citrangequat

N/A: Bred as hybrid cross

Heat Requirements

Citrus climates can generally be divided into three categories: cool Mediterranean zones (coastal California), warm or hot Mediterranean zones (Santa Rosa and Los Angeles to San Diego, California), and humid sub- and semitropical zones (Gulf Coast states and Central Florida).

In cool Mediterranean zones (coastal California), it is doubtful that you can grow and successfully crop true limes. You *may* be able to grow but not crop kumquats. But limequats and orangequats are excellent. And while pomelos and grapefruit will grow and crop, the quality of the fruit is such to make it a Pyrrhic victory. Additionally, in these cooler climes, some mandarins will not develop full sugar content. In hot and subtropical climes, lemons are problematic—they develop too much sugar and not enough acid.

As always, check with your local authorities about what grows best in your area.

Citrus species' relative heat needs

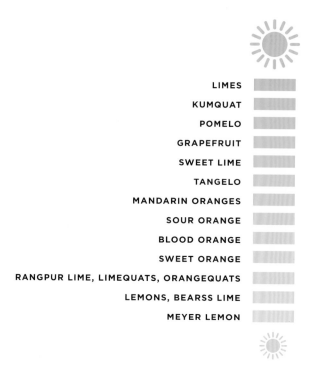

LIMES

KUMQUAT

POMELO

GRAPEFRUIT

SWEET LIME

TANGELO

MANDARIN ORANGES

SOUR ORANGE

BLOOD ORANGE

SWEET ORANGE

RANGPUR LIME, LIMEQUATS, ORANGEQUATS

LEMONS, BEARSS LIME

MEYER LEMON

GROWTH PATTERNS

Citrus exhibits all stages of growth simultaneously throughout the year, although this phenomenon is more pronounced (and problematic) in the tropics. Lemons (especially in cooler climates) are the most extreme in this regard, having succulent new growth, flowering, and young and mature fruit ever present on the tree. Citrus are rambunctious, even exuberant growers, making multiple growth spurts during the growing season. Typically, they throw long, gawky shoots in the spring—it then takes awhile for leaf growth to catch up and fill in. So, although many citrus trees have pleasing natural shapes—columnar (kumquats), pyramidal (tangelos), or dome shaped (oranges, most mandarins, and Meyer lemons)—it takes a while for them to get there.

PLANTING

The planting season for citrus is midspring through early summer. Optimum growth in the first year is linked to spring planting, which gives the tree the maximum amount of time to develop during the warm months. Planting nursery-purchased budded or grafted 5-gallon trees will produce the best and easiest results.

When siting citrus, pay particular attention to microclimates (as discussed in Chapter I, Getting Started. Realistically, you live in one climate, and yet there are often many microclimates on your property. Citrus needs a minimum of 10 hours of direct sunlight year-round. More is better. Also look for spots away from the wind, which is tough on plant growth and makes a site cooler. As usual, the top of a gently south-facing slope trumps all. Planting against the south side of a building or wall can also help boost the microclimate for citrus. The wall absorbs daytime heat and radiates it slowly at night, warming the immediate microclimate.

Citrus root systems require excellent drainage. Lighter-textured soils (sands and silts) and improved, well-drained clays grow good citrus trees.

FEEDING AND CARE

The evergreen nature of citrus leaves give them a slightly different function than that of deciduous tree leaves. With citrus, nutrient production and storage occur almost exclusively in the leaves and young twiggy branches.

Citrus roots are fibrous (branching), shallow, and extensive, displaying a vibrant burnt-orange color. Most of the effective feeding roots are very near the surface down to a depth of 1–2 feet. They often extend one to two times beyond the distance from the trunk to the drip line. Thus, surface applications of nutrients and frequent, shallow waterings beget the best growth response. To foster root growth, practice minimum tillage or cultivation and use mulch. Raised beds and dark-colored mulches afford a little more frost protection than lighter-colored mulches.

Citrus (particularly young trees) respond readily to nitrogen and to a lesser degree to phosphorous and potassium. Nitrogen assists in establishing the vegetative canopy. At maturity, nitrogen is important because citrus bear flowers and fruit on new wood and nitrogen promotes new growth. Too much nitrogen too late in the season encourages sappy growth prone to frost damage; it can also delay fruit maturation. Phosphorous is a great tool for encouraging flowering, fruit set, and sweetness. It also promotes root growth.

Micronutrient deficiencies, especially iron, zinc, and manganese, tend to express themselves during cold, wet periods of the year. They are often tied to a lack of nutrient transport due to suppressed soil temperatures rather than to soilborne deficiencies.

If your trees don't green up by late spring, an application of composted horse manure with bedding (usually straw), kelp products (liquid or meals), or Azomite will usually do the trick. In this instance and in general, citrus respond to foliar nutrient sprays—compost, manure teas, all types of guano, fish emulsion, and sea products (kelp or seaweed).

As citrus are evergreen, they grow continuously throughout the year when soil temperatures are above 50°F. And as citrus often exhibit many phases of function (root and shoot growth, flowering, immature and mature fruit growth) simultaneously, they require frequent fertility inputs in quantity.

A suggested prescription for citrus fertilization is every 4–6 weeks starting when new leaves appear in the spring, running through late July:

- Skim weeds from trunk to out beyond the drip line (a couple/few feet).

- Apply compost over the skimmed area. With young trees, use two or three shovels full; with established trees, apply half to two-thirds of a 5-cubic-foot wheelbarrow.

- Work the compost into the soil surface 3–4 inches deep with a tilthing fork.
- Apply a concentrated, granular, OMRI-approved high-nitrogen fertilizer (greater than 7 percent N). Options include the following:

  > Blood meal, 12 percent N
  >
  > Sustâne, 8 percent N
  >
  > Fish meal, 8 percent N
  >
  > Soybean meal, 7 percent N
  >
  > California Organic Fertilizer Phyta-Grow Citrus
  >   Avocado Mix, 8-5-4
  >
  > Dr. Earth Organic Fruit Tree Fertilizer*, 7-4-2
  >
  > Gardner & Bloome Organics Citrus and Fruit Tree
  >   Fertilizer*, 8-4-2
  >
  > *These products are also inoculated with mycorrhizal fungi,
  >   which aid in nutrient and water uptake.

- Irrigate to activate dry fertilizers. This should prevent any chronic problems.
- Mulch between the trees with 3–6 inches of ramial wood chips (see page 153).

If your citrus have acute problems due to low soil fertility (such as stunted growth, small fruit, and extremely yellow leaves), here's a possible prescription:

- Mix 8–10 ounces Alaska fish emulsion (OMRI approved) and 1 ounce liquid kelp in 5 gallons water and apply evenly to root zone of tree. Follow with light watering.

PRUNING

For citrus, pruning is confined to shaping the trees' general form and limiting height, rather than creating articulated tree forms as with deciduous trees. (Note that the lower portion or skirt of the tree is a very productive and accessible portion and should not automatically be pruned off.) Citrus bear fruit at the tip of the current season's growth. In pruning, you are removing this year's crop. Do as little as possible. The maximum nutrient storage period for citrus is late winter to early spring, just prior to spring bloom, fruiting, and growth cycle. Therefore, if you do need to prune, late summer is better.

The dormant season for evergreen citrus occurs when temperatures drop below 55°F for a good portion of the 24-hour daily cycle. At these temperatures, there is virtually no growth, and the tree hardens itself to deal with the threat of frost.

ROOTSTOCKS

Unlike deciduous trees, where tree size is controlled by a combination of rootstock, scion (a.k.a. variety), and pruning and training systems, citrus tree size is primarily a function of rootstock and secondarily of scion vigor. Citrus on standard (full-size) rootstocks are large trees, often 30 feet tall with a spread of 20 feet. Riverside and Orange Counties in Southern California still sport isolated plantings of 80- to 100-year-old Valencia and Washington navel oranges on standard rootstock. While they are a sight to behold and offer much-appreciated dense shade, they are not practical trees.

Sometime after World War II, semidwarfing rootstocks were developed. The most commonly used is the seedling-raised trifoliate orange (*Poncirus trifoliata*). A Valencia orange that is 30 feet tall on standard rootstock will top out at 12–15 feet on trifoliate semidwarf rootstock.

Truly dwarfing citrus rootstocks, sometimes referred to as Cuban or Shaddock, have been introduced in the last 25–30 years. They will keep oranges at 6–8 feet and weaker scions of mandarin oranges at 4–6 feet. These dwarf stocks offer far greater fruit productivity per area of tree canopy than larger rootstocks. They will also impart precocity to the tree, causing it to bear fruit in the first 3–4 years. The major drawbacks to these truly dwarf rootstocks are that the rootstock suckers (the branches growing up out of the base of the plant below the graft line) are frequent and often overtake the scion. Additionally, dwarf citrus trees are more easily stressed by cold, heat, and drought, which cause suckering and die-out.

FLAVOR CATEGORIES

Citrus flavors can generally be divided into three basic categories:

SWEET oranges, tangelos, mandarins

ACID lemons, limes, grapefruits, Rangpur lime, kumquats and their hybrids, calamondin, pomelo

SOUR OR BITTER Seville oranges, citron, chinotto, Bouquet de Fleurs

The following varietal descriptions offer an idea of the wide range of citrus available to the home orchardist. When choosing among the many citrus varieties, keep in mind scion vigor and growth characteristics, flavor and juice content, season of harvest, ability of mature fruit to hold on the tree, ease of peeling, seediness, and, of course, your climate zone.

> All citrus is self-pollinated and does not require another variety nearby to produce fruit.

SWEET CITRUS VARIETIES OF NOTE

TANGELO (*Citrus paradisi* × *C. reticulata*/mid- to late-spring ripening) Semidwarf: 8–12 feet. Dwarf: 6–8 feet. A bred hybrid cross between a grapefruit and a mandarin orange. The trees are vigorous and productive, but tend to be heavily alternate bearing (large crop one year, small crop the next). Fruit hangs on the tree well for 3–4 months. Varieties of note:

- **ORLANDO** Sweet like a mandarin.

- **SEMINOLE** and **SAMPSON** Acidic like a grapefruit.

- **MINNEOLA** Hybrid cross between a mandarin and a grapefruit, with mandarin predominating. Small tree, 4–5 feet on dwarf rootstock, 6–8 feet on semidwarf. Large bottleneck-shaped, easy-to-peel fruit. Rind is a deep red-orange—a thing of beauty. As for taste, it has a firm texture and a tart (grapefruit parentage) semi-sweet tang. Also has a distinctive, aromatic aftertaste.

MANDARIN ORANGE (*Citrus reticulata*/late-winter to early-summer ripening) Probably the largest group of citrus, also with the most common names—Satsumas, tangerines, slip-skin, or kid-glove oranges (reference to puffy, loose skin that makes peeling literally child's play). Dwarf to medium tree vigor is the rule in this grouping, with Owari Satsuma being the most dwarf scion. Mandarins are very cold hardy, tolerating temperatures into the low 20s before frost damage starts. Perform adequately in coastal areas and can tolerate desert heat. By selecting three or four varieties, the home gardener can have a 6- to 8-month harvest period. There is basically no such thing as a bad-tasting mandarin. Knock yourself out. mandarin varieties of note:

- **OWARI SATSUMA** Earliest-ripening sweet citrus I know of, often commencing at Thanksgiving and in full swing by Christmas. Eat quickly (shouldn't be a problem) as fruits only keep their quality on the tree for 4–5 weeks. The tree is a natural dwarf with a weeping form. Size options:

  1. On the true dwarfing (Cuban/Shaddock) rootstock, mere 3–4 feet, suitable candidate for a half wine barrel

  2. On semidwarfing (trifoliate) rootstock, 5–6 feet

  3. On standard rootstock (recommended choice, if you want a tree-sized tree and not a shrub), 6–8 feet

  Owari is the classic slip-skin or zipper-skin citrus—a favorite with the kids in the crowd as it is easy to peel. Seedless, sections easily, and brings a mildly acidic sweetness that is sprightly, with a zingy vitality. Skins can be boiled and sugared, dried, and kept indefinitely. Juice content is moderate. Tried and true down to the coastal strand.

- **CLEMENTINE** Also known as Algerian tangerine. Introduced as a seedling found and bred by French monk Clément Rodier. Along with the Murcott tangerine, clementines are the subject of highly successful branding efforts; you may know them as Cuties. The two varieties look and taste alike, and serve to extend the harvest season for this seriously trending product. Clementines are intermediate between Owari and Encore in terms of vigor. The tree form is round mounded, the foliage is a dark green, and as the fruit is held out toward the periphery, it makes an outstanding landscape tree. The season of ripening is on the heels of Owari in February to April. It is seedless (as a rule) and produces heavier crops with a pollinator: Dancy, Minneola tangelo, or Kinnow. Prefers inland, even desert heat (consider its North African roots); does passably well in downtown Santa Cruz. Relatively easy to peel, pretty sweet, very juicy, small but beautiful fruit.

Clementine (Algerian) mandarin orange

- **TANGO, SHASTA GOLD, YOSEMITE GOLD, GOLD NUGGET** The last three are UC Riverside patented varieties. My citrus mentor, friend, and UCSC apprenticeship alum Daniel Paduano of Abounding Harvest Mountain Farm in the Santa Cruz Mountains recommends these tangerines. If they're good enough for Daniel, they're good enough for you and me.

- **KARA** Large tree; full-flavored fruit with high juice content. Extends ripening season from March to June. Does best in interior valleys, although not in desert, and is adequate on the coast.

- **ENCORE** If I were restricted to a single citrus variety, this would probably be the one. Its virtues and merits far outweigh its demerits. It is one of the few summer-ripening citrus. Because of its historically late maturation and long hang-time, its sugar development is beyond category. Tree grows vigorously, yet tops out at 7–9 feet on dwarfing rootstock in fertile soils. Heavy yielder, 200–300 fruits on an 8- by 8-foot mature tree. Yes, it's sweet and often a virtual juice bomb, but what seals the deal is its aromatic/oily aspect. Harvest season is extremely long. While a few passable fruits can be "pinched" in June, sugar development begs waiting until July to begin harvesting. Fruit can hang on the tree until December without deterioration. I like to leave a few unharvested and on New Year's Eve at sunset ascend a ladder and pick and eat from on high; a good way to finish off the year. Now for the demerits: the skin develops green-brown spots. While this limits its commercial viability, it is merely cosmetic. Don't let it deter you. The rind (peel, skin) is moderately adherent, but still easily peelable. Encore, like most mandarins, is seriously alternate bearing—heavy crop one year, often light crop the next. There are no cultural remedies for this malaise; it's genetic.

SWEET ORANGE (*Citrus sinensis*/late winter to midsummer ripening) Best known of all citrus. Varieties of note:

- **WASHINGTON NAVEL** Chance mutant from a seeded fruit in Bahia Brazil in 1860s, introduced to Riverside, California (where one of the three parent trees still lives) in 1873, thus starting the citrus industry in California. Ripens from December to May. The classic eating orange. Fruits poorly in high heat of desert and only adequately in cooler areas. Reaches its peak in interior valleys of California.

- **TROVITA** Navel-less seedling of the Washington navel. Reportedly does better on the coast (but that has not been this writer's experience).

- **SKAGGS BONANZA** Early-ripening navel type; large fruit that sections easily. My fave.

- **SUMMER NAVEL** Extends ripening season from March to May.

- **VALENCIA** Most prominent commercial orange in the world, accounting for more than 50 percent of Florida's orange crop. Quintessential juicing orange, although cut into wedges and eaten out of hand, it is sweet, refreshing, and certainly juicy. While Valencias don't peel as easily as navels, both sugar-acid ratio and amount of juice are greater. Late-ripening variety, spring into early summer; as such, benefits from long hang-time on tree. Fruit does not deteriorate and continues to get sweeter. Sometimes if left on tree into summer, fruit manufactures chlorophyll and regreens. This is not a problem, as it is also an indicator of increasing sugar. I like to leave Valencias on the tree until June, even July.

BLOOD ORANGE (*Citrus sinensis*/late winter to midsummer ripening) Unique, attractive, and tasty orange. Depending on cultivar and climate (heat causes more intense coloring), pulp is red. Rich and distinctive taste, with hint of raspberry. Varieties of note:

- **TAROCCO** Large tree and large fruit with high juice content.

- **SANGUINELLI** Small tree with small fruit, best external rind coloring, best on coast.

- **MORO** Medium spreading tree, does well in interior and on coast, fruit in clusters.

ACID CITRUS VARIETIES OF NOTE

KUMQUAT (*Fortunella margarita*/almost everbearing, with concentration in spring) Semidwarf: 6–8 feet. Dwarf: 3–4 feet. Small to medium shrub from China with small (1–2 inches), oblong orange fruit. Flavor is opposite of normal citrus: sweet, edible rind and sour, acidic flesh. Most cold hardy of citrus (18°F–20°F, even down to 8°F–10°F), but also has nearly highest heat requirement for flowering and fruiting. Kumquat hybrids include limequat (kumquat × lime), orangequat (kumquat × orange), and citrangequat (kumquat × orange × citrange). These hybrids are very dwarf (3 by 3 feet), spreading shrubs. Small fruits, kumquatlike. Rinds taste similar to nonkumquat parent. Flesh sour/acid like kumquat. Hardiness midway between kumquat and other parent. Very productive and attractive.

IMPROVED MEYER LEMON (*Citrus × meyeri*/almost everbearing, with concentration in spring) Full size: 6–8 feet. Semidwarf: 5–6 feet. Dwarf: 3–4 feet. Thought to be natural or bred cross between orange and lemon. Spreading shrub almost always covered with flowers, young fruit, and mature fruit. Thin skinned with mild (some say insipid) lemony taste. Among the most cold hardy of citrus and one of the few successfully propagated from stem cuttings (loses dwarfness at 6–8 feet).

Improved Meyer lemon

LEMON (*Citrus × limon*/everbearing, with concentration in spring) Semidwarf: 12–18 feet. Dwarf: 6–8 feet. Because they are an acid fruit, these vigorous growers have a low heat requirement (heat equals sugar content). They are also extremely frost sensitive. Varieties of note:

- **EUREKA** Rangy, open growth habit, few thorns, moderate vigor.

- **LISBON** Thorny, vigorous tree, fruit indistinguishable from Eureka.

POMELO (*Citrus maxima*/early-summer ripening) Also known as pummelo, pommelo, and shaddock. Tall, stately parent to the grapefruit. Largest fruited of all citrus. Sour with low juice content. Marginal in cool growing areas—will fruit, but quality is variable.

LIME (*Citrus aurantifolia*/early-summer ripening) Also known as true lime, Mexican lime, or bartender's lime. Semidwarf: 6–8 feet. Dwarf: 3–4 feet. Along with lemons, the most commonly known acid citrus fruit. In general, the most cold-sensitive citrus, with flower damage occurring at 30°F–32°F. True limes, along with kumquats, have highest heat requirement of all citrus; they also need high humidity and high nighttime temperatures to produce a vibrant tree and quality fruit. True limes are actually small shrubs that have a limited successful range, including Florida, portions of the Gulf Coast states, the Caribbean, and Mexico. Will not grow and fruit in the cooler citrus areas—they become a chlorotic, twiggy, often fruitless shrub that defoliates in cold weather. If you live in a cooler Mediterranean area, short of moving to say, Havana, New Orleans, or Maracaibo, try Bearss limes, Rangpur limes, or Tavares limequats.

BEARSS LIME (*Citrus × latifolia*/fall through spring ripening) Also known as sweet lime, "sweet" being relative, as this type is slightly less acidic than lemon. While not a true lime, the Bearss is an outstanding specimen. The full, round-headed tree with dark green foliage can serve as a focal point in any landscape. Heavy and regular bearer, with fruit from October to April. Used green, it's more limelike; at maturation (yellow), more lemony. But in truth it is unique—not a lemon, not a lime. Juice and aroma are unsurpassed. I find it superior to either a lemon or a lime.

RANGPUR LIME (*Citrus limon × C. reticulata*/spring to summer ripening) Semidwarf: 6–8 feet. Dwarf: 4 feet. Not a true lime, but a natural cross between a lemon and a mandarin. Naturally dwarf tree with a drooping habit. Small fruit has appearance and loose peel of a mandarin. Taste and acidity somewhere between a lemon and a lime. Great in lemonade-like drinks. Good lime substitute in cool growing areas.

TAVARES LIMEQUAT (*Fortunella* × *Citrus aurantifolia* / early-summer ripening) Distinctive, small, oblong yellow fruit. As good as a Mexican lime in margaritas. Tree is allegedly a dwarf (mine now runs to 12 feet— on dwarf rootstock!) and is perpetually loaded with fruit. Fruit can also be cut in half, boiled for 15 minutes in a simple syrup, and then dried in a food dehydrator, and is a divine blend of sweet-tart. But in the end, any lime or lemon is simply best squeezed into a tall glass of ice water.

GRAPEFRUIT (*Citrus* × *paradisi* / late-winter to early-summer ripening) Semidwarf: 8–12 feet. Dwarf: 6–8 feet. Natural hybrid between lemon and pomelo. Large trees with a high heat requirement. Fruit can (and should in cooler areas) be left on the tree to sweeten for up to 18 months. In hot interior areas, it will mature quicker (5–6 months). Trees often carry two or three crops simultaneously. Main varieties:

- **MARSH SEEDLESS** From Florida, white flesh.
- **REDBLUSH** Pink flesh.
- **DUNCAN** Grown primarily in Florida.
- **OROBLANCO** Sweeter variety that produces passable fruit in cooler areas.

CALAMONDIN (*Citrus mitis* / winter through spring ripening) Semidwarf: 15–20 feet. Dwarf: 8–10 feet. Very attractive upright, columnar tree, amazingly productive and very cold hardy (20°F). Loose-skinned fruit with very sour pulp; preferred citrus for marmalade. High juice content. Good mixed with oranges to make a more balanced juice. Fruit hangs on tree almost year-round.

SOUR OR BITTER CITRUS VARIETIES OF NOTE

BOUQUET DE FLEURS (*Citrus aurantium* / spring ripening) Semi-dwarf: 6–8 feet. Dwarf: 3–4 feet. Very sour fruit for marmalades. High essential oil content make this a truly bitter fruit. Strongest scent of any citrus flowers. Dark green, waxy leaves. Attractive tree.

SEVILLE ORANGE (*Citrus* × *aurantium* / summer ripening) Semi-dwarf: 15–20 feet. Dwarf: 8–10 feet. This large, upright tree makes a striking ornamental. Deep orange fruit is rough skinned, bitter, and juicy—great for marmalades.

CHINOTTO (*Citrus myrtifolia* / spring to summer ripening) Also known as myrtle leaf orange. Semidwarf: 4–6 feet. Dwarf: 3–4 feet. Very dwarf, dark-foliaged shrub, always covered with small, bitter fruit that holds on the shrub year-round. Can be used as a hedge. Native to Italy. Used in marmalade.

CITRON (*Citrus medica* / winter ripening) Not technically a variety, but rather a category that encompasses several types of citrus that can be loosely grouped as "citron." Ancient species, first citrus introduced to Europe from Mideast. Rangy shrub that has oblong, lemonlike fruit (citron); warted, fingerlike fruit (Buddha's hand), or knobby, globular fruit (etrog). Somewhat alien looking in appearance. Very fragrant, sour fruit, virtually all pulp and no juice. Etrog is used in the Jewish Feast of the Tabernacles. These days, citron-infused beer is all the rage with microbreweries across the nation.

Pomegranates: The Mythological Fruit

Punica granatum

The name *pomegranate* derives from the word *pome*, meaning small-seeded. (The root word also gives its name to the small-seeded pome fruits.) The old Latin name for pomegranate was *Malus* (the genus for apples) *punicum*. This translates to "apple of grain" or "multigrain." Pomegranate seeds are small, highly edible, glowing ruby gems, imparting

a sweet-tart taste along with a high juice quotient. Pomegranate flowers are also beautiful—persistent, waxy, and pendant. They seem to glow at a distance, orange-red in color. In addition to being visible to pollinators, they often attract hummingbirds. So now you have flowers, fruit, and birds—a good trifecta.

Pomegranates are easy to grow! Pomegranates are wonderful! "Wonderful" is actually the name of the leading commercial variety. And it is probably one of your best varietal choices, especially in hot summer areas. Pomegranates are a superfood! And trending! Everyone says they are loaded with antioxidants! (Interestingly, the reason that commercial pomegranate juice is touted for its antioxidant powers is because the rind is also pressed with the fruit, which expresses high-antioxidant tannins. But don't worry, the fruit is nutritious, too.)

The pomegranate is a fall fruit that has ancientness stamped all over its DNA. It is probably one of the oldest of all cultivated fruits, dating back 5,000 years or more. Pomegranate imagery and symbolism are ubiquitous in many countries, cultures, and cuisines along the Mediterranean rim and throughout the Mideast stretching eastward to Afghanistan and northern India. For example, the Spanish city of Granada derives its name from the word *pomegranate*, and to this day the surrounding countryside is dotted with commercial plantings. In and around Granada, the image of the pomegranate is everywhere: on fountains and murals, street signs, fronts of buildings, the city insignia, and even manhole covers. In Turkey, on New Year's Eve, families throw a pomegranate to the floor to crack it open. If many of the two to four hundred seeds spill out, the coming year will be prosperous.

In Greek mythology, the pomegranate and its seeds (actually just six seeds) play a pivotal role in the tale of Persephone and her mother, Demeter, the goddess of agriculture, harvest, and fertility. The upshot is that Persephone was tempted and abducted by Hades, the god of the underworld, who offered her a pomegranate. She ate six seeds, thereby being condemned to revisit the underworld every year, against her will, during fall and winter (6 months of the year). Demeter was inconsolable during that time, and consequently her attention strayed. Thus the earth and its crops took on a seared, brown, withered, even forlorn look. The story was a reasonable construct by the early Greeks to explain the four seasons.

CLIMATE

Present-day thinking by archaeobotanists places the pomegranate's center of origin in a wide geographic band from northern Iran eastward to Turkmenistan and into the northern mountains of India. The leading producer of pomegranates worldwide is Iran, then the United States (California produces 98 percent of the domestic crop). China, India, Israel, Egypt, Spain, Turkey, and Afghanistan follow suit. In the United States, pomegranates can be grown successfully in USDA zones 7–10 and maybe in a limited and sketchy manner down to zones 5 and 6. In these zones, they will grow and possibly mature fruit in some years. They will probably suffer cold injury in some winters. But with both winter mulch and selection of a good microclimate, they are possible, even doable in zones 5 and 6. Across the nation, they are grown in portions of California, southern Nevada, South Texas, across the Gulf states, and even in northern Florida and the Southeast, although summer rain, heat, and humidity can induce a number of fruit diseases in the South.

Pomegranates grow well in areas that have long, hot summers and cold, somewhat wet, but not frigid winters. The cutoff low temperature for survival is 10°F–15°F, although they may be able to survive down to 0°F. Temperatures below that will sound the death knell. Even at

0°F or thereabouts, the plant can probably recover, spring back, issue new shoots, and begin again. They need a frost-free growing season of more than 120 days; 122–150 days are best. If a majority of those days feature temperatures 80°F–85°F or even hotter, so much the better. Texts often state pomegranates can tolerate heat. The real deal is that they demand it for quality fruit.

Pomegranate flower

GROWTH PATTERNS

The flowering period begins shortly after the plant leafs out in the spring and sometimes continues well into the summer and ridiculously so into the fall. This is especially true in cooler growing districts. Ain't nothin' wrong with this tendency. And as they say in basketball, "no harm, no foul." (If, however, these late blooms result in fruit, thin them off. They won't have time to mature before fall frosts and the season's end, and they will simply drain nutrients away from other potential quality fruit.)

Toward season's end, the fruit size will increase rapidly. The exterior skin will become leathery. Internally, seeds are sizing (enlarging) and the juice quotient rapidly rising. This is an important time to make sure you are applying water about every 7–10 days as your soil dries down.

If you live in an area that features a quick drop in temperatures as fall arrives, accompanied by early frosts, don't let the fruit linger on the bush too long. And while a heavy frost can wither mature fruit on the vine, a touch of light frost is not all bad. Even several light frosts. These light frosts will actually sweeten the fruit. This is an adaptive survival strategy that many crops have—root crops, brassicas, even leaf crops like lettuce, spinach, and arugula. With the threat of cold, the plant senses its death (in an anthropomorphic manner of speaking). So the plant produces sugar, which lowers the freezing point, thus staving off frost damage or even death. Gardeners reap this dividend with sweet, not bland, brussels sprouts and carrots and parsnips packed with sugar. The same applies to pomegranate fruit as well as late-ripening apples, and it is why New England McIntosh apples are superlative.

PLANTING

The planting of pomegranates is similar to that of deciduous fruits; they are planted as bare root stock in the dormant season.

FEEDING AND CARE

Doesn't every gardening book state that every crop does best in a deep, rich loamy soil? Well, it's true of pomegranates as well. But the pomegranate can grow reasonably well on less than ideal soils, even shallow sandy soils—that is, if water and fertility are attended to with both greater amount and frequency. If you have 2–3 feet of a reasonably fertile topsoil, soil conditions shouldn't be a barrier to growing pomegranates.

The usual Rx for soils—an annual application of compost and mulch—should suffice. And if a green manure can be worked into the mix, so much the better. While generally pomegranates are efficient feeders, you can help to establish the tree with a high-nitrogen fertilizer annually (6 percent nitrogen or more) such as ½ pound blood meal (12 percent N), ¾ pound Sustâne (8 percent N), or 1 pound Down to Earth Citrus Mix (6 percent N). Commercial growers choose to pour the nitrogen on annually throughout the life of the plant, but continued nitrogen fertilization at maturity should be confined to the early and mid-season. And you can make one or two incrementally spaced applications. However, be wary of mid- and late-season nitrogen application. This can have a number of negative effects; it can delay fruit maturation, retard coloring of the fruit, diminish the zestful vitality of the taste of the fruit, and even lead to internal rot and subsequent storage issues. Don't do it.

Pomegranates are amazingly efficient at getting by with minimal fertility and water, but if you want a good crop, you should be attendant to both. Most of the pomegranate's feeding roots are confined to the top foot of the soil. Monitor at that depth for dry down. Then apply water. This will probably be every 7–10 days. Always make sure your trees are well watered going into a heat wave, as lack of water will wither the fruit. One thing that pomegranates are not tolerant of is wet feet. So, practicing reasonable restraint with each irrigation is important; you want enough, but not too much. Always allow a good dry-down between irrigations. As always, long-term soil practices that promote good soil structure will aid with drainage.

PRUNING

The pomegranate tree is more properly called a shrub. It can be grown as a single-trunk tree in the open center form or in a multistemmed, informal, arching bush with five or six main branches. The latter is probably your best bet in cold climates, as undoubtedly you will lose some branches to winter cold injury. These multiple stems are a hedge against winter die-out. And even frosted back, damaged stems can regenerate in the spring. Simply cut away the damaged wood as soon as all danger of frost has passed.

Unbidden, whether you like it or not, new stems will spring from the base of the plant. This is good in terms of helping regenerate cold-damaged shrubs, but a total pain in the neck in that you are constantly thinning out these suckers throughout the years.

Growing the pomegranate as a multistemmed bush requires little or no annual pruning, other than lightly heading back the main branches at the end of the dormant period. This induces further growth of these branches (enough, but not too much or too vigorous), and as always, heading cuts induce lateral branches that bear fruit. In addition, annual thinning of weak, unproductive branches or any branch that crosses into the center of the bush or shades in any manner is required. That's about all that is required in pruning pomegranates. If you choose to grow the pomegranate as a single-trunk open center tree, just follow the instructions in the tutorial on page 204. One note: Row spacing for the bush form needs to be 12–15 feet apart; for the open center form, spacing can be 10–12 feet apart. Although pomegranates are naturally tall and rangy, they can easily be kept at 8–10 feet. They certainly are long lived; specimens have been reported to live up to 200 years.

> Pomegranates are self-pollinated and do not require another variety nearby to produce fruit. There are more than two hundred varieties, but only a precious few worth growing. Pomegranates require 100–300 chill hours.

VARIETIES OF NOTE

AMBROSIA Ginormous fruit, up to three times the standard size of other varieties, even the big ones. Pale pink skin.

EARLY WONDERFUL As you might guess, simply an earlier-arriving Wonderful. Probably a better bet to yield the wonder of Wonderful in cool areas.

GRANADA First its praises: Yes, the fruit is large. It is a mutation of Wonderful and resembles it in its red blossoms and regular bearing. And it ripens a month earlier. The fruit is less tart, more sweet, and yet . . . don't plant it. I have never seen a Granada that wasn't riddled with an interior black rot. What it amounts to is 4–5 months of tending and growing, weeding, and watering, only to yield a bitter disappointment.

SWEET And sweet it is. Large fruit with orange-red flowers in spring and pink-skinned fruit in fall. Flesh is also pink and not as deeply dark as other varieties. Also early ripening.

WHITE Again, a large fruit, almost white-pink fruit in fall, with almost transparent white flesh. Very sweet and juicy, perhaps too much so, but still good. Early ripening.

WONDERFUL It is indeed wonderful. Leading commercial variety for good reason. It probably meets more of the criteria for a good pomegranate than any, or even all, other varieties. It is big. It is robust. It is certainly red. It is a heavy bearer. It has many good-sized seeds. And a sweet-tart taste (although tart predominates a bit). Wonderful can take the heat. Consequently, it may not be the best-suited variety for cooler growing regions. Only of passable quality in cool coastal areas.

The "Common" Fig: Decadent and Nuanced

Ficus carica

Ficus carica is known as the common fig, but in looking at the tree and its fruit, I would beg to differ. In the aggregate, the nature and performance of figs belie the word *common*. I'm going with *exceptional*—in botany, growth patterns, shape, taste, and rambunctiousness.

Figs are probably the most vigorous of all deciduous fruit trees. They are members of the Moraceae family, along with mulberries. Other prominent members of this family include the banyan tree, the houseplant ficus, and *Ficus elastica*, the rubber tree.

And, of course, the fruit of the fig tree can in no way be classified as common. It has an intense, jamlike texture, and the syrupy honey-like flesh hints at raspberry. Figs ask and answer the question, *Can something be both decadent and nuanced?* Uncommon indeed!

Figs are thought to be native to the fertile plains of southern Arabia, although their productive hearth and home is considered to be in the area around southern Turkey. Early fig orchards dotted the shores of the Mediterranean Sea and spread to the Fertile Crescent of Mesopotamia (now Iraq). Archaeobotanists now speculate that figs may have predated even wheat, barley, and other ancient grains that propelled our species into farming some 10,000 years ago. Fruit remains that resemble culti-vated figs have been found in an area near Jericho in Israel. Radiocarbon dating put the age of these fruits at 11,500 years old. The speculation is that fig orchards blanketed the area around southern Turkey and into the valley of the Euphrates and Tigris Rivers in Mesopotamia. I can dig it, as it were.

CLIMATE

Turkey is still the leading producer of figs worldwide, although most of the crop is offered dried not fresh. Egypt, Morocco, Iran, Algeria, Greece, Syria, Spain, Tunisia, and the United States are also big fig-producing countries. Stateside, California produces 99 percent of all figs grown for commerce. But in truth figs can be grown widely across the continent: coastal Oregon and Washington State (Seattle has figs!), even coastal southern British Columbia, the Gulf states, Florida, the Southeast, and up into Washington, DC, and New Jersey. New York City proper and Chicago are not out of the question. The variety Chicago Hardy probably originated in Sicily, but was found growing wild in an abandoned garden outside Chicago (go figure). Not all these areas will grow figs as well as a Mediterranean climate or a mild temperate climate will, but one of the things I love about gardeners is that they love to stretch the boundaries, literally and figuratively. They seem to have an utter disregard for the impossible embedded in their DNA. Plant figs!

Figs can be grown easily in USDA zones 7–10. They can be grown with some certainty in zones 5 and 6. But their preference is for a climate that is hot and dry in the summer with little or no rain, low humidity, and wet but cool (not cold) conditions in the winter. Dormant mature fig trees are reliably hardy down to 15°F–20°F. Temperatures colder than that will see some cold injury and dieback of the branches. But they will probably rebound with new growth in the spring. The cutoff point is 0°F—it's lethal. Some varieties are genetically more cold hardy than others (see varietal listings). Note: Large bodies of water mitigate temperature in the surrounding areas, warming in winter and cooling in summer. So the fact that figs can be grown as far north as coastal southern British Columbia makes some sense. For the Chicago area, there is that large body of water, Lake Michigan. Manhattan, you say? Surrounded by water.

Tips for growing figs in marginal climates:

- Choose your varieties carefully.

- Choose a warm microclimate, a gentle south-facing slope, perhaps a planting against a wall, facing south. If the building is heated, you will gain a temperature boost from radiation. If the siding of the building is dark, it will absorb heat in the day and radiate it back at night.

- Grow figs as a loose, very loose multistemmed shrub, not as a single trunk tree. This multistem shrub should have at least ten to fifteen branches. Some of these may be partially or fully winter killed. In the spring, cut back damaged branches into new healthy wood. Cut the dead branches all the way back to the ground. Do this after the threat of frost has passed. In all likelihood, the pruned damaged branches will just resume growth in the spring and summer. The ones that are killed to the ground will sprout new branches from the root mass.

- A heavy mulch, even up to a foot thick, of straw or wood chips helps protect the basal crown of the plant. Even if your fig dies completely to the ground, there is some hope that it will resprout anew in the spring. Occasionally you see photos of figs cut back to head height and elaborately wrapped in burlap. This is for frost protection. But it is cumbersome and imparts a ghoulish look to the home garden.

GROWTH PATTERNS

The fig tree can be rangy, even rambunctious, growing in excess of 25–30 feet tall and almost as wide. The roots are as vigorous and aggressive as the shoots. They are branching and fibrous, and produce an incredibly dense, fibrous mat. They are generally confined to the surface of the soil, sometimes even protruding above the soil surface. The roots often wander or meander, sometimes as far as 20 feet beyond the canopy, if you let them. Not your average tree.

Figs are capable of producing two crops a year, a rarity in fruits. They leaf out in the spring (temperatures greater than 60°F) with a crop of fruit that has set the previous fall. This fruit ripens in midsummer. Figs show vigorous shoot growth spring into early summer and often set a second crop during this period. This second crop can ripen in the fall.

PLANTING

Figs can thrive on a wide range of soils, from improved heavy clays to the more droughty light sandy soils. Probably more important than soil textural class—sand, silt, or clay—is the need for good drainage. Like many fruit trees, figs resent wet feet. As for the depth and richness of the soil, deep, rich alluvial valley or river bottom soils can be problematic. They sometimes impart too much vigor to an inherently vigorous species. There are no dwarfing rootstocks for figs; they don't have rootstock at all. Even commercially, they are simply propagated from cuttings.

Consequently, you only have horticultural means to try to restrain their vigorous nature. By growing figs on less than ideal soil, you can actually rein them in a bit.

Figs are easy to propagate. All that is involved is to take a 12- to 18-inch dormant, leafless hardwood cutting at the end of the dormant season, just prior to leafing out and the resumption of growth. Simply plunk it in the ground where you want a new fig tree, and in 8–10 weeks it will root and sprout new shoots. If you plant such a cutting every 15 feet in row with alleys between the rows of 10 feet, you will have yourself a fig orchard. And so it probably went in southern Turkey 11,000 years ago.

FEEDING AND CARE

The standard package of compost and fertilizer (see page 152), ideally with a green manure (see page 150), is requisite for young (1- to 4-year-old) figs, but it would be wise to totally refrain from nitrogen fertilizer thereafter, as this will encourage unwanted shoot growth at the expense of fruit growth. As fig trees mature into their productive middle years, annual applications of fertilizer are optional.

In the early years, figs should be watered as aggressively as any other young fruit tree. As they mature, though, water can be greatly reduced. In mild summer areas, it is even possible to semidry-farm figs, once established. Simply apply water every 3–4 weeks. Be careful— too little water will result in small, dry, mealy figs, which are not what you're looking for.

PRUNING

Encourage fruiting by growing figs to a loose fan shape or espalier form with spreading, arching main branches growing up and out at an angle of 45–60 degrees above horizontal. Take four to six main branches and train them horizontally. Spread them so that so that they are equidistant from one another—create a fan shape. Winter prune them with heavy heading cuts in each of the first three or four winters, or until the tree has achieved the height and spread you desire. Training and then heading them in this manner will promote the formation of lateral fruiting branches along their run.

Each winter, stub approximately every other lateral back to one or two buds. Leave the others unpruned. The laterals left unpruned will bear an early crop (called the breba crop) in midsummer, on last year's wood. These fruits actually form in the fall, look to be little bumps on the branch, overwinter, and grow and mature the next summer. The stubbed laterals grow back quickly and bear in late summer or early fall. While two crops a year are possible, certainly desirable, in cool and/or short growing season areas, one is much more likely. The second crop on figs or the main crop forms on current season's wood.

The aggressive, rambling nature of fig roots can be contained, somewhat, by root pruning. Once the tree is fully established, on a semiannual basis, simply slice down vertically into the soil 15–18 inches with a sharp spade around the tree's drip line.

There are more than 200 common varieties of figs. Below are some "cream of the crop" recommendations.

Fig flowers are distinctive in their botany: they are contained and hidden within the fruit itself. *Ficus carica* has no need of pollination, as they set fruit parthenocarpically. *Parthenocarpy* is the ability to produce fruit without pollination and to produce seedless fruit. It derives from the Greek—"virgin fruit." These figs require 100–300 chill hours.

VARIETIES OF NOTE

BLACK MISSION (late-summer to fall ripening) Standard for fresh home-garden figs. It is widely adapted. With great reliability, it produces sweet, rich figs. Fruit is a purple-black on the outside with pink flesh on the interior. Very heavy cropper.

BROWN TURKEY (late-summer ripening) One of the more widely adapted figs for cool or warm regions. Subtle but strong coppery brown skin with pink flesh. Naturally small tree, very size manageable. With little or no effort, it can be kept at 10–12 feet tall. Very good winter cold tolerance. Nutty taste, like that of dried figs, even when fresh off the tree.

CELESTE (mid- to late-summer ripening) Second to Chicago Hardy in high winter cold tolerance. Naturally compact, 12–15 feet. Goes by the epithet "sugar fig," an apt nickname. Violet-skinned fruit with warm rose–tinged interior.

CHICAGO HARDY (mid- to late-summer ripening) The king of the north. Brownish purple fruit with rich, sweet flavor. I have seen photos of snow-dusted fruit of this variety.

DESERT KING (mid- to late-summer ripening) Adaptable to all growing areas but, ironically, does best in cool coastal areas, even in the Pacific Northwest. Green skin with red interior. As a rule, it only bears one crop a year, but it is an early crop. Very cold tolerant.

KADOTA (mid-summer ripening) Also called White Kadota. Greenish yellow fruit with slightly tough skin but exceedingly sweet interior flesh. Thrives in the heat and humidity of Hawaii and does equally well in hot interior Central Valley of California.

OSBORNE PROLIFIC (late-summer to fall ripening) Another performer in cool regions. Large, attractive dark purple, almost black fruit with amber flesh. Super sweet and virtually melts in your mouth.

PANACHE (late-summer ripening) Also called Striped Tiger. Striking-looking fruit, a fig lover's fig. Indeed, it has panache. Small size but big taste. Exceedingly sweet and a little dry, an interesting taste sensation. What sells this variety is its looks: greenish yellow background with dark green stripes in foreground. Requires long, warm growing season.

PETER'S HONEY (mid- to late-summer ripening) Originally from Sicily. Needs sustained high heat to ripen properly, but can be cropped in mild summer areas if grown in a favorable microclimate. Yellowish green skin and amber-colored flesh.

VIOLETTE DE BORDEAUX (mid- to late-summer ripening) Also called Negronne. It's not just the French-sounding name that recommends this variety. Yeah, it's got panache, but this is a utilitarian variety that is to die for in the taste department. As for the look of the fruit, it won't hurt your eyes either. Very cold-hardy variety with violet-black skin and a purple interior. Virtually dripping with sugar when you bite into it. Tree is a natural dwarf, topping out at 8–10 feet. Among the best at tolerating winter cold and bouncing back in spring.

WHITE GENOA (late-summer ripening) Very old variety. Does well in warm summer areas and is one of the most reliable figs in cool, short-summer areas and in coastal districts. Almost white greenish skin with strawberry hue to flesh. Tree is easily capped at 6–8 feet by growing the primary scaffold branches at an almost horizontal angle once the tree has reached head height. Minimal pruning at full tree canopy also helps reduce tree height. Sometimes called the strawberry jam of figs.

Persimmons: Fall Bounty

Diospyros kaki

The persimmon is a striking tree. Strikingly beautiful in the landscape and strikingly productive as well. Generally a large, round-mounded specimen, it can serve as a source of shade when seeking shelter from the midday summer sun. But it really comes to the fore in the fall. With pomegranates and late-ripening pears, it comprises a trio of sustained and satisfying crops in the home orchard. In the kitchen, these three offer intriguing and satisfying combinations of hardy autumn fare. Try Alice Waters's all-star salad of Fuyu persimmons, pears, and pomegranates from *Chez Panisse Fruit*. The persimmon and pear slices are thrown in with pomegranate seeds, a head of radicchio, hearts of endive, and a red wine vinaigrette.

Persimmons belong to the Ebenaceae family, the ebony family. Other members feature unusually dense, dark black wood. The persimmon trunk bark is somewhat black, with a fissured and cracked pattern that is a distinctive visual treat. (No need for alarm; it's normal.) Most tree species have bark patterns that run vertically or horizontally with stripes and striations. Not so with the persimmon. Persimmon bark pattern is rectilinear and pronounced, quite a visual mosaic.

Certainly persimmons are a distinctive fruit. Their flavor is unique. While many comparisons are made to other fruits, I believe it was the character Dogberry (a sketchy chap) in Shakespeare's *Much Ado*

About Nothing who quipped "comparisons are odorous." And so it goes with persimmons.

The Japanese persimmon, *Diospyros kaki*, is actually native to China, where it has been grown for more than 2,000 years. It is, however, the revered national fruit of Japan, where it has flourished for more than 1,200 years and is called *gaki* or *kaki*, meaning "persimmon" in Japanese. There are two main types of Japanese persimmons: Hachiya and Fuyu. There is also an American persimmon, *Diospyros virginiana*, which is native to the eastern United States, from southern New England to Florida and west beyond Missouri. The American persimmon is much more cold hardy than the Japanese types. It is a bigger tree with much smaller, more astringent fruit than the Japanese persimmon. When ripe, the fruit is truly sweet, but mealy. It is more of a homesteader's tree with little or no commercial value. I don't recommend growing it, as the Japanese varieties are so much better, if you can grow them in your area.

CLIMATE

Japanese persimmons prefer areas with warm summers and moderate, wet winters. They are grown in California, the Pacific Northwest, warm regions of the South, and generally throughout USDA zones 7–10. Dormant trees are cold tolerant down to approximately 0°F.

GROWTH PATTERNS

The Hachiya tree is tall and vigorous, often 15–20 feet tall and as wide. The fruit too is large, 3–4 inches wide, and heart or acorn shaped. It has a warm, deep orange color and an almost subtle glow. Hachiyas are extremely astringent, laced with tannins, until fully ripe. Then they are like a sugar-water balloon—translucent skin encases innards that are a sweet mushy jelly with lots of sugar. A treat to eat! But, the fruit must be fully ripened and soft to eliminate the tannins and bring up the sugar content. You must wait. Be patient.

When I first came out to California from Boston some 50 years ago, I grabbed a few seemingly ripe Hachiyas from an unsuspecting roadside tree. When I bit into one, what I tasted was the equivalent of one part quinine, one part sandpaper, and one part cement mix, with

Hachiya persimmons

a dose of paint thinner thrown in for good measure. Not exactly a divine fruit. Little did I know what pleasure the fruit acquired after ripening.

Hachiyas can be left on the tree to soften, sweeten, and ripen. Or they can be picked at full color but not mature and laid out in a single layer in a box and ripened in a cool room. They also can be refrigerated and kept for up to 3 months, then brought out and ripened incrementally. When ripe, they can be eaten out of hand, although they are a bit messy. It's easier to cut them in half and spoon the sweet flesh, or just cut the top off the fruit and spoon it. In a sense, Hachiyas are a bit like zucchinis: once they are ripe, you've got way too many. As with zukes, you can make bread or cookies and give them away. They also make a good pudding.

Fuyu, the second type of Japanese persimmon, is also called apple persimmon. Both the fruit and the tree are smaller than the Hachiya. The fruit is four lobed, oblate, and squat, not unlike the shape of a tomato or perhaps an apple, though its taste and texture in no way resemble an apple, thankfully. It is applelike in that it is nonastringent, a bit crisp and crunchy, and can be eaten out of hand. But the flavor is something else . . . Fuyus needn't be soft to be ripe and sweet, just richly colored. The Fuyu tree is a bit more timid and well behaved than the Hachiya. It usually tops out at a modest 8–12 feet tall. It fits nicely into the small home landscape.

Persimmons leaf in the spring and set green fruit in the summertime. As summer turns into autumn, the innocuous dull green fruits start to color, eventually achieving a warm orange-red at maturity. The fruit has an almost subtle glow. In a similar vein, the green leaves ignite with fiery tones of red, yellow, and orange. Then suddenly, often aided by a windblown autumn day, the leaves are on the ground, and the tree's silhouette stands dormant with light fawn-colored branches and orange fruit. It is unusual to see a tree dormant, leafless, and still bearing fruit, but so it is with the persimmon. The tree has an almost mythological look at this point.

Once the tree drops all its leaves, you had better get busy and harvest the fruit. Yes, it could be left to ripen on the tree, but the scavenging trifecta of crows, raccoons, and squirrels bid you to harvest. Use hand pruners when harvesting, and take a short stem with the fruit, about ½ inch long. With fruits and vegetables, a stem is simply a buffer between the item and desiccation or rot. Stems on fruits are important and extend the postharvest shelf life (a protective cloak).

If you're growing Hachiyas, a good way to make sure squirrels don't get more of your harvest than you do is to preserve your persimmons. You can do this with a food dehydrator, or look into the much more laborious (and incredibly cool) traditional Japanese method of making delicious Hoshigaki.

PLANTING

A soil with moderate fertility and reasonable drainage is most preferable, but persimmons are not fussy. In fact, growing them on only moderately fertile soil with minimal fertilization and little or no water can help keep the tree size under control. Persimmons, particularly Hachiyas, have a deep taproot that can drill down greater than 10–15 feet to reach water deep in the soil.

Persimmons are purchased and planted at the end of the bare root season. Assuming moderate soil fertility, they require no fertilization at planting or subsequently. Irrigation is helpful the first three years and virtually unnecessary thereafter. Persimmons have no real dwarfing rootstocks, so at best you can only hope for a midsized, not dwarf, tree. The Fuyu is more of a naturally dwarfed tree than the Hachiya. Plant the trees where they will get 8–10 hours of sunlight a day, although persimmons can tolerate some slight, light shade and still remain productive. Give Hachiyas 12–16 feet between trees; Fuyus, 8–10 feet between trees.

FEEDING AND CARE

If ever there was a fruit tree whose care could be dubbed "managed neglect," it would be the persimmon. Not to be too reductive, but the basic care package runs along these lines: purchase a tree, plant it, prune it for a few years to a loose open center, wait at least 5–6 years, pick the fruit, and enjoy the tree for decades to come. Persimmons are truly indestructible. They require virtually no irrigation, no worries about soil type, no fertilization, no spraying for pests and diseases, no worries about pollination, no thinning fruit, no worries at all. Don't worry; be happy. Really, seriously, no nothin'.

At the UCSC Farm & Garden, we have a persimmon planting dating to the early 1970s. To my recollection, the trees have never been irrigated or fertilized. We pruned them at the outset and only rarely since then. They are marvelous 15- to 20-foot specimens, loaded with fruits year in and year out. Nearby, down in a wet draw on an old abandoned ranch dating to the early 1900s, is a stand of wildings 30 feet tall. These trees fruit abundantly and annually. Both are a welcome example of benign neglect.

I recommend you water the tree in years one through three or four. Irrigation is optional thereafter. Fertilization is absolutely optional at all times. Pests and diseases? There are virtually none.

PRUNING

Prune the tree gently for a few years, forming a loose open center form. Establish a firm framework for the tree canopy in years one through four. Do this with winter heading cuts. Thereafter, little or no annual pruning is required. In subsequent years (actually, decades), all that is needed is simply cleanup pruning. Some thinning at the top can keep the interior of the canopy open to sunlight and keep tree height reasonable.

A word of advice: I know *never* is a strong word, but once a persimmon tree is established, I would never prune it with stimulating winter heading cuts. The resultant growth is crazy, unruly, even delinquent. It features upright, forking, ultravigorous, unfruitful branches. These branches have a narrow crotch angle (see illustration, page 173). Thus they are structurally weak and prone to breakage. Often they grow rampantly, fruit minimally, shade the tree's interior, and eventually snap and break.

> Most persimmons—including the ones recommended below—are parthenocarpic, meaning they can set fruit without pollination and have no need for a pollenizer variety. In fact, cross-pollinated fruits may contain many irritating seeds. Consequently, it is best to only plant one variety of Hachiya and one variety of Fuyu to avoid seeds. All these varieties ripen in a relatively compressed period— mid- to late fall. Persimmons require 100–200 chill hours.

HACHIYA PERSIMMON VARIETIES OF NOTE

CHOCOLATE Bit of a crossover, possessing looks and shape of a Hachiya, but like a Fuyu it can be eaten out of hand when only slightly soft. Generally nonastringent. Yes, it has a hint of chocolate, a taste that goes with the somewhat unappealing chocolate-colored flesh. The chocolate tinge accompanies the typical spicy-sweet, slightly crunchy sensation associated with Fuyu types.

HACHIYA Both a specific variety and the general name for the class of astringent persimmons. Standard of its type for shape, taste, texture, and overall performance. Generally ripe from early October through early December. Large vigorous tree and reliable annual cropper.

TAMOPAN Large, blocky fruit with constricted band two-thirds up the fruit, giving it the appearance of a large acorn. Mature in midseason and especially rich and sweet tasting. Flavor is unique and intriguing.

Hachiya persimmon

FUYU PERSIMMON VARIETIES OF NOTE

FUYU Standard for its class. As with Hachiya, both a variety and the generic name for the type. Distinctly smaller fruit than Hachiya. Four lobed, blocky, and squat. Skin color is a little less showy than Hachiyas, with a mattelike surface.

GIANT FUYU Yep, it's a bigger, but no less tasty, Fuyu.

IZO Exceedingly sweet Fuyu type. At full maturation, flesh is soft and even syrupy. Tree is a natural true dwarf, topping out at a mere 6–8 feet. Fruit ripens early, even as early as September into mid-October. Dependable annual cropper.

Fuyu persimmon

JIRO Large, square fruit with excellent Fuyu-like taste and texture. Often the Fuyu of commerce, especially in California. Stores and ships well, while maintaining integrity of eating experience.

Coda, or Go Forth and Ace It

Somewhere past the end of the growing season, approaching the year's shortest day, day dreamin' about the way things sometimes are, there are cherished quiet moments in the garden. One might get melancholy. But then there are reflections.

By a strange confluence of chance and choice, I have lived most of my life at the UCSC Farm & Garden where I teach. And I don't remember a time when I didn't know this place, this land. I know it intimately, and from a dirt gardener's perspective.

This farm and garden is a place where we have taken a stand, developed systems and strategies for growing and teaching, and, in many cases, made an attempt to pass those systems on to others for the betterment of the world. This work is successful, restorative, even progressive: we teach people to grow plants organically; the applications are many and varied. The effects are measurable, even palpable.

For 40 years, I have seen a cadre of young (and not so young), superintelligent, intrinsically motivated people come to the Farm & Garden. Their jeans are torn, no money in their pockets, but their hearts are huge. They learn the rudiments of organic farming and gardening, and they subsequently go out and change the world. For the better. They work in food systems from postage-stamp-sized to midsized farms and even the occasional large farm—sections of wheat in Kansas (a section equals 1 square mile), large tracks of rice in the Sacramento Valley—to feed the world. They're teaching urban youth the value of food through programs like Pie Ranch and Food What?! in California; developing inmate training programs and rooftop gardens in Mexico City and Farm School NYC; helping preserve seed libraries in the heartland. The apples they grow can be found on the shelves of acclaimed markets like Bi-Rite in San Francisco—and also in pantries in towns you've probably never heard of. Basically, they connect the people who grow food with the people who consume food. These "kids" dare, and usually succeed, at endeavors I wouldn't and couldn't even dream of undertaking. I am, however, privileged to play a role, daily, in assisting them with their endeavors.

As gardeners, as growers, whether you grow fruit or flowers or feed, at home and in the world, you are part of this cohort—a group of people with a similar feature and focus, certainly, but also in that other definition of cohort: one-tenth of a Roman legion (3,000–6,000 soldiers, a force with both discipline and thrust). Only in a more gentle and peaceable manner, one hopes.

And as you go out and garden in the "real" world, sometimes guiding principles are helpful. Occasionally, one consults a book, or a teacher. Or a muse. In this instance, I'll consult Eddie Vedder, a man whose music can shred your soul if you are not careful, who has single-handedly made playing the ukulele cool, who is also a strong voice for social justice. He's got this song, "Rise," where he talks about having faith in the world, even if it seems like folly. You never know what's going to rise up after you plant your trust in something. And so I say, *yeah!* Throw down your ace in the hole—and expend love and effort on a seemingly intractable world.

And all at once the heavy night

Fell from my eyes and I could see,—

A drenched and dripping apple-tree,

A last long line of silver rain,

A sky grown clear and blue again.

And as I looked a quickening gust

Of wind blew up to me and thrust

Into my face a miracle

Of orchard-breath, and with the smell,—

I know not how such things can be!—

I breathed my soul back into me.

—EDNA ST. VINCENT MILLAY,
  from "Renascence," 1917

Nurseries

Below are excellent places to keep in mind as you source and tend your trees. In addition to selling trees, many of the nurseries listed here send out mail-order catalogs. I recommend you start receiving them; nursery catalogs are an invaluable resource, not just for shopping, but as reading material. By reading a diversity of fruit tree catalogs, you will be well informed with snippets of vital information.

SMALL SCALE

Burnt Ridge Nursery and Orchard
432 Burnt Ridge Road
Onalaska, WA 98570
(360) 985-2873
www.burntridgenursery.com
bare root trees, mail order

Cloud Mountain Farm Center/Nursery
6906 Goodwin Road
Everson, WA 98247
(360) 966-5859
www.cloudmountainfarmcenter.org
resources, education, mail order

Grandpa's Nursery
PO Box 773
Coloma, MI 49038
(877) 800-0077
www.grandpasorchard.com
mail order, bare root trees

One Green World
6469 SE 134th Avenue
Portland, OR 97236
(877) 353-4028
https://onegreenworld.com
mail order, bare root trees, mason bees

Trees of Antiquity
20 Wellsona Road
Paso Robles, CA 93446
(805) 467-9909
www.treesofantiquity.com
organic, bare root trees, mail order; specializes in heirloom varieties

MEDIUM SCALE

Adams County Nursery
26 Nursery Road, PO Box 108
Aspers, PA 17304
(800) 377-3106
www.acnursery.com
bare root trees, pollination charts

Cummins Nursery
1408 Trumansburg Road
Ithaca, NY 14850
(607) 269-7664
www.cumminsnursery.com
mail order, bare root trees

Raintree Nursery
408 Butts Road
Morton, WA 98356
(800) 391-8892
www.raintreenursery.com
good pollination charts; will source just about any variety of cherry, apple, plum, or pears

LARGE SCALE

Boyer Nursery
405 Boyer Nursery Road
Biglerville, PA 17307
(717) 677-8558
www.boyernurseries.com/bare-root-plants/
bare root trees; mail order

C&O
1700 N Wenatchee Avenue
Wenatchee, WA 98801
(800) 232-2636
www.c-onursery.com
mail order, ripening chart

Dave Wilson
PO Box 429
Hickman, CA 95323
(800) 654-5854
www.davewilson.com
mail order, bare root trees, resources

Stark Brothers
PO Box 1800
Louisiana, MO 63353
(800) 325-4180
www.starkbros.com
mail order, bare root trees, resources

Vanwell
PO Box 1339
Wenatchee, WA 98807
(509) 886-8189
www.vanwell.net
mail order, pollination information,
spacing charts

Educational Resources

**Clemson University Home & Garden
Information Center**
https://hgic.clemson.edu/category/tree-fruits/
articles, resources

Cornell University Fruit Resources
https://fruit.cornell.edu/
articles, resources

Michigan State University Extension
www.canr.msu.edu/fruit/index
articles, resources

North Carolina State Extension
https://horticulture.ces.ncsu.edu/comprehensive-
resources-for-fruit-trees/
articles, resources

Orange Pippin
www.orangepippin.com and
www.orangepippintrees.com/
    pollinationchecker.aspx?a=0&v=1086
pollination charts

**UC Davis Fruit & Nut Research
& Information Center**
http://fruitsandnuts.ucdavis.edu/datastore/
articles, resources

UMass Extension Fruit Program
https://ag.umass.edu/fruit
articles, resources

University of Georgia Extension
http://extension.uga.edu/topic-areas.html#f
articles, resources

University of Missouri Extension
https://extension2.missouri.edu/mg6 and
https://extension2.missouri.edu/g6001
articles, resources, pollination charts

**University of Oregon Solar Radiation
Monitoring Laboratory**
http://solardat.uoregon.edu
sun charts

University of Vermont: UVM Fruit
www.uvm.edu/~fruit/
articles, resources

USDA National Resources Conservation Service
www.nrcs.usda.gov/wps/portal/nrcs/site/soils/home/
information on soil moisture assessment

Soil Testing Labs

A&L Canada
www.alcanada.com

A&L Great Lakes
https://algreatlakes.com

A&L Plains
http://al-labs-plains.com

A&L Western Labs
www.al-labs-west.com

Waypoint Analytical (formerly A&L Eastern,
with labs in CA, IA, LA, MS, NC, TN)
www.waypointanalytical.com/HomeOwners

RECOMMENDED READING

As a gardener, you may find your curiosity only grows as you learn more; thus you will amass many gardening books on many topics, sometimes at great expense, but in reality priceless. You often draw a little from this title and a little from that title and slowly, the learning creeps forward. . . . Here are a few of my own favorites accumulated over time. I recommend patronizing independent booksellers, either online or in person, when possible; the value of human booksellers and their knowledge is not to be underestimated. If a title is out of print, I've indicated "OOP," and I encourage you to seek out used copies of these gems at used bookstores or libraries. The hunt can be half the fun.

Textbooks

Deciduous Orchards by W. H. Chandler (Leigh and Febiger, 1942)

Dwarfed Fruit Trees for Orchard, Garden, and Home by Harold Bradford Tukey (MacMillan, 1964; reissued by Cornell University Press, 1978)

Modern Fruit Science by Norman F. Childers, Justin R. Morris, G. Steven Sibbert (Horticultural Publications, 10th edition, 1995)

Temperate-Zone Pomology by Melvin N. Westwood (Timber Press, 2009)

The following educational guides are invaluable. These are all published by University of California Agricultural and Natural Resources and available to order at anrcatalog.ucanr.edu:

Peaches, Plums and Nectarines: Growing and Handling for Fresh Market (publication #3331) by James H. La Rue, 1989

Integrated Pest Management for Apples and Pears (publication #3340) by Barbara Ohlendorf, 1999

Integrated Pest Management for Stone Fruits (publication #3389) by Larry Strand, 1999

Organic Apple Production Manual (publication #3403) by Sean Swezet, 2000

Home Orchard: Growing Your Own Deciduous Fruit and Nut Trees (publication #3485) by C. Ingels, P. Geisel, M. Norton, 2007

Pests of the Garden and Small Farm, 3rd Edition (publication #3332) by Mary Louise Flint, 2018

Laypersons' Books

All About Citrus and Subtropical Fruits (Ortho Press, 2008)

The Apple Grower and *The Holistic Orchard*, 2nd edition by Michael Phillips (Chelsea Green, 2001)

Apples by Roger Yepsen (Countryman Press, 1994)

Apples for the 21st Century by Warren Manhard (The North American Tree Company, 1995)

Apples of North America by Tom Burford (Timber Press, 2013)

Apples by Frank Browning (North Point Press, 1998)

Apples of Uncommon Character by Rowan Jacobsen (Bloomsbury USA, 2014)

The Backyard Orchardist by Stella Otto (OttoGraphics, 1993)

The Book of Pears by Joan Morgan (Chelsea Green 2015)

The Fig by Ira Condit (Chronica Botanica, 1947; OOP)

Fruit Trees in Small Spaces by Colby Eierman (Timber Press, 2012)

The Great Citrus Book by Allen Susser (Ten Speed Press, 1997)

Growing Fruit Trees by Jean-Marie Lespinasse and Évelyne Leterme (W.W. Norton & Company, 2011)

How to Select, Plant, and Grow Citrus by R. Ray and L. Walheim (HP Press, 1980; OOP)

The New Book of Apples by Alison Richards and Joan Morgan (Edbury Press, London, 2002)

Storey's Guide to Growing Organic Orchard Fruits by Danny L. Barney (Storey Publishing, 2013)

Pruning

The Lorette System of Pruning by Louis Lorette (M. Hopkinson and Co Ltd., 1925; OOP)

The Simon and Schuster Step-by-Step Encyclopedia of Practical Gardening by Christopher Brickell (Simon and Schuster, 1979) Originally published with the Royal Horticultural Society, Brickell's guides have been repackaged and sold in various ways over the years. Seek them out; they're good stuff.

Soils

The Nature and Property of Soils [a.k.a. the soil bible] by Nyle C. Brady and Ray R. Weil, 15th edition (Prentice Hall, 2016) There are 15 editions of this book, with many additions and deletions over time. Each edition has value; I have most of them, and I am partial to the 8th.

The Soul of Soil, 4th edition by Joe Smillie and Grace Gershuny (Chelsea Green, 1999)

Start with the Soil by Grace Gershuny (Chelsea Green, 1993)

Bees, Pollinators, and Biodiversity

Attracting Native Pollinators by The Xerces Society (Storey Publishing, 2011)

The Bee-Friendly Garden by Kate Frey and Gretchen LeBuhn (Ten Speed Press, 2016)

How to Manage the Blue Orchard Bee As an Orchard Pollinator by Jordi Bosch and William P. Kemp (Sustainable Agriculture Network, USDA National Agricultural Library, 2001)

ACKNOWLEDGMENTS

Some things take time, much like soil formation—
1 inch every 500–1,000 years. And some things take
time and are melded by multiple factors, much like
the interplay of parent rock, climate, topography,
vegetation and time in soil. And so it goes with both
this book and this gardener. Acknowledgments at
the intersection of time, place, and people . . .

Time and place:
My decades spent living, learning, working, and
teaching at the UCSC Farm & Garden formed the
basis of this book. It is the sweetest spot.

People over time:
Foremost gratitude and respect to anyone who has
ever worked at, or on behalf of, the UCSC Farm &
Garden apprentice program—such a cohort!

To the Rosetta stone, Alan Chadwick, master gardener, stage actor, and charismatic visionary—the
man who planted seeds aplenty that in turn ushered
in the organic gardening movement and catapulted
it from nascent to the flourishing entity we now call
sustainable organic agriculture. To his founding of
the UCSC Farm & Garden on a steep and forebod-
ing hillside.

To Steve Kafka and Pierre Ott, UCSC early farm
managers, who took on a fledgling apprentice in
1974.

To "Big" Jim Nelson and Dennis Tamura, comrades
in arms. In the early years at the Farm & Garden
there was virtually no one to teach us. We had to
figure it out ourselves, and so we did. Jim taught me
trees and soils and Dennis taught us all two things:
how one conducts oneself in the world, and how to
grow quality crops.

To the more than 1,500 apprentice program grads,
a.k.a. our agents of change. Such an exceptional

cohort; they are my inspiration and I have profited
immeasurably from our interactions.

And here's to modern-day visionary Daniel Press,
associate dean of social sciences, professor of environmental studies, executive director of the Center
for Agroecology and Sustainable Food Systems at
UCSC. Daniel is my boss and about as good a boss
a person could ask for. Thank you for your stalwart
support.

To Martha Brown, a special person in all regards,
and her jogging partner Ann Lindsey. For over
30 years, Martha has taken my countless tattered,
fragmented jottings on yellow legal pads and trans-
formed them into impressive broadsides. She has
also served as a lively conversationalist regarding all
things sports, especially baseball. Much respect.

To some of the farmers with orchards who have
allowed me to help them with their trees: the boss
crows at 5th Crow Farm in Pescadero, CA: Mike
Irving, Teresa Kurtak, and John Vars, the hardest
working farmers on the central coast. Nancy Vail
and Jered Lawson, owners of Pie Ranch, who bring
social justice to farming and to farming with youth.
Rich and Laura Everett of Everett Family Farm in
Soquel, CA—Rich with his Honeycrisp orchard and
dedication to bringing back the Yellow Newtown
Pippin, and Laura with her cider orchard and righ-
teous brand, Soquel Cider.

To a special subset of the apprentices I have had the
pleasure of instructing, many of whom are now my
colleagues: Evan Domsic and Ella Fleming, my
present-day sidekicks. Albie Miles and Christof
Bernau, a couple of characters with character.
Matthew Sutton, a true tree whisperer with good
business sense to boot, someone who defines the term
equanimity. Ryan Silsbee, a talented orchardist who is
sweet, smooth, and skilled beyond his meager years.

And his running mate, James Nakahara—well, just for being James, a brother. Aaron Delong, a man with a strong moral compass and an insatiable thirst for garden work, day in and day out, and a gifted writer. Doron Comechero: if any of us had half your energy, intelligence and wit, this world would be a far better place. Thank you for your dedication to youth in farming. Lyn Garling: flat-out the smartest woman on the planet, ergo the smartest person on the planet. Kirsten Yogg and Darryl Wong, managers of the UCSC Farm and the two most thoughtful farmers I have ever encountered. And last but definitely not least—in fact, dearest to my heart—Zoe Hitchner and Sky DeMuro, farmers, gardeners, talented flower growers, and charter members of the "roving band of nomadic orchardists." How many trees have we pruned together, how many people have we taught to prune? True partners in grime.

A heartfelt thanks to all.

Thank you to Lisa Regul, Chloe Rawlins, Jane Chinn, and all the talented and patient folks at Ten Speed Press; to Liz Birnbaum for your lens and eye; and to Kate McKean. Words written on yellow legal pads do not make a manuscript; for typing services, gratitude to Caroline Martin, Stephanie Martin, Manjula Martin, and Ella Fleming. Thank you to Samin Nosrat for your generous advice at a crucial time. Thank you, Alice Waters, for doing all you do, and in an intergenerational manner.

To my family: The "kids"—Niranjan, Manjula, Katie, and Caroline (now a flower farmer herself with Wild Moon Flowers). Here's to all the good times growing up, in, and at the Farm & Garden. It has been a pleasure to grow and pick good apples for you, for life is too short to eat lousy apples. And you are, of course, the apples of my eye.

And especially in this instance, gratitude to my eldest daughter, Manjula. She wrote me a promissory note as a birthday card in 2009 that said, "This piece of paper entitles the holder to one (1) hand-tailored, expertly researched, savvily crafted book proposal. Courtesy of your eldest daughter." Manj, look what you've done! But without your persistent, yeoman-like, indomitable efforts, intelligence, and humor, there would be no book. And to Max Bell Alper for supporting Manjula, digging holes, and cooking for us during our writing intensives—a true gentle-man.

To my wife, Stephanie, a woman possessed of many attributes, including but not limited to intelligence, artistic capabilities, and a caring nature,

"To whom I owe the leaping delight
That quickens my senses in our wakingtime . . .
No peevish winter wind shall chill
No sullen tropic sun shall wither
The roses in the rose-garden which is ours and
ours only . . ."

—from "A Dedication to My Wife,"
T. S. Eliot, 1958

INDEX